THE NECESSARY DREAM

THE NECESSARY DREAM
New Theories and Techniques of Interpretation in Psychoanalysis

Giuseppe Civitarese

Translated by Ian Harvey

Routledge
Taylor & Francis Group

LONDON AND NEW YORK

First published in Italy in 2013 as *Il sogno necessario: Nuove teorie e tecniche dell'interpretazione in psicoanalisi* by FrancoAngeli, Milan

First published 2014 by Karnac Books Ltd.

Published 2018 by Routledge
2 Park Square, Milton Park, Abingdon, Oxon OX14 4RN
711 Third Avenue, New York, NY 10017, USA

Routledge is an imprint of the Taylor & Francis Group, an informa business

Translated by Ian Harvey.

British Library Cataloguing in Publication Data

A C.I.P. for this book is available from the British Library

ISBN-13: 9781782200659 (pbk)

Typeset by V Publishing Solutions Pvt Ltd., Chennai, India

To my brother

CONTENTS

ABOUT THE AUTHOR

Giuseppe Civitarese, psychiatrist, Ph.D. in psychiatry and relational sciences, is a training and supervising analyst in the Italian Psychoanalytic Society (SPI) and a member of the American Psycho-analytic Association (APsaA) and of the International Psychoanalytical Association (IPA). He lives and is in private practice in Pavia, Italy. Currently, he is the editor of the *Rivista di Psicoanalisi*, the official journal of the Italian Psychoanalytic Society. He has published several books, which include: *The Intimate Room: Theory and Technique of the Analytic Field*, London 2010; *The Violence of Emotions: Bion and Post-Bionian Psychoanalysis*, London 2012; *Perdere la testa: Abiezione, conflitto estetico e critica psicoanalitica* [*Losing Your Head: Abjection, Aesthetic Conflict and Psychoanalytic Criticism*], Firenze 2012; *I sensi e l'inconscio* [*Senses and the Unconscious*], Rome 2014. He has also co-edited *L'ipocondria e il dubbio: L'approccio psicoanalitico* [*Hypochondria and Doubt: The Psychoanalytic Approach*], FrancoAngeli, Milano 2011 and (with H. Levine) *The Bion Tradition*, London, 2015.

INTRODUCTION

After a hundred years of psychoanalysis, what has the psychoanalytic interpretation of dreams now become? Are what Simic calls the films of our lives still the royal road to the unconscious or do we now have a different concept both of dreams and of the unconscious? What is the meaning of dreams in the analytic dialogue? Do they still have a key role to play in clinical practice or not? These are just some of the questions I shall seek to answer in this book.

We perceive Freud's theory of dreams as essentially unchanged. We have the impression that everything there is to say about the subject has been said.[1] Nothing could be more false. It is true that many analysts work according to the principles established by Freud, but it is equally true that there have been radical innovations in this field—we no longer work on dreams but with dreams.

Freud explores the way residues of infantile neurosis become unconsciously inscribed in dreams. The paradigmatic example in this regard is the Wolf-Man's famous dream. Freud seeks tirelessly to return to the real scene reflected in it. Initially he takes a realistic approach to the dream, but is then forced to abandon this need for concreteness. Psychic reality has an effectuality that can only be explained by postulating the existence of primal fantasies, of organising patterns of experience that are transmitted phylogenetically.

This is where Melanie Klein starts from. Klein takes up Freud's challenge and undertakes to clarify how this inner world is formed and what role it plays in people's lives. She comes to think of it as a theatre full of actors, whom she calls internal objects and whose task it is to act out the dark dramas of unconscious fantasies. This inner theatre gives meaning to the things of the world. Its plots are expressed in dreams and in children's games. Primal fantasies thus transform into unconscious fantasies. Both, however, give the impression of innatism and fixity. More than Freud, Klein emphasises the role of the object and of the life environment, but then in effect she depletes it of meaning. Gradually material reality becomes evanescent, almost to the point of disappearing.

Winnicott and Bion make up for the deficiencies of a theory that was still too unipersonal. For Winnicott and Kahn the "dream space", unlike dreaming as a neurophysiological activity, is not given at birth but develops in the relationship with a caregiver. For Bion, a mind cannot exist alone, but needs another mind. The mother dreams the child, and thanks to her capacity for reverie, the phenomenological expression of an invisible α function of the mind, she receives and transforms his most violent emotions after having first absorbed them by means of projective identifications. She then passes on the method, which thus enables the child to accomplish this task by himself. Moreover, we dream both while awake and asleep. It is the dream that creates the contact barrier and thus separates the conscious from the unconscious.

Meltzer emphasises this aspect of symbolic creation that Bion attributes to the dream and equates dream and aesthetic experience.

With Ogden the dream becomes more and more of a social product.

By using the similar but different notion of "analytic field", derived from Bion, the Barangers, and Langs, Ferro extends the concept of the dream to encompass the entire analytic dialogue. There is no communication on the part of the patient (or analyst) that cannot be seen as the story of the dream of the session itself.

From these few lines one can already see how the theory of the dream has been greatly enriched. Depending on the various authors, the dream performs several functions: it testifies to the patient's history, it reveals the geography of the unconscious, it gives meaning to experience.

Each of these perspectives is based on an analytic model and has its own validity. Not to admit this would be to betray the ambiguous spirit of the dream. Dreams are fascinating precisely because of their inexhaustible richness and because, more than any other psychic production, they embody the game of points of view that is essentially the game of the unconscious and of analysis.

However, today we no longer regard the dream as the royal road that helps reveal the disguises dream-work imposes on latent thoughts; rather, we valorize its function of transformation and symbolic creation. The ambiguity of the manifest text of the dream no longer arouses suspicion. We consider it instead the expression of its poetic function. In clinical practice the recounting of the dream no longer occupies the privileged position it once always held over the other contents of the patient's discourse, even simply the banal retelling of the events of everyday life. But we should not deceive ourselves. If this happens, it is because, when we hear them recounted within the framework of analysis, we also interpret the events of material reality and the past as if they were waking dreams.

In this way the paradigm of the dream takes on an even more central role than in classical theory. Understood as the result of a communication between one unconscious and another, it is something we listen to as an intersubjective production. We read every session as if it were a long shared dream and conceive the whole of analysis as an exchange of reveries. In principle, it would be difficult to tell what belongs to one and what belongs to the other. In interpretation, also the associations and reveries of the analyst rightfully come into play, and they too help us understand the patient's dream.

Actually what I should say is *not* understand it. The essential thing is not so much deciphering the images of the dream in order to lift the veil of censorship and to reconstruct the original text that speaks of the infantile wish; rather, we use the dream and its characters as we would use toys in the treatment of a child. The aim is not so much to translate the unconscious into the conscious—"Where id was, there ego shall be" ["*Wo Es war, soll Ich werden*"], wrote Freud (1933, p. 80)—as to develop the narrative competence of the mind. That's why we say working *with* dreams and not *on* dreams.

Obviously, however, working with dreams often means playing the game of working on dreams by using the traditional method of circumstantial evidence (Ginzburg, 1979). If Bion, the principal architect of this change, has taught us one important thing, it is never to trust commonly used conceptual oppositions; and among these, if they are taken in a static and not dynamic way, not even the binary pairs of instinctual/relational, intrapsychic/interpsychic, past/present, censorship/caesura, depth/surface. At the heart of the change there are, as it happens, quite a few factors of continuity. To name one, with Bion's concept of α-dream-work and then α function, the dream becomes the very model of thought. The transformations brought about by the α function of primitive emotions/feelings, or β elements, which represent the start of the symbolisation process, can only be thought of as a way of giving meaning to experience that operates within the analogical-differential regime, that is to say, the regime of metaphor and metonymy, identified by Freud in the mechanisms of dream work: displacement, condensation, figurability, and secondary elaboration.

The new paradigm pays less attention to psychic contents and more to the mind as container and to its functioning, because in the meantime psychoanalysis has become more and more relational. For example, we perceive in a notably different way the role of the analyst as a person and of his subjectivity. But if present-day psychoanalysis is no longer that of Freud—and likewise nor is the theory of dreams—this is due to the fact that the general cultural framework has changed. Today, no one would defend hyper-positivistic theses, such as those of early Wittgenstein, and if many regard him as one of the greatest philosophers of the last century, it is on account of his later period, when he formulated the theory of "language games" and of the *as if* character of perception. Needless to say, with his radical critique of the status of the subject of psychology and classical philosophy, Freud contributed perhaps more than anyone else to the emergence of so-called post-modern thought and the philosophy of deconstruction.

In this book I say something about the fascinating trajectory of the theory of dreams and the relative technique of analysis. In Chapters Two to Seven I illustrate the contributions of the authors I regard as most important, while at the same time being aware that I should have dedicated at least as much space to Jung, Ferenczi, Winnicott, and Kohut. I also pay constant attention to the concept of image, a problem which sees philosophy and neuroscience as the natural interlocutors of psychoanalysis. This framework is also meant to serve as a point of connection with the world of cinema.

The book started life in some seminars on clinical work with dreams held at the Cesare Musatti Centre of Psychoanalysis in Milan in 2008. To illustrate the ideas of an author, at every meeting I would show some short clips from films. Showing these scenes, which here of course I can only describe, was a way of evoking the raw material from which dreams are made—the films of our lives as Simic calls them. It was also a way of recreating the magic of their images, of stimulating new perspectives, emphasising some theoretical points, making certain points more vivid, and finding a new way of investigating the lively, challenging, intriguing, or distressing fabric of dreams. As it happens, we do not yet have a DC-Mini, the device that in *Paprika* (2006—the Italian version adds the tagline *I Dreamed a Dream*), an animated film by Kon Satoshi, allows the analyst to participate concretely in the patient's dream, to record its images, and then, frame by frame, to review them together with the patient.

Both born in the last decade of the nineteenth century, cinema and psychoanalysis often intersect; they wink at each other, they imitate each other and are reflected in each other. For various reasons there is an objective link between them that is worth exploring. However, rather than taking the usual path of interpreting films from a psychoanalytic point of view, here I ask myself the question about what cinema can reveal to analysts about themselves and their theories. I am interested more in movies that interpret psychoanalysis and less as is usually the case, in taking the opposite approach. In this way I also avoid venturing too far into the difficult terrain of the Freudian-style aesthetic criticism (on this point, see Civitarese, 2012a). I use cinema in an allegorical way to help clarify the meaning of a key concept of the dream theory of a certain author: for example, the final scene of *They* (Harmon, 2002—the Italian title adds the tagline *Nightmares from the World of Shadows*) in relation to Bion's β screen.

In most cases, these are films that in one way or another speak of psychoanalysis, are inspired by psychoanalysis, or films in which one of the characters is a psy-something. The exceptions are *Raising Arizona* (Joel & Ethan Coen, 1987) and *Rashomon* (Kurosawa, 1950)—unless one wishes to see the medium in *Rashomon* as being a similar figure. There, I feel empowered by the authors I deal with in the relevant chapter; they themselves mention it.

It matters little if at times the films are mediocre and certainly far from being masterpieces. I mention some films, when the context warrants it, only because of associations or reveries, to highlight what is present in the subtle weave of our imagination and how they represent an important filter—which has become so pervasive as to be barely visible—for interpreting reality.

The reference to movies is also justified from another perspective, which is the one I most care about. There is a basic element that unites dream theory and film theory: the relationship that they entertain between simulation, or falsification, and reality. I regard this as the true thread of the book. I raise this point in the first chapter and then in the ninth, taking my cue from a story by Borges and a small footnote on dreams within dreams that Freud added to *The Interpretation of Dreams* in 1911.

Indeed, in the penultimate chapter I address the theme, which is already enthralling in itself (but even more so when seen as a model of dreams in general, of analysis and representation), of the dream within a dream.

I have ordered the other chapters like entries in a dictionary of thinking about dreams: "fiction" for Freud, "concreteness" for Klein, "ambiguity" for Meltzer, "reverie" for Bion, "dialectic" for Ogden, "narration" for Ferro.

Some concepts have been passed on from one author to another, each time becoming inscribed within a new context. Often they are themselves rather ambiguous, so it is inevitable and even necessary to approach them from multiple perspectives. However, we can achieve a certain precision in the use of concepts that are both so powerful and fragile only if we make the effort to constantly redefine them and look at them each time as if for first time.

In the last chapter I attempt a conclusive synopsis, partly inspired by some of the most reliable theories in neuroscience. It is interesting to look at this discipline against the background of psychoanalytic theory and to see how it contextualises the fascinating and unsolved problem of the transition from the material to the psychic and how images are formed in the mind.

Finally, I put forward the hypothesis that dreams are the connecting thread between the body and the mind, a way of giving back the body to the mind every night, of giving a personal meaning to experience and thus regenerating the psychic skin that protects us from the traumas of life. Thus I reaffirm the value of Freud's intuition of the dream as the guardian of sleep, while at the same time extending it to embrace the "sleep of reality".

Note

1. Karl Abraham expressed such an idea in 1908: "*The Interpretation of Dreams* is so well rounded and finished that there remains nothing for any of us to do" (Freud & Abraham, 2002, p. 67).

CHAPTER ONE

Dark contemplation*

Traumfabrik

The world, on the contrary, has once more become "infinite" to us: in so far we cannot dismiss the possibility that it contains infinite interpretations. Once more the great horror seizes us—but who would desire forthwith to deify once more this monster of an unknown world in the old fashion?

—Friedrich W. Nietzsche, *The Gay Science*

The space of dreams is a private and inaccessible sanctuary. When dealing with dreams we always and only have to do with stories—that is, with words, and never with images. One way of remedying this lacuna is to borrow images from the cinema. One traditional interpretation of the cinema is the idea that it is a "dream factory" (*Traumfabrik*) (Ehrenburg, 1931), or vice versa, that dreams are a cinema of the mind.[1] Film images are different from dream images in that

---

*On film and psychoanalysis, see Gabbard and Gabbard (1999), Sabbadini (2003), Riefolo (2006), Campari (2008).

we can contemplate them together. For that matter, curiously, while in novels I find almost all dreams annoying—perhaps because I feel them to be artificial—I cannot say the same about dreams in films. This is because when we watch a movie we are already dreaming, we are already inside the screen. The images are more evocative and unsaturated than words, they are less abstract. They seem to be endowed with a power words do not possess. They are closer to the deep, bodily bedrock of our sense of ourselves, and maybe that is why they excite us more.

This is why it is always rather frustrating to talk about dreams since from the very first retelling of a dream its vibrant hallucinatory quality is reduced to a matter of words and one loses sight of the thing itself. And this is not even the first transformation of the dreamed dream because recollection organises the memory of the dream experience even before it is verbalised. Without falling into the trap of some naive identification between dream visions and film visions, which are obviously artistic products, we expect films to render something of this experience. Like dream images, the images of films are "appearance, a distant image of the truth. They are all connected to the idea of pretending something that is not there, and do not enjoy [...] any transference from the reality of things to their reproduction" (Bertetto, 2007, p. 16). In this pretence, film and dream are both "subject to Freud's 'considerations of representability'" (Albano, 2004, p. 11). As Lou Andreas-Salomé already observed in 1913, cinematic technique is "the only one which permits the rapid succession of pictures which approximates our own imaginative faculty; it may even be said to imitate its erratic ways" (1987, p. 101). This view is echoed today by, among others, Damasio:

> Movies are the closest external representation of the prevailing storytelling that goes on in our minds. What goes on within each shot, the different framing of a subject that the movement of the camera can accomplish, what goes on in the transition of shots achieved by editing, and what goes on in the narrative constructed by a particular juxtaposition of shots is comparable in some respects to what is going on in the mind, thanks to the machinery in charge of making visual and auditory images, and to devices such as the many levels of attention and working memory. (1999, p. 188)

It is no accident that in Italian when we want to express the idea of fantasising or daydreaming we use the expression *"farsi un film"* ("making a film inside your own head"), and not *"fare teatro"*. Films are more immersive and mesmerising than plays. The term *"fare teatro"* (being melodramatic) is used instead to refer to histrionic behaviour. To a much greater extent than theatre, movies regularly enter the narratives and associations of patients and analysts. They shape our imagination and undoubtedly enrich our modern mythologies.

The infinite world

Films and dreams are works of darkness. In the images we see projected on to the movie screen we have the systematic alternation of lit frames of exposed film and black frames. Moving pictures are fake, contrived, already divided at their origin, discontinuous, constructed, not at all natural. Darkness is intrinsic to watching the film. Blackness is rooted at the very heart of the visible, the element that makes it possible. The manufacturing process of a film is a concrete metaphor of the way in which we falsify or perceptually construct the real. All the tricks and special effects—the lights, lenses, different camera distances, and so on—suggest the "manufacture" of reality by the mind. Editing a film is equivalent to dream-work and then also to α dream-work, Bion's first name for the α function, which for him is also active while we are awake.

Films and dreams are born from the darkness of sleep and both are simulacra of reality. Dreamer and spectator both experience a state of immobility, passivity, of relative closure to other sensory channels, and live through an experience where the focus is on images. They create the meaning of the dream and the film only at that moment of waking up, which is repeated ad infinitum, when they again move from a form of primary consciousness to full self-consciousness, and thus realise the fiction of the frame, of the margins of experience. Letting themselves go in a dizzying back-and-forth movement between multiple levels of reality, they play the highly serious game of participation and distance on which self-consciousness is founded. We are reflected on the cinema screen as on the dream screen. Both cinema and dream confront the subject with the crisis of naive realism. Descartes knew all about this— the idea that the experience of the dream as a subversion of the status of the subject can only be opposed by faith in the infinite goodness of a transcendent entity.

Films have a strong illusionistic quality; dreams are indeed even hallucinatory. While on the one hand, they both produce intense involvement, on the other, they demystify reality: they show its illusory face, leading straight to the *as if* of perception in wakefulness. Indeed, what films and dreams have in common is artifice, pretence, arbitrariness. This is why they are able to go beyond the "realistic" illustration of reality, to get closer to reality.

Activity and passivity are two differing but equally present aspects of both dream and film experience. The dream is active, because there is an ego who is both director and producer, who sets up a scene; but it is also passive, because there is a self that suffers the vicissitudes of a plot that is constantly new and surprising (Bollas, 1987).

As at the cinema, we can regard the dream as an aesthetic object. The wonder we experience during the dream as an aesthetic experience adds to what we gain from its value as a revelation, from its traditional receptive divinatory side—or, to put it in Vitale's terms (2005), from its apocalyptic character.[1]

Dreams are the most intimate revelations by which we come to know about ourselves, but, also, the images we receive passively at the cinema (and perceptions in general) are the object of identifications and transferences, which we use to construct them actively and make them "personal" or significant.

Not only film and dream, but also the "dream of the session" is a work of darkness. The declaredly artificial setting of analysis borrows the fictionality of the dream to decentre the subject, to show the subject that the ego is not master in its own house, that there is an unbridgeable gap between words and things, and that reality is only an effect of reality (Barthes, 1984). Just as when you see a film at the cinema the lights are turned off, within the perimeter of this space, so as to see better in a dream, analysts invite their patients to close their eyes.

We can only see if we blind ourselves artificially. For Saint John of the Cross, in a sort of "dark contemplation", the closer the soul comes to God (an approach which could be translated in Bion's terms as "becoming O", or philosophically as thinking Being, the real), the more it sees the darkness surrounding it. The more it is sheltered in the dark, the better it can proceed safely. By analogy, dreams and films, in short, can be seen as forms of contemplation of the divine understood as the real. They can live alone in the darkness, but precisely for this reason they reveal the darkness that is in the light, the black frames that alternate with the exposed frames, making for a vision of the world that is not overexposed.

Dreams are dark, and hence they need to be interpreted, just as the sleep that encloses them is dark; but, in fact, they are also contemplation. Etymologically the word comes from *cum* and *templum*, where *templum* stands for the space in the sky within which the augur observed the flight of birds. It was later extended to mean fixing one's gaze or thinking about something that arouses wonder or reverence. This is why the expression "dark contemplation" gives the idea of the state of enchanted receptivity in which we find ourselves when we dream, or when we dream at the movies because we are fully absorbed. After all, from where else if not from the mother's body as real, from our "first home", must we extricate ourselves in order to become human, while at the same time always yearning to rejoin it?

You are requested to close the eyes (or an eye)

Dreams partake of a non-logic, they are outside of any economy of usefulness. They are mysterious, shadowy, enigmatic. They appear fragmented, impalpable, elusive. They are like the theatre of the absurd, a one-man show for only one spectator. They unfold in the digressive and purposeless manner of conversation and with the disinterestedness of contemplation, wonder, and sensual aura. The dream is solitary, but it is still a dialogue with someone because at birth the self develops in a social dimension, before the unconscious becomes a linguistic unconscious and there is a glimmer of self-awareness.

The dream is made up of figures, images that do not tell the truth as such but show it, approximating to it, making it obliquely visible. Dream images are indefinable, they belong more to the order of sense rather than meaning. This is why they resist the grip of language. In terms of visionary quality, syncretic functioning, and constitutive ambiguity, perhaps only film and poetry are able to render the dream in some way.

The dream ferries us between worlds. It is the metaleptic device of choice for crossing borders, potentially also the most feared. It is an ongoing conversation with the shadows of this radically different world, each time a nocturnal *nekyia*, as Borges emphasises in poems and stories dedicated to the dream, and Foucault too in his introduction to Binswanger's *Dream and Existence*: "In the depth of his dream what man encounters is his death" (1994, p. 54). Dreaming is not acting, but contemplating an afterlife of consciousness, transcending the waking self, overcoming the basic splitting of the ego. You discover a duality, a separate and illusory reality. You sense the existence of a distant extraneous world where you can get in touch with reality, "O" (Bion), the thing (*das Ding*), and return to a sort of "aquatic communion" with the cosmos (ibid., p. 36). In the modern age, psychoanalysis gives back to rationality the space of this transcendence, the unconscious, as the possibility for consciousness that has become unhappy, as well as infinite, to be reconciled in a secular sense with one's own gods, thus making it possible for the subject to acquire a true self.

Freud considers the death of one's father to be the most important event in a person's life. In his case, it gave him the impetus to self-analysis and the writing of *The Interpretation of Dreams*. The night before his father's funeral, or, according to the letter to Fliess dated 2 November 1896 (Masson, 1985, p. 202), the day after, he dreams of entering into a barber's shop and reading a printed notice, similar to those found in railway station waiting rooms, with the words "'You are requested to close the eyes' or, 'You are requested to close an eye'" (Freud, 1900, p. 317). There is a precise context for this dream. His family is unhappy. They accuse him of not having organised the funeral properly. He had decided on a service that was too simple. What's more, he arrives late at the ceremony because he has been to the barber's.

Freud presents this dream—John Huston has provided a fascinating film version in his *Freud: The Secret Passion* (1962)—as a failed dream. The dream-work had failed to create either a unitary text of the dream thoughts or an ambiguous text. To us this "failure" appears instead as the glowing core of the dream, as the expression of Freud's painful emotional ambivalence towards his father. The dream alludes to the custom of the son closing the eyes of the deceased, but it is as if Freud were asking him, since he has survived him and senses the arrival of an unconscious feeling of guilt, to forgive him, to be lenient, in short, to turn a blind eye; but also, to close his eyes and not come back to haunt him as a ghost.

Now, "You are requested to close the eyes (or an eye)", from being the inaugural moment of Freud's self-analysis and of psychoanalysis, becomes the moment that marks the start of each analysis. We ask patients to free associate, to dream, to set aside external reality and to focus on psychic reality. The analyst too turns a blind eye because he forgoes any judgemental attitude. And he closes his eyes. Analysis consists in an exchange of states of reverie, in the creation of a shared dream space in which the communication between one unconscious and another takes place in ideal conditions.

Through the intuition of the unconscious movements of the relationship, the analyst builds new symbolic forms to help the analysand express hitherto unthinkable emotions, to make the superego less ruthless, and thus to be more fully human. The assumption behind this approach is that when a patient enters analysis, he loses his mind (Ogden, 2009) or, in other words, enters an intermediate psychological area, or one shared with the analyst. The way in which each generates the meanings of his or her own experience is affected by the presence of the other. What is created is an unconscious emotional field that the couple share. In short, for a mind to develop, when it is born, or to resume psychic growth that in some areas may have been arrested, there have to be at least two people.

The very device of analysis (an unprecedented form of relationship, a new way of being human that was invented by Freud) is therefore an example of voluntary blindness, like turning off the lights to focus on the theatre of the inner life or the phantasmagoria of the cinema of dreams. In one of his sonnets Shakespeare speaks of "darkly bright" eyes, "bright in the dark directed", that contemplate dream images, and it seems to me the best definition possible that metonymically can be given of the visions of the dream and of the dream itself. Similarly, in a famous passage in a letter to Lou Andreas-Salomé, who was also a friend of Nietzsche and Rilke, Freud (Freud, E. L., 1961) writes that when he wants to solve a problem in his work, he needs to project a beam of darkness on to the problem. And luminous mist ("*neblina luminosa*") is the oxymoronic expression that Borges uses (2010, p. 275) in a poem when speaking of his blindness, which reduces "all things to a single thing/with neither form nor colour. An idea, almost".

Bion also expressed this very same need in a new formulation that is both fascinating and scandalous: the analyst must listen "without memory or desire". What he really means is that the analyst must allow memory our desire to visit him as in a dream, in his reveries, and only after having passed through the unconscious. This is nothing other than a radical version of Freud's idea of maintaining "evenly suspended attention". Bion links this suggestion not only to the hyperbolic recourse to the practice of systematic doubt as theorised by Descartes, but also to the thinking of Saint John of the Cross (who wrote: "As I rose to higher reaches/Dazzled, blinded was my vision,/And in an utter darkness won/The hardest of my victories"; Brenan, 1975, p. 175). We proceed with safety, in short, only under the cover of darkness ("In the midst of this darkness, the soul is illuminated and the light shines forth upon the darkness"; St. John of the Cross, 2005, p. 103).

The basic juxtaposition, which is modelled on the traditional opposition between reason and passion, is between knowing (K/knowledge) the real and becoming the real ("O" as origin or zero), between using arid abstractions and achieving a form of disciplined intuition; between assuming oneself and the other as given human beings and focusing instead on a dialectical view of self-with-other. In the consulting room this means between understanding things about the other, in a kind of translation that often becomes mechanical, detached, and lifeless, and becoming "the other" and participating in dreaming his undreamed dreams. This is what Ogden (2009) metaphorically called night terrors (in the sphere of psychotic pathology) or, if things are working better, interrupted dreams, nightmares (in the non-psychotic sphere). Whatever happens, analyst and patient will share an emotional experience which will inevitably transform both.

In psychoanalysis, darkness also corresponds to the systematic exercise of doubt, a scepticism which, however, with Roland Barthes I would call "sweet." In his seminar on *Le neutre*, he quotes an old Pyrrhonian definition according to which sweetness is the ultimate iteration of scepticism (*"la douceur est le dernier mot du scepticisme"*; 2002, p. 66), which I like to interpret as not imposing oneself on the other in a dogmatic way and as the expression of an ethic of hospitality. But why do we need scepticism? Because as analysts, from Freud onwards, we are painfully aware of the fact that we have no direct or privileged access to the truth and that all we can do is mourn this loss.

It is in this spirit that in *Si prega di chiudere gli occhi. Esercizi di cecità volontaria* [You are requested to close the eyes. Exercises in voluntary blindness], Vitale (2007)—see also de Man (1971) and Derrida (1990)— composes an unexpected eulogy to fog: "in the subtle landslide of identity that it causes in the heart of reality, the gaze finally regains its primitive original state, when seeing was only perceiving, always an instant before any heightening of thought or language". He then describes it as the formless "original womb inside which all things are held together, surfacing and plunging into the foam of being, unaware of any established hierarchy, insensitive to any appeal to expectation" (Vitale, 2007, pp. 12–13).

Fog becomes a metaphor for an outlook on things without memory or desire, unburdened by knowledge, which, when excessive, obstructs the view. In the deformation produced by the voluntary limitation of vision there is the same tension that in Bacon and many other painters motivates the rejection of everything that is illustration in painting, that which only renders reality, not the real, and which, as we have seen, Borges considered the origin of the idea, of thought. Fog is the price paid to the analogy that blurring differences somewhat enables us to get rid of the undecidables of binary caesuras of logical thinking— either A or B.

Because of its inherent metaphorical nature, as Nietzsche pointed out so well, in itself language is generally obscure. All language is woven out of the transferences of primary metaphors. The *as if* signals the indissolubility of signifier and signified, gives form to the zero degree of representation and marks the analogical structure of thought. Once again, it cannot be put better than in the words of Vitale: "the consistency and truthfulness of a world, as emerges from the metaphorical fabric, are in no way visible, and cannot be commensurate with the ability to reproduce rigorously a state of affairs that one supposes exists outside. Rather, they are resolved in the darkness of a system of relationships and references—made up of sounds, echoes and refractions— acting from within a given language, and to which we can only listen" (ibid., p. 34).

What binds us to reality escapes us.

The fact is, however, that one important philosophical tradition identifies knowledge with light (with *phôs*), and not with the darkness. The basic idea is that knowledge is seeing, that we can grasp the world mimetically, in an accurate, objective way, according to the paradigm that regards representation as a mirror of nature.

Psychoanalysis is the expression of critical thinking that places at its centre the metaphor of oedipal blindness as a prelude to insight or vision. Accordingly, the paradigm of the psychoanalytic method is the dream, both divine and ghostly, evanescent and as sensorially intense as hallucination. But does not the relative opacity of consciousness in the dream correspond in analysis to the intermittent blindness of focused suspended attention? To the temporary hypnosis of reflexive logic?

To the darkness in the auditorium that throws light on the theatre of the unconscious?

Note

1. Vitale (2005) identifies three major paradigms at work in psychoanalysis: circumstantial, archaeological, and apocalyptic. Regarding the first, also investigated by Ginzburg in his classic essay of 1979, he recalls that Freud was an avid reader of detective stories. In a letter to Jung he compares himself to Sherlock Holmes in his ability "to guess the real situation on the basis of subtle clues". Freud's maid, Paula Fichtl, reported that he always kept one of Conan Doyles's books on his bedside table and that he used a snapped matchstick as a bookmark. The archaeological paradigm is all too well known: writing to Stefan Zweig, Freud admitted that he had "actually read more archeology than psychology" (E. L. Freud, 1961, p. 258). The apocalyptic paradigm, inspired by Biblical exegesis, corresponds to the pervasive idea that the (secret, hidden) truth is given as retrospective unveiling, as *apokálupsis*, a Greek word that translates the Hebrew *galeh*. There is the idea that the end becomes *immanent* rather than imminent, in short, the confident expectation that there will be a moment of "absolutely profane illumination" (ibid., p. 105).

CHAPTER TWO

Dream fictions

Final analysis

In the first scene of *Final Analysis* (Joanou, 1992), Diane Bayler, alias Uma Thurman, recounts a recurring dream to her analyst, Dr Isaac Barr, alias Richard Gere:

DIANE: ... I had the dream again. I'm arranging flowers on a table ... for a centerpiece. I decorate the flowerpot with fancy paper ... It feels like velvet ... There are three different kinds of flowers. There are lilies ... and there are ... By the way, did you reach my sister?

ISAAC: Wait a minute ... Let's go back to your dream. Tell me more about these flowers.

DIANE: There's nothing more to tell ... Besides, aren't you gonna tell me that we're out of time?

ISAAC: We have a few more minutes. You were late today.

DIANE: I'm late for everything these days.

ISAAC: What's going on in your life? ... What's making you late?

DIANE: Whenever I leave my apartment, I have to go back and make sure the stove's off. Then after I check it, I have to go back and make sure the pilot light didn't blow out when I closed the oven door. Today I went back eight times. I didn't get to the store till ten.

ISAACS: And what happens when you are late?

DIANE: Nothing. I mean ... I don't get into trouble or anything. My supervisor's been trying to get a date with me.

ISAACS: Interested?

DIANE: In you? ... Ehm ... I ... I mean, in him? ... Oh ... I don't know.

ISAACS: It could be that ... you perform this ritual in order to be late to avoid a prospective lover or anger him.

DIANE: You mean I'm passive aggressive? ... You really should talk to her, Dr Barr.

ISAACS: To who?

DIANE: My sister. She says she knows some things ... about my mother and father. Might shed some light ...

ISAACS: Maybe those are the kind of things that we'd do best to uncover in our work here.

DIANE: You should really talk to her. You won't regret it. She's ... she's a very interesting girl.

In this opening, *Final Analysis* ironically plays on the Freudian concept of erotic transference, and indeed the title itself alludes to the concept of the interminability of analysis. Shiny and glossy, the film features an impressive all-star cast: alongside Uma Thurman and Richard Gere, we have Kim Basinger playing the role of Heather, Diane's sister. The genre it belongs to is a hybrid of courtroom drama, murder-mystery, and thriller. *Final Analysis* aspires to being a new *Vertigo* (1958) but is more like a remake of *Fatal Attraction* (1987). "Things get weirder and weirder, until it's clear scriptwriter Wesley Strick's the one who needs analysis," writes Desson Howe, one of the *Washington Post's* most caustic critics (7 February 1992). He concludes: "for videotape audiences only".

When the film came out the reviews were negative ("middle-grade trash", according to *Entertainment Weekly*, February 14, 1992). Nevertheless, it was a great success with the public. Many critics found the situations implausible and the characters unbelievable. From the point of view I am taking here—an attempt to study the gradient that goes from lie → falsity → fiction → as-if → truth of dream → truth of representation—this is interesting. It is as if the film, taken in itself, were just like a *matryoshka* doll, the nth version of the theme of what is credible or not in analysis and perception.

The film is set in San Francisco. Two sisters set a trap to kill off the elder sister's (Heather-Basinger) husband—a mentally unstable gangster—so as to pocket his sizeable life insurance. As part of their plan, they use the unwitting analyst who is treating the younger sister, the exotic Diane Baylor (played by Uma Thurman). Isaac Barr-Gere—I shall keep the double-barrelled names because the relationship between actor and character is an effect of figure/background, as Brecht knew very well—is an authority in the field of forensic psychiatry and regularly gives evidence in court cases. He is also a charismatic therapist. He seems to have come straight out of *American Gigolo* (Schrader, 1980). His one flaw, however, is that he has been on his own for some time. In the script, Dr Barr is persuaded to "violate" professional ethics by going to bed with his patient's sister. A lawyer friend of his tries to warn him about Heather's husband—"Fucking around with his wife is like teasing King Kong," he says—but his warning goes unheeded.

Heather is very much the "bad girl", and what's more, she has a "stunning" wardrobe (*Variety*, 1 January 1992); in short, she is a *femme fatale*. For this reason, under the pretext of helping her to reconstruct her life story (the father had abused his eldest daughter and had lost his life in a mysterious fire), Diane has no difficulty in luring Dr Barr into the trap. Insidiously she suggests he meet her sister: "You should really talk to her. You won't regret it."

If he had known his classics, Barr-Gere would have remembered this passage from Freud:

> Information of this kind may, as a rule, be employed as absolutely authentic material. So it may seem tempting to take the easy course of filling up the gaps in a patient's memory by making enquiries from the older members of his family; but I cannot advise too strongly against such a technique. Any stories that may be told by relatives in reply to enquiries and requests are at the mercy of every critical misgiving that can come into play. One invariably regrets having made oneself dependent upon such information; at the same time confidence in the analysis is shaken and a court of appeal is set up over it. Whatever can be remembered at all will anyhow come to light in the further course of analysis. (1918, p. 14, footnote)

In the interests of dramatic tension, "Gere and Basinger go at it, of course" (Desson Howe, *Washington Post*, 7 February 1992); and then in the sixth scene of the film, just before recounting a variation of her dream, Diane asks the analyst mischievously how things worked out:

DIANE: Isn't she beautiful, Dr Barr? She said you guys met.
ISAACS: Yes, we did.
DIANE: Compared to Heather, I always felt like a caterpillar, creepy and crawling.
ISAACS: A caterpillar turns into a butterfly, doesn't it?
DIANE: Heather's the butterfly. Isn't that obvious? ... I had the dream again ... I'm arranging flowers on a table as a centerpiece. Lilies, carnations ...
ISAACS: What was the third?

Meanwhile, Heather-Basinger makes Dr Barr believe she is suffering from acute pathological intoxication. When she drinks, she becomes violent but once the crisis is over she cannot remember anything. This is how she sets up her trap (the term "set up" alluding to setting, the idea of framing, staging a play at the theatre, and positioning the camera to shoot the scene). During one of these episodes Heather kills her husband, but is exonerated by the psychiatrist who by now has fallen in love with her. She also procures some false evidence so that she can blackmail him if necessary: during a romantic trip to the San Francisco lighthouse, Barr leaves his fingerprints on the murder weapon, a dumbbell used for weight training. But things don't go according to plan. Heather dies and in the last scene of the film, in a kind of (conscious?) repetition compulsion, we see the younger sister who has fully identified with the criminal role of the elder sister. In the end the caterpillar has become a butterfly.

What went wrong with Heather-Evans's diabolical plan? It was down to the dream! Let's look at another version, in the eleventh scene.

DIANE: I had the dream again. I'm arranging flowers on a table as a centerpiece. I decorate the flowerpot with fancy paper. The paper ... The paper feels like velvet. I have three kinds of flowers. Lilies, carnations ...
ISAACS: And the third kind?

ISAACS: And the third kind?
DIANE: Violence.
ISAACS: Violence?
DIANE: I didn't say violence!
ISAACS: What did you say?
DIANE: I said violates! I said violets ... Violets ... They're just flowers.
           I once did floral arranging. Does everything have to be
           about sex?

The story of the dream punctuates the film repeatedly. Only later
in the story do we understand the reasons for this insistence. In the
twenty-fourth scene there's a surprise. Barr is at a symposium. We see
him sitting diligently in the audience listening to a colleague's paper on
psychoanalysis and female sexuality:

> Everyone has heard Freud's rhetorical question: "Women ... what
> do they want?" Elsewhere, Freud refers to the female sex as "the
> dark continent". In his *Interpretation of Dreams* the man who gave
> the world "penis envy" declares that women's libido is essentially
> masochistic. The evidence? Well, it's buried deep in Chapter Six.
> A patient, dreaming about arranging a floral centrepiece has the
> poor taste to mix violets with lilies and carnations. The lilies rep-
> resent purity; the carnations, carnal desire. And of course last, but
> not least, the violets, standing in for a woman's unconscious need
> to be violated. Violently ... wouldn't you know? But I would like to
> paraphrase the good doctor and say that sometimes a violet is just
> a violet. And what of the table on which these flowers were laid?
> Forgive the expression.

Clearly the screenwriter has read *The Interpretation of Dreams* very carefully, including the formidable last hundred pages in which Freud gives
a theoretical summary of his work. The first section of the famous seventh chapter begins with a dream that a woman patient recounts to
Freud after hearing it at a conference. It made such an impression on
her that she dutifully went so far as to "to 're-dream' it, that is, to repeat
some of its elements in a dream of her own" (Freud, 1900, p. 509).

This dream is not only moving, it is also especially significant
because it reverses the pattern of Freud's own dream about his father's
funeral. In that dream a dead child rises up out of his coffin and goes
into the adjoining room where the father, exhausted after the long vigil,

is asleep. As a result he does not realise that a candle has set fire to the sheets and that the flames are already licking the arm of the corpse. *"Father, don't you see I'm burning?"* is the child's heartbreaking reproach (ibid., p. 509).

The position of this dream at the beginning of the seventh chapter of *The Interpretation of Dreams* must give pause for thought. The fact that it is not a dream of Freud's, and not even of the patient who tells it, could reflect a distancing from something that, appropriately enough, scorches. This may be the same mechanism of denial at work that affects the fragment of reality contained in a dream within a dream (see below, Chapter Eight). On the one hand, the interpretation of the dream follows a "realistic" pattern, in other words, a physical stimulus (the glow of the fire) is incorporated into the dream; on the other, it depicts the obvious, all too obvious, desire of the father to bring his son back to life. We should not forget that the theory of infantile seduction was like a terrible accusation that Freud was directing at the generation of the fathers, including his own (Anzieu, 1959).

To return to the movie. We have already realised that Barr is not very knowledgeable about his classics, but this time he gets suspicious and runs off to check the quotation. This is perhaps the most far-fetched scene in the film: an analyst having to go to a library to consult *The Interpretation of Dreams*! It may just have been the place closest to the conference hall, but any unkind viewer might think that Barr does not have a copy of his own.

At a superficial reading it may seem that the dream is Freud's, as explained by the speaker at the conference. When I read it in *The Interpretation of Dreams* and saw that the text of the dream is given in English, at first I thought of a foreign patient, only to realise later that the passage is within quotation marks. Indeed, as stated in the previous paragraph by Freud (1900, p. 373), it is a supplement added in 1914,[1] describing a dream already published two years earlier in *Zentralblatt für Psychoanalyse* by a rather obscure student, one Alfred Robitsek. So the "plagiarism", so to speak, has already been committed and Freud is the culprit!

In the book Freud puts Diane's dream in the tenth paragraph of Section E of Chapter Six, and offers it as a contribution to the question of symbolism in dreams by healthy people. This is his response to the objection raised by Havelock Ellis, namely that dream symbolism is the exclusive product of the mind of neurotics. Freud takes the view that the mechanisms of the dream are identical in healthy and neurotic people. Indeed, since in healthy people censorship and distortion of dreams are less frequent, the symbols are usually also more naive and transparent, as is the case with children.

In order not to fall back into a mechanical or arbitrary reading, following a kind of "book of dreams", initially Freud interprets dreams relying on context and associations—paradoxically, it is as if the dreamer were the only person authorised to interpret his dream—and in no way does he force a symbolic reading. Only later does he make room for symbolism, and in particular sexual symbolism, perhaps the element of his theories that has entered most deeply into popular culture. If we put the various fragments together, this is the dream in full: "I'm in a house where I do not at present live and I feel a sense of happiness. I prepare the centre of a table with flowers for a birthday. They are expensive flowers, which you have to pay for: lilies of the valley, violets, and carnations. I decorate the flowers with green crepe-paper, to hide things that are not clean, not beautiful to look at, a crack, a small gap between the flowers."

Plagiarism

Robitsek's text deserves to be read in its entirety (Freud, 1900, pp. 373–377), for one thing because it brings us face to face with the problem of mistrust or suspicion of the analyst and of the dishonesty of the patient:

> One objection which is frequently brought forward by opponents of psycho-analysis, and which has lately been voiced by Havelock Ellis [...], argues that though dream-symbolism may perhaps occur as a product of the neurotic mind, it is not to be found in normal persons. Now psycho-analytic research finds no fundamental, but only quantitative, distinctions between normal and neurotic life; and indeed the analysis of dreams, in which repressed complexes are operative alike in the healthy and the sick, shows a complete identity both in their mechanisms and in their symbolism. The naive dreams of healthy people actually often contain a much simpler, more perspicuous and more characteristic symbolism than those of neurotics; for in the latter, as a result of the more powerful workings of the censorship and of the consequently more

far-reaching dream-distortion, the symbolism may be obscure and hard to interpret. The dream recorded below will serve to illustrate this fact. It was dreamt by a girl who is not neurotic but is of a somewhat prudish and reserved character. In the course of conversation with her I learnt that she was engaged, but that there were some difficulties in the way of her marriage which were likely to lead to its postponement [a typically Manzonian theme] ... Of her own accord she told me the following dream.

"I arrange the centre of a table with flowers for a birthday." In reply to a question she told me that in the dream she seemed to be in her own home (where she was not at present living) and had "a feeling of happiness".

"Popular" symbolism made it possible for me to translate the dream unaided. It was an expression of her bridal wishes: the table with its floral centre-piece symbolized herself and her genitals; she represented her wishes for the future as fulfilled, for her thoughts were already occupied with the birth of a baby; so her marriage lay a long way behind her.

I pointed out to her that *"the 'centre' of a table"* was an unusual expression (which she admitted), but I could not of course question her further directly on that point. I carefully avoided suggesting the meaning of the symbols to her, and merely asked her what came into her head in connection with the separate parts of the dream. In the course of the analysis her reserve gave place to an evident interest in the interpretation and to an openness made possible by the seriousness of the conversation.

When I asked what flowers they had been, her first reply was: *"expensive flowers; one has to pay for them"*, and then that they had been *"lilies of the valley, violets and pinks or carnations"*. I assumed that the word "lily" appeared in the dream in its popular sense as a symbol of chastity; she confirmed this assumption, for her association to "lily" was *"purity"*. *"Valley"* is a frequent female symbol in dreams; so that the chance combination of the two symbols in the English name of the flower was used in the dream-symbolism to stress the preciousness of her virginity—*"expensive flowers, one has to pay for them"*—and to express her expectation that her husband would know how to appreciate its value. The phrase *"expensive flowers, etc.",* as will be seen, had a different meaning in the case of each of the three flower-symbols.

"*Violets*" was ostensibly quite asexual; but, very boldly, as it seemed to me, I thought I could trace a secret meaning for the word in an unconscious link with the French word "*viol*" ["rape"]. To my surprise the dreamer gave as an association the English word "*violate*". The dream had made use of the great chance similarity between the words "*violet*" and "*violate*"—the difference in their pronunciation lies merely in the different stress upon their final syllables—in order to express "in the language of flowers" the dreamer's thoughts on the violence of defloration (another term that employs flower symbolism) and possibly also a masochistic trait in her character. A pretty instance of the "verbal bridges" [...] crossed by the paths leading to the unconscious. The words "*one has to pay for them*" signified having to pay with her life for being a wife and a mother.

In connection with "*pinks*", which she went on to call "*carnations*", I thought of the connection between that word and "carnal". But the dreamer's association to it was "*colour*". She added that "*carnations*" were the flowers which her *fiancé* gave her frequently and in great numbers. At the end of her remarks she suddenly confessed of her own accord that she had not told the truth: what had occurred to her had not been "*colour*" but "*incarnation*"—the word I had expected. Incidentally "*colour*" itself was not a very remote association, but was determined by the meaning of "*carnation*" (flesh-colour)—was determined, that is, by the same complex. This lack of straightforwardness showed that it was at this point that resistance was greatest, and corresponded to the fact that this was where the symbolism was most clear and that the struggle between libido and its repression was at its most intense in relation to this phallic theme. The dreamer's comment to the effect that her *fiancé* frequently gave her flowers of that kind was an indication not only of the double sense of the word "*carnations*" but also of their phallic meaning in the dream. The gift of flowers, an exciting factor of the dream derived from her current life, was used to express an exchange of sexual gifts: she was making a gift of her virginity and expected a full emotional and sexual life in return for it. At this point, too, the words "*expensive flowers, one has to pay for them*" must have had what was no doubt literally a financial meaning.—Thus the flower symbolism in this dream included virginal femininity, masculinity and an allusion to defloration by violence. It is worth pointing out in this connection that sexual flower symbolism, which, indeed, occurs very commonly in other connections, symbolizes the human organs of sex by blossoms, which are the sexual organs of plants. It may perhaps be true in general that gifts of flowers between lovers have this unconscious meaning.

The birthday for which she was preparing in the dream meant, no doubt, the birth of a baby. She was identifying herself with her *fiancé*, and was representing him as "arranging" her for a birth—that is, as copulating with her. The latent thought may have run: "If I were he, I wouldn't wait—I would deflower my *fiancée* without asking her leave—I would use violence". This was indicated by the word "*violate*", and in this way the sadistic component of the libido found expression.

In a deeper layer of the dream, the phrase "*I arrange ...*" must no doubt have an auto-erotic, that is to say, an infantile, significance.

The dreamer also revealed an awareness, which was only possible to her in a dream, of her physical deficiency: she saw herself like a table, without projections, and on that account laid all the more emphasis on the preciousness of the "*centre*"—on another occasion she used the words, "*a centre-piece of flowers*"—that is to say, on her virginity. The horizontal attribute of a table must also have contributed something to the symbol.

The concentration of the dream should be observed: there was nothing superfluous in it, every word was a symbol.

Later on the dreamer produced an addendum to the dream: "*I decorate the flowers with green crinkled paper.*" She added that it was "*fancy paper*" of the sort used for covering common flowerpots. She went on: "*to hide untidy things, whatever was to be seen, which was not pretty to the eye; there is a gap, a little space in the flowers. The paper looks like velvet or moss*".—To "*decorate*" she gave the association "*decorum*", as I had expected. She said the green colour predominated, and her association to it was "*hope*"—another link with pregnancy.—In this part of the dream the chief factor was not identification with a man; ideas of shame and self-revelation came to the fore. She was making herself beautiful for him [for Dr Robitsek?] and was admitting physical defects which she felt ashamed of and was trying to correct. Her associations "*velvet*" and "*moss*" were a clear indication of a reference to pubic hair.

This dream, then, gave expression to thoughts of which the girl was scarcely aware in her waking life—thoughts concerned with sensual love and its organs. She was being "arranged for a birthday"—that is, she was being copulated with. The fear of being deflowered was finding expression, and perhaps, too, ideas of pleasurable suffering. She admitted her physical deficiencies to herself and overcompensated for them by an over-valuation of her virginity. Her shame put forward as an excuse for the signs of sensuality the fact that its purpose was the production of a baby. Material considerations, too, alien to a lover's mind, found their way to expression. The affect attaching to this simple dream—a feeling of happiness—indicated that powerful emotional complexes had found satisfaction in it.

This is what Robitsek—or rather the pseudo-Freud from the film—has to say for himself.

Dr Robitsek

What kind of analyst is Dr Alfred Robitsek? With the young woman Robitsek carefully avoids referring directly to the meaning of the symbols. He respects her reserve, seeks to arouse her interest, formulates hypotheses to himself and waits for them to receive gradual confirmation. He has a technique and a strategy. He deconstructs the dream into its various component parts and proceeds delicately to a systematic and careful translation of all the symbols contained in the manifest text. Thus, *lilies* stands for purity, *valley* for women, *lily of the valley* for virginity, *violets* for *viol*, in other words, defloration (behind this lies the theory that a masochistic trait is typical of the female gender), *hope* for the hope of a pregnancy, velvet and moss for *crines pubis*, flowers for the male genitals organs, birthday for the birth of a child, *centre-piece of flowers* for virginity, *gap* for vagina, etc.

At last the analyst gets round to formulating the latent dream thoughts: "'If I were he, I wouldn't wait—I would deflower my *fiancée* without asking her leave—I would use violence.' This was indicated by the word '*violate*', and in this way the sadistic component of the libido found expression" (ibid., p. 376).

Readers who know a thing or two may wonder who, apart from the patient, makes the identification with her boyfriend, but for now we'll leave that open. Implicitly what Robitsek prescribes for the girl is patience, seriousness, honesty. In this way, he indirectly draws a picture of the ideological and cultural background of the period, one of whose features is the exchange economy that regulates interrelations between the sexes: virginity in exchange for bourgeois well-being and maternity. Every now and then he takes risks by daring to interpret. Then he shows us a twist: after she has finished speaking, he tells us, all of a sudden the girl spontaneously confesses that she has not told the truth about an important detail, the association between colour and incarnations. Of course, Robitsek interprets her lack of honesty as a symptom of intense resistance, and hence as the temporary outcome of a never resolved conflict between libido and repression.

Robitsek gives an account of the patient's associations, even though, according to Freud, this work is rather negligible. He mentions almost all the essential concepts that make up Freudian vocabulary; "every word was a symbol," he writes. The translation of the unconscious meaning of the symbols allows the latent dream thoughts to surface. In this way the deformation imposed by psychic censorship is averted, resistances are overcome ("her reserve gave place to an evident interest in the interpretation"), and the veil that repression had placed over the expressions of the libido is removed. The Freudian theorem is fulfilled: the dream is the hallucinatory realisation of a repressed wish whose nature is largely sexual and whose origin is childish. During the waking state the counter-cathexis of the ego keeps the unacceptable desire away from consciousness. At night this pressure is lowered in order to protect sleep. Desire can then emerge and express itself in a disguised form. Censorship selects what content to allow to pass through and what to bar. The dream always stands on two legs: one is the present with its latent thoughts and the day's residue, the other is the past of infantile unconscious desire. The need for sleep and rest is based on the psychological necessity to satisfy drive demands. Indeed, dreaming "discharges the *Ucs* excitation, serves it as a safety valve" as Freud points out (ibid., p. 579). There is a striking similarity between Robitsek's conversation with his patient and a detective with a suspect. The fact is that, in order to save himself, Dr Barr is forced at some point to suddenly play the role of detective. But before we go back to the film, let us focus once again on the Freudian model and point out its essential features.

The guiding principle of Freud's interpretation is that the dream is the disguised satisfaction of a repressed infantile wish. Later, in a note added to his autobiographical study (1925), he plays down this formula by specifying that the dream is only an *attempt* at wish fulfilment. This allows him to include in his explanatory scheme even dreams of anguish.[2] Most often dreams take inspiration from something that happened the day before, just as, writes Freud, the ruins of ancient Rome were transformed into new buildings. However, they enact desires from the infantile period. Transferred on to the more or less indifferent material of the so-called day residues, in fact, only the indestructible infantile desire can be the engine of the dream. The dream protects sleep by neutralising potentially disturbing stimuli (somatic, external, internal, psychic) and it does so by partially satisfying them. It is the same mechanism—a certain obscurity/dishonesty as the price to pay for partially legitimising desire—that according to Freud explains the compromise formation of symptoms in neuroses.

Dream-work, the subject of the sixth chapter of *The Interpretation of Dreams*—regarded by Meltzer (1984) as the most extraordinary and advanced chapter in the book—deploys four mechanisms: compression or condensation (*Verdichtung*), displacement (*Verschiebung*), considerations of representability (*Rücksicht auf Darstellbarkeit*), and secondary revision (*sekundäre Bearbeitung*). The first two, as Lacan was to point out, correspond to the most important tropes of language, metaphor and metonymy, which in turn merely express the elementary modes of psychic functioning and the creation of meaning. Secondary revision (basically, editing) is the first self-interpretation of the dream in a search for coherence, order, and intelligibility. It's the "illusionist" of the dream, which is followed by a second self-interpretation when the dream is recalled and recounted (these are, in fact, two different stages).

Freud interprets the dream guided by the associations of the patient—the "mother-liquor" that contains latent dream thoughts (Freud, 1933, p. 12)—and only subsequently does he translate the symbols of the text. He is in fact wary of symbols and typical dreams. He regards the interpretation of the symbol or of a typical content as merely an "auxiliary method". To encourage the patient to associate freely, Freud invites him to close his eyes and rests his hand on his forehead, a technique which he was later to abandon. He asks what events of the day before may have provided inspiration for the dream images. He pays attention to the narrative continuity of several dreams from the same night, focusing also on dream materials within a single session, associations and non-dream materials, and from several consecutive sessions. He uses supplementary dreams to look for the key to stories already told. A fragment of a dream that the patient adds or suddenly remembers during interpretation work indicates that he has overcome a resistance, and this makes it the most significant: "These subsequently added portions regularly turn out to provide the key to the dream's interpretation" (Freud, 1900, p. 155, footnote). The annotation is interesting because it can be taken as a rule for the ever recursive movement of understanding: the interpretation of the dream never reaches a true stopping point.

In trying to break down the process of secondary revision, Freud follows a chronological order. He proceeds from the most superficial level to the most profound, from the present to the past, and from the egosyntonic to the egodystonic. He appraises carefully all the details of the dream, but sometimes starts from those that are sensorially most intense because this clue may indicate the lurking presence of a particularly high degree of condensation. He analyses in minute detail the various segments and avoids giving a global interpretation. He warns against focusing attention on the dream as a whole. If the dream seems confused, Freud asks for it to be repeated and looks more closely at the points in the story where he sees variants or parts left out. There he identifies the weaknesses in the dream's disguise: "But the parts of the dream which he describes in different terms are by that fact revealed to me as the weak spot in the dream's disguise: they serve my purpose just as Hagen's was served by the embroidered mark on Siegfried's cloak" (1900, p. 515). Sometimes in order to circumvent the resistance of the analysand, he has him recount past dreams as if they had been dreamt the night before.

Various elements are relevant when interpreting dreams: the associations, their number and quantity, the location of the dream, and the use the patient makes of it, whether exploratory or defensive. In itself, the dream has a natural propensity to transference (Grinstein, 1983, p. 59). A dream can even supply diagnostically useful information: "There seems to be no reason why any such pathological idea should not be transformed into a dream. A dream may therefore quite simply represent a hysterical phantasy, an obsessional idea, or a delusion—that is, may reveal one or other of these upon interpretation" (Freud, 1922, p. 230).

In Freud's eyes, dreams (in actual fact, the interpretation of dreams; Schneider, 2010) are of scant value in themselves, but they are useful as the instrument that can give an idea of the unconscious life of the dreamer. This is the famous image of the *royal road*. On the one hand, Freud reassesses the dream as an object of scientific investigation, a revolutionary fact to which his name is forever linked; on the other, he fails to rid himself completely of the residues of his original belittling of its value. These are reflections of the two traditional schools of thought about dreams that Freud summarises in the literature review that serves as the introduction to *The Interpretation of Dreams*. The dream is a message from the gods, or an incoherent psychic production, utterly meaningless, pure noise. Then, when Melanie Klein establishes the equivalence between dream and play, and Bion that between dream and thought, paradoxically they perhaps bestow more value on the dream than even Freud had done.

Drawing several times on an expression of Nietzsche's, Freud affirms that dreams embody a "transvaluation of all psychical values" (1900, p. 330, p. 507, p. 516). Dreams transform (*hallucinate*) stimuli and concepts mostly into visual images, and on the basis of associative relationships dramatise them as figures that occupy space and time and follow "the rules of causality" (ibid., p. 36). Two thoughts immediately following one another are bound together by an objective connection, and the same goes for the relationship between most dreams: "absurdity in a dream signifies the presence in the dream-thoughts of *contradiction, ridicule and derision*" (Freud, 1901, p. 662).

As we can see, in order to describe dream work Freud employs a fascinating metaphorical apparatus—again, a further, intriguing effect of "falsification". Not even in scientific discourse are metaphors considered spurious elements; rather they contribute more or less secretly to the organisation of meaning. Originally any literal expression is nothing but a metaphor, that is, a "dream", a visual image. One of the most compelling examples regards latent dream thoughts:

> If doubt attaches to an indistinct element of the dream content, we may, following the hint, recognise in this element a direct offshoot of one of the outlawed dream thoughts. It is here just as it was after a great revolution in one of the republics of antiquity or of the Renaissance. The former noble and powerful ruling families are now banished; all high positions are filled by upstarts; in the

> city itself only the very poor and powerless citizens or the distant
> followers of the vanquished party are tolerated. Even they do not
> enjoy the full rights of citizenship. They are suspiciously watched.
> Instead of the suspicion in the comparison, we have in our case the
> doubt. (Freud, 1900, p. 409)

Another example regards censorship. *"Dreaming is a piece of infantile mental life that has been superseded,"* says Freud (ibid., p. 566). For this reason, if censorship did not intervene, anxiety would develop, but because it is not as strong while one is asleep, one can dream. In the same way as a river in spate—this is the image—blocks the main lines of connection and forces it to take difficult side roads, so censorship only breaks the most superficial chains of associations. He suggests an image: "We may picture, by way of analogy, a mountain region, where some general interruption of traffic (owing to floods, for instance) has blocked the main, major roads, but where communications are still maintained over inconvenient and steep footpaths normally used only by the hunter" (ibid., p. 530).

So the analyst is this hunter who takes the "inconvenient and steep footpaths" of associations that have no purpose, that are secondary and superficial. The recruitment of the dream elements is like "election by *scrutin de liste*" (ibid., p. 284). The dream wish grows up like a mushroom out of its mycelium, in other words from the "intricate network of our world of thought" (ibid., p. 525). The dream itself is "like a firework, which take hours to prepare but goes off in a moment" (ibid., p. 576). For the *"entrepreneur"* of the day's residue, infantile desire is the *"capitalist"* that gives him the means to realise his projects, or for the "American dentist" it is the "legally qualified medical practitioner" who provides him with professional cover (ibid., pp. 561–563).

Let us now return to Phil Joanou's film. In *The Interpretation of Dreams* the talk is often of flowers. The insertion of Robitsek's dream in his book says what Freud keeps silent about or, rather, what he only alludes to when he comments on his famous dream about the "botanical monograph". This is in fact a remarkable dream, because it condenses an incredible number of autobiographical elements. One amazing sentence stands out: "Cyclamens, I reflected, were my wife's *favourite flowers* and I reproached myself for so rarely remembering to *bring* her *flowers*, which was what she liked" (ibid., p. 169). One wonders whether this might not be one of the clues that suggests to Meltzer (1978) that at the time, somewhat like Gere-Barr in the film, Freud was not satisfied with his married life. This at least is the point Anzieu makes in his comment on the dream in his book on the subject of Freud's self-analysis. I quote his observation because it is a further reverberation emanating from Robitsek's dream of flowers. Anzieu (1959, p. 281) writes:

> Freud makes three interpretations of the dream. One of them is a mere outline. Another is fully elaborated. The third is deliberately concealed by him from the reader, but can easily be pieced together [...] The first interpretation is offered by Freud at the beginning of his analysis of the dream. Cyclamens were Martha's favourite flowers, whereas Sigmund adored artichokes, which she often cooked for him. "I reproached myself for so rarely remembering to *bring* her *flowers*, which was what she liked." Freud, then, identified with his former patient's husband. One thinks immediately of the symbolic meaning of the expression "to offer one's wife flowers": this would suggest that Freud was failing to give Martha tokens of his virility. True, Freud felt he was growing old—and later said so in a letter to Fliess—but at the same time he had a feeling of "satisfaction". Once again, a dream was enabling him to justify himself in Martha's eyes, by placing her on the same level as young women friends or patients in "the bloom of life", the prototype of such women being of course Irma. We may therefore attribute the following meaning to the dream: I certainly feel less sexual desire for Martha; but I have proved myself capable of writing important monographs (on cocaine, on hysteria, and, in the near future, on dreams, in other words on sexuality); in any case, with six children, I have proved myself.

Within the perspective of our discussion on dreams in Freud, this is no insignificant detail. A complex game of interlocking stories is created, which I shall now attempt to schematise. A girl satisfies her sexual desire (experienced as guilty and hence repressed) for her boyfriend by transforming reality into a dream (a psychic production already steeped in fiction, but not without meaning: Freud emphasises "how sensible a dream can be even when it appears to be absurd"; 1900, p. 591). When recounting the dream to Robitsek, a student of Freud's, she confesses to him that she has been dishonest. Robitsek (the analyst as a character in the account he has written of the meeting) interprets the dream and publishes it in one of his own works. Freud (the "plagiarist") puts it into his most important book (it becomes a "false" dream of Freud's, but one which can also been seen as a supplement [*Nachtrag*] to the "mendacious" (i.e., censored) dream of the "Botanical Monograph"). Diane-Uma recounts a fragment of the dream taken from Freud in a session with Dr Barr within the framework of a false analysis and inside the director's dream-film.

But things don't stop here. *Final Analysis* (with the subtitle *The Making and Unmaking of a Psychoanalyst*) is also the title of a book by Jeffrey Moussaieff Masson published in 1990—two years before Joanou's film came out. Earlier Masson had also published *Assault on Truth: Freud's Suppression of the Seduction Theory* (1984), which has as its central theme Freud's "honesty" about the frequency of the real trauma of incest in neurotics. In his book, Masson, an analyst from Toronto, editor of the important Freud-Fliess correspondence (1985), who for a time was close to Kurt Eissler and Anna Freud and was in charge of the Freud archives in London, accused Freud of having deliberately invalidated the theory of seduction as the explanation of the traumatic etiology of neurosis in order to conciliate his critics. Masson argued that psychoanalysis as a whole is thus based on a falsification. Joanou's film can be seen in the broader context of this controversy. The hall of mirrors is dizzying. But what is most interesting is the way dreams and their interpretation pose the problem of the dishonesty or falsity of representation itself and the multiplicity of points of view—a world that once more becomes "infinite".

Exercises in style

Now, having looked at the dream in the original text, it will be useful to change our angle of vision and to examine some other interpretive perspectives. I shall focus on these at greater length in the coming chapters. We might imagine a series of exercises: how would a Kleinian read the dream? What about an interpersonalist or a self-psychologist? How would Barr interpret it? What kind of analyst is he? What is he looking for in the dream? Traces of historical reality, given that he asks for information about the patient's sister, or something else? What if the "dream" were the story of the film in its entirety? What would we say then? How would we look at it from a field perspective?

For a Kleinian, the dream and the girl's associations may be seen as actors in a drama that is performed on the virtual stage of the patient's inner world, with the analyst as a spectator; or as figures that appear in a child's drawing or play. The actors give body and voice to characters from scripts of unconscious fantasies.

A Kleinian would read the dream as Freud does (who looks more to the past), taking into account both the associative context and the symbols, indeed accentuating this latter aspect. He or she would relate it to the vicissitudes of the primary relationship with the mother. If, for Freud, the central myth of psychoanalysis is the story of Oedipus, for Klein it becomes that of Orestes, the matricide.

Dream life takes place without interruption and is manifested in dreams, in waking imagination, and, in children, in play. As we can see, we are on the threshold of Bion's concept of waking dream thought. Psychic reality becomes a concrete world, a place where meaning is generated, which then pervades life in the material world. Neurotics are no longer people who suffer from memories, but people who live in the past, as this past is represented in the inner world (Meltzer, 1984). The Kleinian model maps a complex geography of mental space that corresponds to the world-body of the mother, or rather, at various times, to a particular place in it (as if there were various possible worlds): "The state of mind engendered in a part of the personality inhabiting each of these different compartments," explains Meltzer, "constitutes living in very different worlds" (ibid., p. 40).

In the Kleinian model, transference is immediate, but it is still seen as a projection of the patient's phantasies on to the white screen of the analyst. Although the concept of projective identification is poised to overcome it, the Kleinian model is essentially a unipersonal psychology. In the foreground is the theatre of the mind, but it is still a private theatre. The analyst is present at a Shakespearean drama between characters and parties engaged in a bloody struggle for power. The final outcome of the conflict decides the nature of the regime that will be established in the mind: totalitarian (paranoid-schizoid) or democratic (depressive).

From a field perspective, the account of Robitsek's session, for example at an imaginary supervision, would be regarded as a dream by the analyst about himself with his patient. From the very beginning there are hints of the presence of opponents. There is an objection to refute, attributed to Havelock Ellis, but that also might suggest some intimate resistance by the analyst to differentiating between the sane and the neurotic, as one might gather from the insistence on the normality of the woman. She is a little inhibited; she does not feel at home in this setting, with this therapist. There is an obstacle to the marriage or to the coupling or the attunement of minds that might make the meeting creative. This is the general context of the session. The patient then recounts a dream. She is preparing the table, decorating it for a festive gathering, a birthday, an anniversary (the session?). These are the rightful desires of a bride, but the analyst does not relate them to the treatment. Transference is still understood only as the fire at the transference theatre of love.

Robitsek appears to be a capable analyst and knows how to translate the unconscious, but he pays little attention to his own. He focuses on the associative work of the patient, but gives the impression of knowing all the answers from the outset. He translates, but does not seem to be aware that translation is impossible or is, at most, negotiation. He is far from being without memory, will, and desire—the state recommended by Bion. He tends to saturate meaning. He organises what he says to prove a point. He must overcome the resistance of the "patient", cunningly make her give in. He does not think that she is "dreaming" the session, or that she is posing the question of the sincerity or insincerity of the analyst's feelings (and hers towards him). This is the bottleneck through which we pass in each analysis and which essentially reproduces the aesthetic conflict (Civitarese, 2010a, 2011a; Meltzer, 1981). He does not see *viol* as also being an allusion to the "violence" of interpretation. And indeed in the end Robitsek manages to extort a confession from her.

The clarification of the symbolic significance of the various elements of the dream can be seen as a defence of symbolisation in the immediate situation, as a refusal to participate in the patient's dream. The analyst declines to play the role of her shy or all too respectable boyfriend, and cannot imagine that, if nothing else, the girl is at the very least asking him to be more active. He does not seem aware of her sexual fantasies, or possibly the lack thereof. It may be that he finds her dull, boring, not very seductive; perhaps, in order to distance himself from his desire, he avoids getting involved. He worries about decorum and scientific seriousness. He does not assume that the real problem of the person he has in front of him is her dull life, the absence of stimuli, in short, her *mal di vivere*—and that he is transmitting it to her. At the end of the text of the session, however, we find the word *hope*: there seems to be some hope for a more intimate relationship.

As a second set of exercises, we might ask: what kind of analyst is Gere-Barr? Compared to Robitsek's account, the context in which the dream is told has completely changed. In the film, the dream is the detail that enables the analyst to unmask the plot against him, and this leads to a situation, one of many, in which it no longer makes sense to maintain the setting. One might think that Uma-Diane is envious of her sister's sensuality and jealous of her relationship with her analyst and her relationship with her father; that, in turn, she has a genuine transference with the analyst and uses a dream taken from Freud, as happens every time a patient speaks of psychoanalysis, to intrigue him and seduce him; that he has given either a very naive or a very astute interpretation of the dream read in Freud's book, etc.

The interpretation Dr Barr offers her is that she was using the dream to save him. The fact that she recounts a dream lifted from *The Interpretation of Dreams* is of some significance, but equally significant is the content of the dream. Diane unconsciously chose that particular dream, and not another. In the course of the film she tells the dream several times. Why? Is it a real choice or does she have no alternative? In any case, professional ethics aside, the analyst-Gere is fairly in line with classical Freud. He endeavours to remove the veil of repression and to give the patient back her memory. He works to reconstruct the past, he plays the part of a police inspector, and he deploys the archaeological-circumstantial paradigm (Ferro et al., 2011). The analysis has the air of a thriller, as is often the case with dream analysis in Freud and also in Sharpe (1937). And at the end of the film Barr the hero is saved by a real detective (possibly, a function of the mind?).

A Kleinian analyst would see all the characters in the film as actors on the dream-stage playing the parts of the objects within the mind of the director-dreamer. Thus, for example, the sister Heather would be a split-off aspect of Diane, and likewise the sadistic husband. The various characters would divide into helpers and opponents. Since the overall climate of the dream is one of persecution, one might think that some destructive parts of the self are trying to lead the good objects astray.

If he had been attentive to the dynamics of field, Barr would not have met Heather and would not have got into trouble. As someone with Kleinian genes in his DNA, he too would have thought of the sister as a split-off aspect of Diane, but also as a possible index of the functioning of the analytic field. He would have asked in what way the King Kong-husband had entered the scene. He would have been less wary and suspicious about her seductiveness, and might have thought of it as a request for more emotional intimacy. The discovery of the false dream would have opened the way to several more interpretive possibilities. After all, somehow or other, Barr and Diane manage to "eliminate" the gangster-King Kong and the evil sister, who is the one who was raped by her father and was also a patricide. Could this mean that the caterpillar has become a butterfly?

But there are still more vertices (fictions) to be considered. For example, perhaps it had really been dreamt or the entire film had been narrated. Something like: "Last night I went to the cinema. I saw a film called *Final Analysis*. Heather, a beautiful and unscrupulous woman, decides to kill her psychopathic gangster husband in order to cash in on his life insurance. To give herself her an alibi, she seduces the analyst who is treating her younger sister, Diane, and tricks him into thinking that she suffers from pathological intoxication. But something goes wrong. The sister falls in love with the analyst and gives herself away. During analysis on several occasions she tells him a recurring dream, but it is not hers, because she has stolen it from Freud. In the end Heather dies, the treatment is suspended, Diane gets away with it and takes up Heather's perverse game with someone else."

I am not going to dwell any longer on the various paths interpretation can take, except to mention that, albeit indirectly, here we are dealing with dreams about therapy and analysis, in other words, with transference dreams (Civitarese, 2006).

The sleep of waking

In using this film—what the caustic Desson Howe might call a home-video *Rashomon*—to introduce the theory of dreams in Freud, my idea was to look at the basic question of the status of psychic reality and the value of symbolisation, that is to say, the act of giving form to the real, which is the task of dream work. We started with the theme of the falsification of the dream—plagiarism (of course, a false plagiarism), insincerity, the deformation imposed by censorship, the pseudo-Freud (Robitsek), but also the dreams falsely reported (or understandably censored) in Freud's *Interpretation of Dreams*, the falsifications of the English-German-Italian translation (as we say in Italian: *traduttore-traditore*—translator-traitor), and those intrinsic to the game of actor-character (it is a commonplace, for example, to point out that many actors, once they reach a certain point in their career, become incapable of doing anything other than acting themselves, regardless of the part they have been asked to play). Now we have reached the meaning of column two in Bion's grid and waking dream thought (and I shall return to this point later). Maybe we have even found out who is the real victim of *Final Analysis*—the reality of common sense—and who is the real culprit: dreams themselves, of course, or rather Freud, the person who revealed their secret.

Meaning always arises out of a context. Reality can only be seen in the dimension of fiction. For Nietzsche, truth starts only from error. Truth is perspective, it is always "relatively false": "If one wants to pull out of the world of prospects, one would perish. Even a *neutralization* of the great illusions already incorporated destroys humanity. We need to approve and accept many things that are false and evil" (1975, p. 264). The falsification of dreams coincides with representation. It is no longer the effect of psychic censorship, but *seeing as*, the *necessary* error that allows you to crystallise an image, illusion as "the one true reality of things" (p. 341).

People do not monitor precisely and comprehensively the context in which they utter their statements, because it is largely unconscious. It is not possible—either when you think you are telling the truth or when you lie intentionally. Any utterance is a *Limited Inc.*, to pick up the play on words contained in the title of one of Derrida's most intriguing books (1988), where he appropriates precisely this concept. The falsification of reality, or rather, of the real, is not the exception but the rule. Precisely when she's lying, Diane-Uma might be telling the truth about her character and her neuroses, about the plot of the film, and also about herself as a woman and an actress (in the autumn of 2007 she appeared in a women's magazine together with her psychotherapist, who also happens to be therapist to many Hollywood stars). As Freud says when talking about Dora: "He that has eyes to see and ears to hear may convince himself that no mortal can keep a secret. If his lips are silent, he chatters with his finger-tips" (1905, pp. 77–78).

Perhaps only psychoanalysis can inhabit this place where the truth produces a sense of vertigo—remember that *Final Analysis*, in defiance of the moratorium requested by one critic, was meant as a homage to

Vertigo—without sacrificing rationality. Joanou's film does nothing other than go through the Freudian drama of the abandonment of the seduction theory and the discovery of the primal fantasies, which is indeed the discovery of each analysis.

Together with his "double", Nietzsche, and, like Oedipus, Freud is both the killer of our naive conception of reality and the detective who turns out to be guilty. How? Through a dream. It could not be otherwise. In this case the dream of a patient in exile from Russia whom he calls the Wolf Man, perhaps the most famous dream in the history of psychoanalysis. In the case of the Wolf Man, performatively Freud goes through the transition from the traumatic theory of neuroses to the more complex psychic temporality and causality established by *Nachträglichkeit*, which is the point to which the discovery of psychic reality and the radical taking into account of subjectivity leads. Murdered reality is not the real, which is something quite different, but the hallucinated reality of *The Matrix* (1999) or *The Island* (2005).

This is the same discovery that Lacan sees in the ever-shifting game of the three registers: the Real, the Imaginary, and the Symbolic. It fully reveals the hallucinatory function of the night dream and waking dream as custodians of sleep, that is, acting as a screens against the trauma of the real.[3] The images of the mind have a vital "useful *irreality* function which keeps the human psyche on the fringe of all the *brutality* of a hostile and foreign non-self" (Bachelard, 1960, p. 20). The real avoids being traumatic only if it filters through stimuli that can be processed and transformed, if it can be assimilated or "digested", or if it becomes "personal" (Grotstein, 2007). Similarly, endogenous or external stimuli are integrated into the dream without waking up the dreamer; they are transformed into images to protect sleep. Dreams are indeed the custodian of sleep, but above all of waking sleep or consciousness and the illusion or the effect of reality that pervades it.[4] Now, the identity of the subject is constructed through the continuous process of defining the borders, margins, and boundaries between psychic reality and material reality, between dream and wakefulness. Becoming a person also implies acquiring the ability to move across these borders and to live quite comfortably and at the same time in the various possible worlds in which we live. This is the prerequisite for conceiving that others have minds and for identifying with them.

For some, the critique of an absolute or metaphysical conception of reality leads to a kind of neo-obscurantism where all values are pitifully relative. We forget that while Freud undermines the notion of the subject, deemed no longer master in its own house, he also radically heightens the sense of ethical responsibility. It is not surprising, then, that *The Interpretation of Dreams* ends with the section entitled "Reality and psychic reality". Hence the immediate link is precisely with the Freud we find in the "Wolf Man", who, unable to come to terms with the documentary value of the dream, utters his famous *non liquet* and formulates the concept of *Nachträglichkeit* and of "primal fantasies"; and with Klein, who dissolves reality completely in the innatism of the death instinct and the dramatic mythology of the primitive world of internal objects.

More than Nietzsche, to whom everything seemed "appearance and will-o'-the-wisp and a dance of spirits and nothing more" (1991, p. 116), nothing more than a dream in a dream, in this paper Freud launches a corrosive attack—definitive, "final"—on the naive concept of reality and its correlative, the truth. Indeed, the subversive force of the Freudian critique, by which I mean the inherent strength and effective impact it has had on the way mankind thinks of itself, is without equal in any philosophical theory. On the one hand, philosophy always tends towards re-composition, towards system, synthesis, totality; on the other, however, it fatally mistakes the abstractions of thought for real life. But there is no absolute perspective on reality. The truth cannot be independent of the frame it fits into, not even the emotional frame.[5] As Grotstein (2007) puts it beautifully in his book on Bion, knowing reality means dreaming it.

The Interpretation of Dreams stops at the edge of this abyss.

Notes

1. *The Interpretation of Dreams* was published on 4 November 1899, but the publisher Deuticke (Leipzig) gives 1900 as the year of publication.
2. For Garma, on the other hand, more than the inclination to fulfil desires, the most important factor in the genesis of a dream is a traumatic situation, however "miniature" (1966, p. 162). All too often, dreams are unpleasant in nature.
3. See Freud (1920, p. 32, my italics): "We may assume, rather, that dreams are here helping to carry out another task, which must be accomplished before the dominance of the pleasure principle can even begin. These dreams are endeavouring to master the stimulus retrospectively, by developing the anxiety whose omission was the cause of the traumatic neurosis. *They thus afford us a view of a function of the mental apparatus* which, though it does not contradict the pleasure principle, is

nevertheless independent of it, and seems to be *more primitive than the purpose of gaining pleasure and avoiding unpleasure* […] This would seem to be the place, then, at which to admit for the first time *an exception to the proposition that dreams are fulfilments of wishes.*" See also Amigoni (Amigoni & Pietrantonio, 2004, p. 179): "If a certain permeability, regulated by censorship, between Inc, Pre and C has been one of the main features that contradistinguish mental health, it then becomes necessary to extend the powers of the dream: from guardian of sleep […] to guardian of the proper functioning of the psychic apparatus, a sort of antidote to psychosis."

4. According to the model described by Freud, the device of censorship could be reformulated in Bionian terms as the mechanism of container/contained. A repressed contained is a content for which there is no containment capacity—either at the level of formation of alpha elements or as dream-thoughts—and which therefore must be eliminated, either through action, abstraction, or symptom.

5. See Bion (1965, p. 73): "Meaning is a function of self-love, self-hate or self-knowledge. It is not logically, but psychologically necessary". And further (p. 77): "something seems real only when there are feelings about it."

CHAPTER THREE

The Cell and the cruel/painful world of Carl Stargher

The Cell

The Cell (Singh, 2000) is shot through with extraordinary dream images. Made after *The Silence of the Lambs* (Jonathan Demme, 1991), but considerably inferior, and also after *The Matrix* (Lana & Andy Wachowski, 1999), *The Cell* came out in 2000—and it also comes across as a remake of *Dreamscape* (Joseph Ruben, 1986)—setting new standards in its visual rendering of dream scenarios. It revisits the triangle (id, ego, superego?) made up of serial killer ("And believe me, the mind of this guy is not exactly a friendly place", William Arnold, *Seattle Post-Intelligencer*, 18 December 2000), (child) psychotherapist, in this case Jennifer Lopez, "who is so beautiful she would send most men into therapy, not out of it" (Stephen Hunter, *Washington Post*, 18 August 2000) and detective (Peter Novak-Vince Vaughn).

The plot. A criminal, Carl Stargher (played by Vincent D'Onofrio), abducts young women and holds them captive in a Plexiglas cell, a kind of automated torture chamber. Before drowning them with studied slowness, he turns them into dolls and rapes them according to a perverse ritual.

37

When caught by the police, the serial killer, who suffers from a rare form of schizophrenia, goes into an irreversible coma. His latest victim, however, is still being held prisoner, and no one knows where. In order to obtain this information, an FBI agent suggests that Dr Catherine Deane (Jennifer Lopez) penetrate the unconscious of the killer. Although still at the experimental stage, the futuristic technology of "neuro-synaptic transfer" now makes this possible.

Prior to this film, there had arguably never been such an impressive depiction of the virtual landscapes of psychic reality. These owe much to Dalí, but critics have also pointed to the influence of many other artists: from Bacon to Buñuel; from the photography of Matt Mahurin to Madonna; from video games to the graphic art of Bill Sienkiewicz; from the glossy world of perfume advertising—the director had a background in music videos and advertising—to post-human art; from the nightmares of cyberspace to REM videos; from Eiko Ishioka to Helmut Newton; and so on.

Andrew O'Hehir (*Salon.com*, 18 August 2000) feels that Lopez perhaps puts on her "Miss Nevada look" a little too often. "Several times in the new sci-fi thriller *The Cell*," notes Bob Graham in the *San Francisco Chronicle* (18 December 2000), "you expect Jennifer Lopez, extravagantly costumed and posturing amid surrealistic sand dunes, to turn to the camera with a bottle of perfume in her hand and whisper, 'Calvin'".[1] Perhaps the film fails to arouse true emotions and it also lacks continuity. However, it sticks in the memory, and not only because of its fascinating leading actress ("What boy doesn't want Jennifer Lopez in his dreams?" asks Elvis Mitchell, *The New York Times*, 18 December 2000).

There are several remarkable things about *The Cell* that justify mentioning it here in a chapter on the development of the Kleinian theory of dreams, but notable among them is the fact that the film effectively portrays the concrete nature of the inner world and the characters that inhabit it. To get an idea of what becomes of the dream in the Kleinian model, we need to become familiar with this world.

The concreteness of the inner world

"Concrete" is the adjective that recurs more than any other and almost obsessively in the writings of Kleinians when they talk about the inner world and inner objects. The dictionary tells us that concrete stands in opposition to "abstract" and means dense, compact, solid, material, real. The word comes from the past participle of the Latin verb *concrescere*, meaning to clot, to condense, to harden. The suggestion is that internal objects are concrete because they are formed by aggluti- nations, conglomerates, incrustations, or sedimentations of early life experiences. There is the idea of autonomous agents felt as having their own reality which actively exist as characters in the internal world[2] or quasi-foreign bodies split off from the ego, not identified with it (although, in fact, the question remains ambiguous, because from another point of view this is how they must be). We might think of them as the place of projection and collection of bundles of bodily sensations so intense as to form stable entities of the mind and to be the expres- sion of a range of relationships with objects. Or as accumulations of β elements, proto-sensoriality and proto-emotions which the infant, not having an α function, is physiologically too immature to process. There are those who, like Grotstein[3] (2007), believe this function is present at birth in a rudimentary state, in the form of stimuli that have been unable to find a capacity for digestion, elaboration, and transformation. Or again, they can be seen as "experiences" waiting to be symbolised as psychic retreats, psychotic parts of the mind, agglutinated nuclei (Bleger, 1967). Each definition is convincing on one level and unsatis- factory on another. In the end, as Hinshelwood himself admits, internal objects remain somewhat mysterious.

In order to form a less abstract idea, one may think of the dis- eased organ of the hypochondriac or psychosomatic patient, which is experienced both as a part of one's body and as a foreign body, a "symptom/solution" that the subject adopts unconsciously by going back along the road that leads from the concrete to the symbolic. In traditional psychology, the term "object" stands in opposition to the term "subject"; it is "in correlation with the perceiving and knowing subject: an object is whatever presents itself with fixed and permanent qualities" (Laplanche & Pontalis, 1967, p. 273). It is a prototype of the superego described by Freud, the internalisation of parental figures.

Traces of the presence of these objects are to be found in common idioms, such as having a lump in one's throat, butterflies in one's stomach, and the like—every time, that is, we use bodily metaphors to describe emotions.

So it is that internal objects are equivalent to unconscious "inter- pretations" of bodily sensations (Hinshelwood, 1989). For example, the feeling of hunger is interpreted as the presence in the stomach of a physical object that provokes hunger and which intentionally attacks and wounds the person from inside; essentially this is the earliest knowledge that, by means of a transfer, the infant has of the object. Later, when one makes more adequate representations of external and internal reality, this concrete quality of internal objects fades, but it never disappears completely. Archaic split objects are always active in one way or another. They originate from the level of experience described by Ogden (1989) as the autistic-contiguous position. While Ogden's concept refers to an even more elementary level, the Kleinian theory of internal objects, on the other hand, implies a dramatic narrative from the very beginning of life. Hinshelwood (1989) makes this point very clear. According to him, internal objects and representations coexist in the mental life of individuals. He maintains, then, that probably there is no representation without a corresponding internal object, and no manipulation of mental representations without a corresponding unconscious fantasy of a relationship that involves the internal objects.

This would amount to saying that there is no mental image that is not the transformation of proto-emotions or proto-sensations, no narration that concerns it because it is related to others, which is not implied in an unconscious fantasy. Elementary sensations immediately enter into phantasy scenarios scenarios in which they are "read" as if they had been produced by internal objects engaged in some sort of action and bond. To put it another way, it is like not being able to go on stage (to create a pure, neutral image of a thing) unless there are actors (internal objects), in other words people already possessors' of the specific moral and physical characteristic necessary for the roles set down in the script. One may think, that is, of internal objects as ideo-affective nuclei which are relatively stable and "inter-dependent" and which influence the processes of conscious and unconscious representation.

Even in adults, every sensation, thought, and feeling continues to have its matrix in unconscious fantasies in which the autonomous internal objects, more or less stable or unchanging and bearers of (proto-) affective loads, interact with each other like actors on the stage of the unconscious. The rudimentary grid of meanings that they set up continues to be determined directly by the materiality of the body. The activity of symbolisation originates in the body and its parts as an attempt by the infant "to rediscover in every object his own organs and their functioning" (Klein, 1930, p. 237). This is primitive or elementary transference, the metonymic substitution of the self for the whole. The symbols come from the child's pre-representational search for knowledge, (which then becomes the desire), leading in turn to the known becoming similar to the unknown, what in Hegel is described as negation-that-preserves or preservation-that-destroys (*Aufhebung*).

At the beginning of life the known—in other words, that which will become the unrepressed unconscious due to the physiological immaturity of the neuro-anatomic systems of memory—can only come from the immediacy of the sensations of the body; a body that differentiates gradually from a state of fusion or syncretic intercorporeality with the mother in a process of primary repression that Kristeva (1980) sums up under the term abjection.

Klein's conception anticipates elements of Merleau-Ponty's phenomenology of perception (1945) and Lakoff and Johnson's major contribution to the study of metaphor (1980). The transference of internal objects or their nature on to other objects, which is what happens in play, marks the start of the activity of replacement we call dreaming and thinking, the beginning of the game of rhetorical figures that correspond to the basic cognitive structures. The characteristic feature of transference is the tendency to fragment and inform several objects.

As in Freud, the object is characterised as the most variable drive element. According to Laplanche and Pontalis (1967, p. 275): "Between these objects symbolic equivalents are established, which Freud brought to light in his article 'On Transformations of Instinct, as Exemplified in Anal Erotism' [...] as a result of such substitutions the life of the instincts passes through a sequence of metamorphoses". In this article, Freud goes back to the origins of the series child = penis = faeces = money = gift: "concordance" or the "organic analogy" gives rise to "unconscious identity" (1915, p. 133). Relations of mutual substitutability, which for consciousness become first symbolic equivalences and then symbols, are set up on the unconscious level between objects that stimulate the body interface. In essence, metaphor comes from the spatial proximity, or contiguity, or the metonymic bond. At birth the infant gets its first information about the object from its own tears (Freud, 1950).

In the section of *The Interpretation of Dreams* devoted to the somatic sources of dream, Freud mentions Scherner and his thesis that the dream work "seeks to give a *symbolic* representation of the nature of the organ from which the stimulus arises and of the nature of the stimulus itself" (1900, p. 225). Although Scherner arrives at schematic interpretations starting from this idea, as if taken from a kind of book of dreams, nevertheless, according to Freud, what Scherner says is not entirely meaningless, and there is a "a kernel of truth" (ibid., p. 227). Scherner's insight is even more compelling in the light of Klein's theories: the dream of the organ or of its function refers to a kind of zero degree of psychic activity, and to the concept, which Klein attributes to Ferenczi, of identification as a psychological process that is the precursor of symbolisation.

For Klein, the dream is the film that chronicles the life of internal objects. But in children the dream is called play. The technique of play that she introduced creates a weld between symbolism and dream. Playing is like daydreaming and at the same time like externalising fantasies on to adequate substitutes, the more or less elaborate storylines that preserve the memory of the child's first vicissitudes with the object. Playing is the way children train to form symbols.

Klein's obsession with the formation of symbols and with the way in which bodily sensations generate internal objects will later become Bion's "ontological epistemology" (Grotstein, 2007), a new psychoanalytic theory of thinking. With Bion, theoretical interest shifts to thinking understood as an activity that binds the emotions that arise from attrition with the real according to the model of the container/contained ($\male$ $\female$). If not connected, emotions can become killer contents, that is, contents that threaten to shatter the container (Ferro, 2002; Mazzacane, 2007). This is what happens, for example, when a person stutters. Bion writes: "The words that should have represented the meaning the man wanted to express were fragmented by the emotional forces to which he wished to give only verbal expression. The verbal formulation could not 'contain' his emotions, which broke through and dispersed it as enemy forces might break through the forces that strove to contain them" (1970, p. 94).

For Klein, then, the inner world has a concreteness fully equivalent to that of the outside world. It is a space populated by natives (different ways and stages of relating to the object, especially understood as part objects; that is, resulting from the sedimentation of interaction with the body parts of the parents) who constantly yearn to be projected outwards. In a child's play, for example, they are the ones that imprint their nature on a given character. Similarly, internal objects appear in a distorted way in dream images. In this drive to assimilate the world by transforming it into terms of one's own bodily self lies the origin of every transference and every activity of symbolisation. This is the reason the Kleinian school more than any other puts such great emphasis on the role of transference and the importance of interpreting it promptly. Melanie Klein's motto is: "First interpret the transference" (King & Steiner, 1991, p. 635).

There is therefore a continual interaction between perception and phantasy, between the conscious and the unconscious. As in the Möbius strip, there is constant slippage from the outside world to inner reality and then back again to material reality. The theory of internal objects changes the interpretive work with dreams. These are seen as an expression of transference in the immediacy of experience. In essence, however, this is still transference in the traditional understanding of the term. Melanie Klein introduces a social model of the constitution of the inner world, but by putting so much emphasis on the nativism of unconscious fantasies, she ends up emptying it of all historicity. For this reason her theory of the mind and the dream was defined as theological. As we know, angels and demons pre-date the subject.

For Freud, the mind develops thanks to the instinctual drive; for Klein it develops from the relationship with the object, which at birth is the infant's relationship with the breast. The father, the mother, the primal scene of the Freudian theory of the Oedipus complex and the parents' bedroom become, respectively, the breast, the penis, the combined parental figure,[4] and the mother's body. To defend himself from anguish, the child projects love and hate on to the breast. If the Oedipus complex, object relations, and the mental operations of splitting and projection are as early as Kleinian theory postulates, it follows that the transference is universal, ubiquitous, immediate, and always imbued with traces of relations with part objects. The classical Kleinian technique is therefore characterised by profound early interpretations that are directed especially at the negative transference. This approach also reflects Klein's adhesion to Freud's notion of the death instinct, reformulated however as primary envy.

In the session, the analyst attacks an inadequate (negative) transference with maddening systematicity, but this begins to take another turn. It is increasingly seen as the mechanism—in fact, it subsumes several others—in which the meanings that are produced continually in the inner theatre of the mind are passed to the outside. Making transferences, "transferring", becomes a bit like digesting. For the analyst, it is not so much a matter of highlighting and resolving the patient's mistakes in perceiving reality as making him discover the importance of internal reality in generating meaning. From being the repetition of something that has remained as a foreign body in the mind, the transference becomes an ever active process of constructing the outside world that emanates from scripts performed in the inner world. Neurotics do not suffer from memories; rather they live in the past (Meltzer, 1984).

To repeat: the dream (and play) puts us in touch with these processes and it becomes symbol-poiesis. Not only that; it appears as a continuous activity of the mind. Internal objects never sleep. One can see how, unlike Freud's diachronic perspective on the dream, Klein has a supremely structural and synchronic vision of it. We can see the outline of the premises for the transition from Freud's theory of dreams, passing through the elaboration of the theory of unconscious fantasy, and up to Bion's concept of the α function of waking dream thought and the unconscious as a psychoanalytic function of the personality. Thanks also to the concept of projective identification, we begin to move from one-person psychology to intersubjective psychology.

Etchegoyen (1986, p. 212) points to another important corollary of Klein's theory of transference: "This is why Klein reaches the conclusion that the transference should be understood not only as comprising direct references to the analyst in the material of the analysand, since the early transference, in that it sinks its roots into the deepest strata of the mind, leads to an appreciation of a much broader and more comprehensive phenomenon." If the world always takes its colours from the palette of unconscious fantasies, because transference is considered active, there is no need to wait for the patient's direct allusions to the analyst. In addition, what is transferred is not an element isolated from the internal world, but its totality.

The continual dream of the mind

At any given moment the mind has at its disposal a company of actors, all of them derivatives of the sensations that resulted from the fragmented experience of the infant in the interaction between parts of itself with parts of the object that are at first blurred but then gradually become more distinct. Internal objects can therefore also be regarded as possessing a procedural type of knowledge. Some are better suited to playing the good parts, others the bad parts, for example, the roles of protective or persecutory internal objects. They then find themselves making films that are designed to contain or to make sense of the emotions-sensations-β-elements activated by internal or external stimuli, mental or physical. However, as in the play based on Karl Kraus' *The Last Days of Mankind* (which was put on some years ago by Luca Ronconi at Turin's Lingotto), in the inner world many plays are staged simultaneously. In each scene what is represented is ultimately the world of fairy tales, with its extreme and pervasive sadism, a world inhabited by ogres, fairies, witches—a theatre of all kinds of cruelty. Here is an example taken from Klein's account of the treatment of Trude, a little girl aged four years and a quarter who has suffered from bouts of *pavor nocturnus* since the age of two:

> she came out of the particular corner which she called her room, stole up to me and made all sorts of threats. She would stab me in the throat, throw me into the courtyard, burn me up, or give me to the policeman. She tried to tie my hands and feet, she lifted the sofa-cover, and said she was making *"po-kacki-kucki"* [*Popo* = buttocks. *Kacki* = faeces. *Kucki, Kucken* = look].
>
> It turned out she was looking into her mother's "popo" for the kackis, which to her represented children. Another time she wanted to hit me on the stomach and declared she was taking out the "a-a"s (faeces) and making me poor [...] At that time she had already wished to rob her mother, who was pregnant, of her children, to kill her and take her place in coitus with the father. These tendencies to hate and aggression were the cause of her fixation to her mother (which at the age of two years was becoming particularly strong), as well as of feelings of anxiety and guilt. (1927, p. 143)

Whereas in Freud, the latent scene of the dream is the space of the primary scene and the parental coitus (the prototype is the famous scene of the dream in the "Wolf Man"), in Klein it is the breast (body) of the mother and the relations between the part objects, and in Bion it is the mind and the relationship between container and contained ($\male\,\female$), or between pre-conception and conception. Freud's is a clinic of desire, Klein's one of anguish, and Bion's one of knowledge. So we have three different authors, "three films", different in the way they see the mind developing and working, three different representations of Oedipus, moving from the scale of direct ocular inspection to the optical microscope, and finally on to electronic microscopy. As we can see, Oedipus remains a myth for all of psychoanalysis, that is to say, a scientific instrument.

With Bion we are attentive to molecular levels of psychic functioning, such as the formation of visual pictograms or α elements. This involves an even more radical extension of the Oedipus myth than suggested in 1928 in *Early Stages of the Oedipus Complex*, and here too, a change in the focus of attention from the contents to the container. Bion writes:

> Although I shall speak of the Oedipal situation as if it were the contents of thoughts, it will be apparent that thoughts and thinking may be regarded as part of the content of the Oedipal situation. The term "Oedipal situation" may be applied to the (1) realization of relationships between Father, Mother and Child, (2) emotional preconception, using the term "preconception" as I have used here as that which mates with awareness of a realization to give rise to a conception, (3) a psychological reaction stimulated in an individual (1) above. (1963, pp. 44–45)

Bion's idea of the Oedipal scene has twofold implications: it sharpens the resolution at which the phenomenon is observed and the perspective contracts ever more from the past to the present. In Sandler's explanation: "The model of container and contained [...] and its fundamental basis, the double arrow—can be seen as an outgrowth that integrates Freud's use of the Oedipal situation and Melanie Klein's theory of positions—as lived by an analytic couple during an actual session, when thinking and a vivid intercourse takes place between two people" (2005, pp. 538–539).

Let us now look at three children's dreams.

The beetle

Here is the account of a dream made by an eight-year-old child which shows the processing of very primitive persecutory anxieties:

> Me and two friends were in a castle. We had walked all over the castle, except for one part. We went into that part and then at some point we hear: "Raul, gather your troops of archers!" Raul was a beetle. At some point we hear steps coming towards us. It was Raul's archers shooting arrows and hitting us, but it didn't hurt too

much. After that, we ran to the castle to avoid the archers and went into a closet. But the closet was a secret passage. We fell into a river. We got out and went home. The river was infested with piranhas.

One may think, along with Klein, of the castle as an inhospitable part of the mother's body because it is owned by Raul-father and his arrows-penises. The closet would then be another safer place in the same body. It would be the secret passage that allows you to be taken safely to a proper home. But first you have to face other hazards, such as swimming in a river infested with terrifying piranhas. The arrows, then, may stand for piercing thoughts. And the beetle's exoskeleton, its strong suit of armour, could stand for a weapon of combat.

The cow

For Freud, children's dreams are of little interest because they are short, simple and characteristically transparent in representing a wish fulfilment. Here as an example the dream of a ten-year-old girl:

> I was with Renzo, Giovanni, Paolo, and Anna. We were eating lunch on a remote island when I heard the cry of an animal. I took my surfboard and followed the source of the noise. Only after reaching the destination did I realise what was making the noise. A cow! I didn't know what to do. I looked around, my gaze fell on my own feet. I immediately thought: "WHERE ARE MY SLIPPERS?" Then I looked at the cow. I lowered my gaze farther until I saw my flip-flops, which at that moment were being worn by the cow! I went into the pen where the cow was, bent down carefully to the level of its knees. But then the owner of the cow arrives, asks me what I'm doing and starts yelling at me. But then Dad comes and starts talking to the man. They fight. But in the meantime with a quick movement I grabbed my slippers. I left the pen. I took my surf board and ran to join my friends. Then the alarm went off, and I heard my mother: "BICE, TIME TO GO TO SCHOOL!" My mother always tells me off for leaving my slippers around.

Bice has the problem of being alone (she is "on a remote island") cut off from the parents' bedroom by a fence. Various elements suggest the primal scene. The mother-cow looks like its rival because it puts on flip-flops. The father has two antagonistic but complementary aspects. The surfboard might suggest Oedipal fantasies that heighten sensitivity to noise.

The ogre

A seven-year-old boy recounts a dream:

> It was me, Giovanni, and a grandmother that I don't have. We were in a gloomy castle, we were asleep and at some point I heard a noise. We were a bit frightened, so we decided to follow the noise. Immediately we spread out, and all the while the noise was getting louder. All of a sudden I saw an ogre. We met up again and hid. I went in a closet and Giovanni under a bed, the grandmother (who I don't have) found no hiding place but we could not find her. THEN, I WOKE UP!

The child has this dream at a time when the paternal great-grandmother and maternal grandmother are in poor health. What is plain to see is the attention to the noises in the parents' bedroom, the loneliness (the eerie castle), the father-ogre, his mother-closet, the double negation of the mother in the expression "non-na that I did not have" [in Italian "nonna", a word that contains a double "no", e.g., "no" and "non", means grandmother], the brother in relation to the bed, and the child going back to the belly-closet.

However, from a Bionian vertex, we would not so much be looking for a hidden meaning, because the manifest text is already the expression of a completed process of symbolisation. The "ogre" could continue to be a metaphor for the father experienced as threatening, without thinking that censorship prevents you from calling him by his name. In short, what we would see is the addition rather than the subtraction of meaning.

The father (Raul, the cowherd, the ogre) is a direct concrete and external presence in Freud's model, indirect and phantasmatic in that of Klein; and he intervenes as difference, that is, as a function, in that of Bion. In Freud, at the centre of everything are the jealousy aroused by the primal scene and the fantasy of patricide; in Klein, the envious attacks inside the mother's body and the bad contents (paternal) that are accommodated there—the prototype is that of the union between penis and vagina in the combined parental figure, namely the fantasy that parents are permanently and mutually absorbed in an exclusive interest; in Bion, the attachment is to the "sexual" link between thoughts (pre-conception + realisation). The attachment is directed at internal reality, self-awareness and one's own perceptual apparatus, that is to say, at the possibility of forming symbols.

Carl Stargher

In the dreamscapes of *The Cell* there is a blinding light; we are projected into a desert. In the opening scene the soft curves of the dunes evoke associations with the maternal body and its beautiful and terrible forms. Craters open up in the landscape that are like the mouths of a volcano. Time seems to be suspended. Everything is still. Then suddenly something appears, a figure starts to move, turns and then disappears as quickly as it came. Dr Catherine Deane, played by Jennifer Lopez, has been chosen to enter into the mind of the killer using the innovative technology of "neuro-synaptic transfer":

> HENRY: Now, this, gentlemen, is the catalyst. The neurological transfer system not only maps the mind, it sends the signal to another party. All you need to do is tune in, but you do much more than tune in. You become part of the show.

She has already given proof of her rare gifts of empathy by being able to penetrate into the locked-in world of young Edward where others had failed. The purpose, as she explains to Detective Novak, is to get in touch with Stargher's more childish and hidden self:

> NOVAK: You think you can change that?
> CATHERINE: Do you believe there's a part of yourself that you don't show anybody?
> NOVAK: I think everybody has that side of themselves.
> CATHERINE: During a session, when I'm inside, I get to see those things. With Stargher, I felt things I never want to feel again. He's not even Carl Stargher anymore. He's this idealised version of himself. A king in a very ... very twisted kingdom. The place for him to indulge every ... You know, I don't want to talk about this in here.

At this point, the images change; the two are still talking to each other, but with roles reversed. The scene can be seen as an allegory of the role play that takes place in therapy between attitudes on the part of the analyst that are empathic and others that are more exploratory and distancing; or in Bion's terms, between becoming O and becoming K.

CATHERINE: I could never do what you do, devote myself to understanding a mind like that.

NOVAK: I don't think we'll ever be able to understand a mind like that.

CATHERINE: But you try. That's your job.

NOVAK: I guess so.

CATHERINE: You don't like what you do?

NOVAK: I like it better than my old job. Used to be an attorney, I was a prosecutor.

CATHERINE: What happened?

NOVAK: I had a case, um, where this little girl was molested. And because of this tiny piece of evidence that was tainted, he walked. Uh, Charles Gish walked away. Nothing I could do about it. The night after he was released, Margaret's parents came home—that was the little girl's name, Margaret Sims. And they found Charles Gish sitting in their living room. He was watching television, and Margaret was sitting next to him, and he had cut her open right down the middle. The parents found Margaret's heart in the freezer. Charles figured they'd probably want to keep it. After that, I left the D.A. and joined the FBI. Figured I'd just try to catch 'em.

CATHERINE: Till now.

NOVAK: Yeah.

CATHERINE: You know, I started to tell you that Stargher isn't Stargher anymore. Well, that's true, and it's not true. The dominant side is still this horrible, but there's a positive side.

NOVAK: Positive side?

CATHERINE: Well, the way he sees himself as a child.

NOVAK: But isn't that him?

CATHERINE: The boy Stargher made contact. He's curious about me. If I could reach the boy, then maybe he'd tell me about Julia.

The venture is not entirely risk free. The perverse world of Carl can enchant in the same way that, according to Steiner (1993), the psychic refuge can capture analysis in its perverse logic. This is how the researcher in charge of the "neuro-synaptic transfer" experiment explains it to the detective:

HENRY: She's had quite a journey. Unlike anything we've ever seen before.

NOVAK: So she's made contact?

HENRY: Oh, yes. She's gone very deep into his world. At times too far … That can be dangerous.

NOVAK: What are you talking about?

HENRY: Well, if she came to believe that Stargher's world is real, then theoretically, her mind could convince her body that anything that was done to it there is actually done. It's like the old wives' tale where you die in your dream, you die in real life.

Transposed into the analytic situation, what Henry and Novak are discussing is the fire in the theatre of transference and the abolition of the internal setting, or the radical dream perspective in the session. From a psychoanalytic perspective it is significant that Henry tells Novak that on this journey into the other the psychologist becomes part of the show because the person of the analyst, as is commonly known, *becomes* part of the show.

When she penetrates Carl's painful, dark, and lavishly perverse world, Catherine comes into contact both with the adult and with the terrified abused child still living inside him, and tries to win their trust. For a time the psychologist remains entangled in Carl's topsy-turvy world. Novak—is he a self-monitoring function helping her retrieve an internal setting? Or does he stand for the usefulness of maintaining an investigative attitude in analysis?—must go to her rescue and fight hard to save her from the monster. Clearly each of these characters—the child, Novak, Carl, the psychologist, the father, the dog, and so on—can be seen as characters of the inner world of the same individual.

In the film, the mind is not depicted as a digital stream of green numbers on a dark screen, as in the famous scene in *The Matrix*, an idea also taken up by Arnold Dreyblatt in his fascinating video based on Freud's essay on memory entitled *Wunderblock*.[5] It is not even present in the tangle of circuits and neural networks glimpsed at the beginning when the "neuro-synaptic transfer" device is turned on. Instead we are in an environment that has physical, material characteristics. You can live in it, move in it, measure it, but it is an unstable space, such as in a video game. The characters and scenarios change at every step. A gentle and sad child turns at the speed of light into a horrible demon and vice versa.

It is a terrible world—paranoid, dark, bloody, primitive. Here reigns an absolute and ruthless binary logic. There are no nuances. Each stimulus is likely to cause a psychic catastrophe. It's like being in the mind of a small child, exposed at every moment to the dramatic swings between the opposing pairs of pleasure and pain, hot and cold, hunger and satiety, anguish and security.

The extreme quality of the emotions that colour this world poised between ecstasy and horror evokes a state of helplessness in the infant. *Hilflosigkeit*, as Freud calls it, makes parental care essential and, thanks to the constraints this establishes, lies at the origin of every moral determination (Freud, 1950). The infant relates to part objects because his perceptual and discriminative immaturity prevents him from bringing together stimuli into a single source. He finds himself in a situation of "double dependence" (Girard, 2010; Winnicott, 1945). This does not mean that at another level of development the adult will not also have to struggle with problems of integration.

Sofia, for example, tells me that she has always felt divided and contradictory in the whole way she behaves. Her two personalities come close to being integrated only when she falls in love with someone. I feel her secret to be so real, and so painful, that I reflect that perhaps I have never fully realised the incredible unifying force that the object of love can have on the divided mind. As soon as I express this thought, I immediately have an image of a magnet that magically orders into a fascinating pattern the iron filings that until a moment before were scattered all around. In an analysis even healthy hate acts as a magnet (Winnicott, 1947) as well as healthy love of the analyst for the patient, as Ogden writes (2009, p. 137) in a commentary on a paper by Searles on countertransference: "in order to successfully analyze the Oedipus complex, the analyst must fall in love with the patient acknowledging that his desires will never be fulfilled."

In nurslings, the split between love and hate is extreme. They are immersed in a universe their experience of which is based on innate patterns or preconceptions. Consequently, the most primitive fantasies form even in the presence of adequate care. In Klein's theory this is where the implicit devaluation of the second term of the pair nature/culture originates and the disquieting effect of the overlap between psychopathology and immaturity that leads us to see the child as if he were psychotic.

As we have seen, the setting in which the storylines enacted by the characters come to life as internal objects is the child's body. However, at the beginning it is almost indistinct from that of the mother, which amounts to saying that it is the mother's body; and then, as the rudimentary processes of differentiation start, it becomes the relationship between parts of the child's own body and parts of the mother's body. This concrete identification will gradually fade or rather be accompanied by mental representations or symbols. The fantasy is no longer seen as the failure of perception resulting from the frustration of the libido, but as the first stage of symbolisation, or in other words, the "falsification" of the real, as what results from an elementary transference.

The dichotomous logic of the world of internal objects sends into crisis the binary vision fantasy/reality or primary process/secondary process which is characteristic of Freud. Reality is *always* pervaded by the dream of the mind.

In one of the most disturbing scenes of the film, which is in keeping with the dictates of its morbid sense of imagination, Carl is suspended from the ceiling by hooks inserted in his skin. This is what the spectators see. Carl, however, sees himself in a hallucination as an almighty king ruling over a perverse kingdom. The victim, but primarily the mother's body-as-parent-monster, is reduced to an inert, inanimate object that Carl no longer fears will abandon him. He controls it absolutely. For a while, but only briefly—because it is a sense of security based only on hatred—the terror clears.

The analyst who interprets the dream from a Kleinian perspective is confronted with worlds that have these characteristics. He feels like the knight who must kill the dragon and vanquish evil, whether it be the death instinct, primary aggression, or destructive narcissism. He is wary. Against the mafia gang one is never sufficiently on the alert. He takes it for granted that the criminal internal objects are false. He fears that manipulation is always lurking. The tone of the interpretations can resonate with blame, coming from the prosecuting attorney, because the analyst automatically puts himself on the side of the patient's weak self under attack from the sadistic and perverse part of his personality. But, as one can see in the film, Carl the child and Carl the serial killer are one and the same thing![6]

In short, a paranoid climate reigns. Those who approach Klein's clinical reports for the first time are struck by the doom-laden, expressionistic, gloomy language. It is clear, however, that the tension that runs through it comes from Klein's striving to express the inexpressible, to render the hyper-dramatic dimension of a primitive life which projects its cruel mythology on to the present, to depict the world of gods and demons which becomes invasive in psychosis, but still remains the background to any dream.

In the long dream sequences, which take up almost half the film, one can see the darkest, most sordid recesses of the psyche. At one point, after an initial failure in the race against time to save the killer's latest victim, Catherine-Lopez asks to reverse the flow of the "neuro-synaptic transfer". She lets the killer into her mind! This is precisely what Klein, engaged in keeping up a continuous barrage of transference interpretations, seems unwilling to do. Translating the language of metapsychology, it is as if, at the risk of her own mental health, Catherine agrees to allow herself to be permeated by Carl's violent projective identifications. One is reminded of Bion's remarks about the need in a genuine analysis to also experience the fear, and the fact that the consulting room always contains two fierce and frightened animals.

Half a page

Kleinian psychoanalytic theory is essentially a psychology of the intrapsychic and the isolated subject. Unconscious fantasies are externalised but in one direction. The sexual symbolism is extreme because the primal scene described by Freud broadens to include the "sexuality" of the pregenital part objects. Here is an example of this extension in a passage by Klein where even the letters of the alphabet lose their innocence:

> For Fritz, when he was *writing*, the lines meant roads and the letters ride on motor-bicycles—on the pen—upon them. For instance, "I" and "e" ride together on a motor-bicycle that is usually driven by the "I" and they love one another with a tenderness that is quite unknown in the real world. Because they always ride with one another they became so alike that there is hardly any difference between them, for the beginning and the end—he was talking

of the small Latin alphabet—of "I" and "e" are the same, only in
the middle the "I" has a little stroke and the "e" has a little hole.
(1923, p. 73)

Brilliant, sharp, ambitious, dogmatic, "ruthless" (Grosskurth, 1980;
Kristeva, 2003; Segal, 1979), Melanie Klein has the courage and the
lucid, passionate determination of the outsider who knows she can
count only on herself. Perhaps it is these qualities that allow her to rev-
olutionise all the traditional Freudian concepts. Much of her strength
also lies in being first and foremost a clinician, and the prominence
given to the clinical aspect will forever remain the hallmark of the whole
school directly and indirectly inspired by her.

To erect her theoretical edifice, in child analysis Klein uses the lever
of the technique of play as the equivalent of dream and free association
in adults. It works so well as to lead to a significant reversal of perspective, as free associations are compared to play, the squiggle game, or to
building with Lego bricks.

In all this, Klein could have been picking up a suggestion of Freud's.
In a note added in 1914 to the seventh chapter of *The Interpretation of
Dreams*, Freud cites a book by A. Maeder from two years earlier in
which the author attributes to dream a recreational function and draws
a "parallel between dreams and the play of animals and children
which may be regarded as practice in the operation of innate instincts
and as preparation for serious activity later on" (Freud, 1900, p. 579).
Arguably this is not only one of the many effects of *après-coup* that per-
vade Freud's work, but the intentional and systematic development of
a specific suggestion.

In her clinical work, Klein uses a rigorous technique. She forgoes
any pedagogical intention. She makes the concept of transference into
a concept of space as well as time and does not rely much on countertransference. She formulates precocious, profound, and direct interpretations, and favours the analysis of the negative transference. She treats
patients by containing their anguish in the here and now rather than
seeking to reconstruct their past or formulating etiological hypotheses.
Ultimately even this can be seen as a development of Freud's technique.
He was the first to say that nothing can be defeated *in absentia* or *in effi-
gie*. For this reason, transference neurosis, a phenomenon that develops
in the present, has been and continues to be the cornerstone of classical
theory.

Klein has a point, then, when she claims to have built her theory on the foundations laid by Freud. It is difficult, for example, not to see some kinship between the concept of unconscious fantasy and that of originating fantasy, which marks Freud's final surrender to the needs of psychic reality—one need only remember the title of the last section of *The Interpretation of Dreams*. The concept of unconscious fantasy, the mental representation of the instincts and physical sensations felt ("interpreted") as relations with part objects, amplifies and extends the notion of primal fantasy.

According to Hinshelwood, Klein began to be interested in psychoanalysis around 1918, when Freud published the case of the "Wolf Man", and she was influenced by this paper. This is an invaluable clue. It is as if the student wanted to take up a challenge laid down by the brilliant teacher. Once again, it all starts with a dream, as it had with Irma's dream in Freud and now with that of Sergei Pankejeff, also known as the Wolf Man. Even the central role reserved for the death instinct, which when excessive can feed envy, masochism, destructiveness, and perversion, ultimately picks up the most controversial concept in the whole of Freudian metapsychology.

The unconscious fantasy is essentially a way of defending oneself from the anxiety that comes from not being able to make sense of the stimuli of the moment. If this is excessive, it can inhibit thought. As a result, the interpretation becomes a way of contributing to the work of shaping experience. This is achieved by building and offering to the analysand good plots, however cruel and violent they may appear, a little like going to the theatre, but designed to integrate the contradictory qualities of the objects, to move from the paranoid-schizoid position to the depressive (SP → D), and thus promote better contact with psychic and material reality.

The inner world is a stage which is always in operation and which moment by moment generates the meaning that it then externalises. The unconscious fantasy is the script which describes the relationships that bind one to part objects, and the dream and daytime fantasy are its expression. The dream is no longer a text deformed by censorship which contains the fulfilment of a desire to protect sleep. The analyst seeks to see everything, dream and non-dream, in the key of transference and in reference to the here and now; he reads every association of the patient as referring unconsciously to him.

Klein reformulates the concept of transference in terms of play and extends the dream paradigm of the session. What the adult says is like a child's drawing or play. Now everything is within this frame. The concrete metaphor of play makes understandable the metaphor of the uninterrupted dream of the session: the dream "represents the unconscious fantasy of object relations as stimulated by the active impulses (good or bad) of the moment" (Bott Spillius, Milton, Garvey, Couve & Steiner, 2011, p. 315).

This is why the psychoanalytic literature that draws inspiration from Klein includes very few works on dreams as a specific topic. The exception is Sharpe who, after initially being a sympathiser, later openly sided with Anna Freud, and who, after Freud's "instinctual" theory and Klein's "theological" theory, anticipates Meltzer's "aesthetic" theory of the dream and Bion's "epistemological" theory. There are of course also the contributions on dreams by Hanna Segal and Salomon Resnik. In Hishelwood's Kleinian dictionary, as Bléandonu notes (1995), the dream receives only half a page. Meltzer is already a *post*-Kleinian, and Bion, despite starting from Klein, took entirely new paths.

The incontrovertible fact remains that Klein implements a first major extension of the role of the dream in analysis because, as someone who treats children, she establishes the equivalence between dream and play. The words and actions of children are their dreams. The analyst interprets play as if he were being told the story of a dream. The more often he has to overcome in some way the inhibition of very young or very sick children, the more frequently he intervenes—another trait that is found in the analysis of adults and the model of the analytic field:

> In their play children represent symbolically phantasies, wishes and experiences. Here they are employing the same language, the same archaic, phylogenetically acquired mode of expression, as we are familiar with from dreams. We can only fully understand it if we approach it by the method Freud has evolved for unravelling dreams. (Klein, 1926, p. 146)

So, also in play there is a hidden text and a manifest text. Compared to the dream, the difference is that in play secondary processing is of more importance (Bléandonu, 1995). The opposite view is taken by Kristeva, who sees play as an access road to the unconscious that is even more comfortable than dreams and free associations because "play is more amenable to the expression of a pre- or transverbal unconscious"

(Kristeva, 2003, p. 50). It produces an effect of haze, but not so much in the sense of the text censored as of the seeing-how, the natural tendency of the mind to know reality through substitutions or metonymic-metaphorical tropes. It seems that the game of substitutions is the only one the mind really knows how to play, both in metaphor (rose means "love") and in the most logical abstraction where every difference is undone in a way that makes it possible to manipulate symbols that are postulated as having an absolute identity (A = A, or 1 = 1). But not even a table, as we are reminded by Kojève (1947), is ever the same as itself in time.

This is the reason Hinshelwood's dictionary has only half a page about dreams, because in all the others it is included in play. Ludic space and dream scene coincide.

Psychic retreats

To return to the movie. *The Cell* is a good illustration of what Steiner (1993) has called the psychic refuge, a complex and rigid organisation of the mind that defends the individual from anxiety and protects him from too much direct contact with reality and with emotions that are likely to annihilate the ego.

Carl has built a shelter for the mind, a cruel place where everything is allowed and where all relationships are impregnated by the sadism that occurs in the relationship between part objects. In his realm he controls the objects, treats them despotically and robs them of their vitality. Reduced to inanimate things, they no longer threaten the more wounded and mortified self and are no longer likely to smash it to pieces. Of course, the sense of security is illusory and is purchased at the price of isolation and partial alteration of the relationship with reality, as Freud describes when talking of fetishism.

Venturing into this world means exposure to two equally dangerous risks: one can either be captivated by its perverse fascination or destroy it and reduce the other to a state of panic. Each contact is followed by an immediate retreat. The alliance instantly transforms into a deadly challenge. This is what happens to those who, once the processes of the synthesis of identifications have failed, and overly influenced by opposite patterns of imago, have too much need for love figures to counter those that threaten (Klein, 1928). Love and hate coincide instantly (Winnicott, 1947).

In this theatre of cruelty, Deane, the psychologist, and Novak, the detective, act as analytic functions, one more immersive and the other more interactive-reflexive. Novak is a superego that is allied to the ego, the source of positivity that comes from the depressive position and love for the total object even if it is an ambivalent love—or perhaps because of it.

For the subject, the refuge of the mind thus has a function of equilibrium, but the lack of emotional nourishment and (emotional) truth that weaves the threads that allow the mental container to expand prevents the development of the fragile part. Fragility is instead denied and turns into omnipotence. If not sustainable, in fact, even an offer of help can be seen as a killer-content ($\male$ k; Ferro, 2002). For the narcissistic organisation of the personality all forms of true intimacy, gratitude, or positive transference are a serious threat. It's like trying to take heroin away from a drug addict. Doing so deprives him of the powerful resource that serves not so much to obtain gratification—this is only the surface of the symptom—as to drive away the intolerable pain which, although sometimes well hidden, is always there. So it is that the desert advances and destroys the fertile soil. The refuge tends to expand, but in the long run the vicious circle of guilt-sadism-guilt is bound to explode.

This comes out in the film, when it is mentioned that the serial killer is committing his crimes at ever shorter intervals,[7] meaning that he is trying unconsciously to get caught and is looking for someone who can put a stop to his agony. Arguably he senses dimly that eventually the ceaseless spread of guilt and anguish will ultimately destroy him physically.

Building a shelter also serves to tie up destructiveness and to liberate other areas of the ego. Sometimes, notes Steiner (1993), a patient who has started therapy after the collapse of his psychic refuge transforms analysis into a new shelter. Here he can become arrogant, angrily omnipotent and dismissive. By triumphing over the analysis and the analyst he reverses the humiliations he has suffered. But this helps very little, because at the same time guilt grows apace. The escalation can lead to the fragmentation of the new container or the new shelter.

A refuge is a kingdom of unchecked hatred, the opposite of the conscious and tolerated hatred Winnicott mentions in his famous article on countertransference (1947). Healthy hatred can also serve as nutrition for psychic growth. The hatred that is not integrated, on the other hand, makes for scorched earth around one. The lack of a suitable psychic container leads to the excessive use of projective identification, a concrete identification that prevents the formation of symbols. The sadistically attacked and damaged objects become spectres that continue to take their toll. Even though it protects patients who are not openly psychotic against more serious collapse, obsessiveness of thought announces their constant return.

Notes

1. Incidentally, (Calvin) Klein's line of *Fragrances* also includes some highly suggestive names: *Secret Obsession, Obsession,* and *Obsession Night.*
2. See Meltzer (1967, p. 85): "In the structural sense, such objects are seen possessed of a portion of the mental apparatus, with all its inherent capacities, even the ability to seize control of the organ of consciousness (as occurs in demoniacal possession, hypnosis and certain types of *folie à deux*). Integration, and conversely dis-integration, of self and internal objects, always moves in parallel rather than in series."
3. In this way Grotstein also explains why, to illustrate the process of mentalisation, Bion reversed the normal alphabetical order by postulating the conversion beta → alpha. For Fornaro (1991, p. 81), however, the reason would be that, although beta is genetically antecedent, it can be investigated only from alpha. Alpha would be genetically second but first on the cognitive level.
4. Thus the terrifying combined parental figure, a fearsome mother-monster, takes centre stage. In the child's unconscious sexual theories, "in copulation the mother is continually incorporating the father's penis via the mouth, so that her body is filled with a great many penises and babies. All these the child desires to eat up and destroy. In attacking its mother's inside, therefore, the child is attacking a great number of objects" (Klein, 1933, p. 273).
5. Available on the Internet at: www.dreyblatt.or/video/Wunderblock.mov
6. For Freud (1900, p. 191) it is obvious that the child continues to live in the adult: "[…] the actual wish which instigated the dream, and the fulfilment of which is represented by the dream, is derived from childhood; so that, to our surprise, *we find the child and the child's impulses still living on in the dream.*"

7. In the work entitled *Criminal Tendencies in Normal Children*, Melanie
Klein gives us a valuable key to help us understand Carl's upside-down
and corrupted world:

> The sexual theories are the basis of a variety of most sadistic
> and primitive fixations. We know from Freud that there is some
> unconscious knowledge which the child obtains, apparently in a
> phylogenetic way. To this belongs the knowledge about parental
> intercourse, birth of children, etc.; but it is of a rather vague and
> confused nature. According to the oral—and anal-sadistic stage
> which he is going through himself, intercourse comes to mean
> to the child a performance in which eating, cooking, exchange
> of faeces and sadistic acts of every kind (beating, cutting, and
> so on) play the principal part. *I wish to emphasize how impor-
> tant the connection between these phantasies and sexuality is bound
> to become in later life.* All these phantasies will have apparently
> disappeared, but their unconscious effect will be of far-reaching
> importance in frigidity, in impotence and in other sexual distur-
> bances. This may be quite distinctly seen in the small child in
> analysis. The little boy who has demonstrated his wishes about
> the mother, showing in this respect most sadistical phantasies,
> tries to escape by choosing instead of the mother-object the
> father-imago; and will then withdraw from this too, if his oral-
> sadistic phantasies prove to be connected with this object of love
> also. Here we find the basis of all the perversions which Freud
> has discovered to have their origin in the early development of
> the child. Phantasies of the father, or of himself, ripping up the
> mother, beating, scratching her, cutting her to pieces, are some
> instances of childish conception of intercourse. I will refer here to
> the fact that phantasies of this nature are really carried into action
> by criminals, to mention only the instance of Jack the Ripper.
> (Klein, 1927, pp. 190–191)

And further:

> We know that Freud called neurosis the negative of the perver-
> sions. An important addition to the psychology of the perver-
> sions was made by Sachs, who arrived at the conclusion that
> the pervert does not simply permit himself, owing to lack of
> conscience, what the neurotic represses in consequence of his
> inhibitions. He found that the conscience of the pervert is not

less strict but is simply working in a different way. It permits one part only of the forbidden tendencies to be retained in order to escape from other parts which seem still more objectionable to the superego. What it rejects are desires belonging to the Oedipus complex, and the apparent absence of inhibition in the pervert is only the effect of a superego not less strict, but working in a different way.

I arrived at an analogous conclusion concerning the criminal some years ago, in the report mentioned at the beginning of my paper, in which I gave details of the analogy between criminal acts and childish phantasies.

In the case of the child I have described and in other not quite so pronounced but yet instructive cases, I found that the criminal disposition was not due to a less strict super-ego but to a super-ego working in a different direction. It is just anxiety and the feeling of guilt which drive the criminal to his delinquencies. In committing these he also partly tries to escape from his Oedipus situation. In the case of my little criminal the breaking open of cupboards and attacks on little girls were substituted for attacks on his mother. (ibid., pp. 199–200)

CHAPTER FOUR

The inability to dream in *They* and *Dark City*

[W]e shall be working towards an explanation of the psychoses while we are endeavouring to throw some light on the mystery of dreams.

—Sigmund Freud,
The Interpretation of Dreams

They

"Every night when I went to bed I had to thump the whole bed with my fists because I was afraid there were snakes hidden underneath it; later, that fear went away," Sara tells me. But now, many years later, the "snakes" are back in the form of depressive anxieties, psychosomatic disorders, and uncertainties. Laura, another patient, describes the following scene:

I was in the bedroom I slept in as a child and I was so afraid because a crocodile was peeping out from the pouf under the bed. A real crocodile! Another time, I was at a party and even there I was frightened because there were wild animals—a tiger, a lion. Someone told

63

me that they were in fact masks and not real animals. But I was still
terrified and ran away. As I dashed off I knocked over a little girl.
A friend of mine screamed at me, "What have you done? You've
killed her!" I apologised and explained that I was really scared and
that was why I hadn't gone back. But I was incredibly upset.

These two scenes, one a memory and the other a dream, are very similar
to the opening scene of the film *They* (Italian subtitle: *Nightmares from
the World of Shadows*; Harmon, 2002).

Julia (Laura Regan), a psychology student who appears to be very
delicate and vulnerable, and who suffers from mood swings ("When
I'm high, I'm very high; when I'm down, I'm very down," she tells her
boyfriend), finds herself once again facing the childhood night terrors
which had led her to being treated by Dr Booth (Jay Brazeau).

The film opens with a scene that has a Proustian flavour. A mother
refuses to give in to her imploring six-year-old boy, Billy, who does not
want to sleep alone because he is afraid the bad guys will come and take
him away. Immediately afterwards he has an episode of night terror
when "they", the monsters, arrive.

Julia and Billy have been friends since they were children. They
met because they were both suffering from the same disorder.
Nineteen years later, Billy (John Abrahams) calls her asking to see her
immediately.

They meet in a diner. Billy is clearly paranoid and terrified and
after a dramatic conversation takes out a gun and kills himself in front
of her.

The whole scene is intercut with images of a small baby who cries all
the time as it sits on its mother's lap at a nearby table, the point being
to suggest the nature of Billy's childhood fears and their origin in the
terrors described by Klein in the early stages of life (but it is also, perhaps, an allusion to Eisenstein). Shortly after this tragic event Julia fails
the final examination for her master's degree in psychology and from
this moment on she starts to have the same nightmares she suffered as a
child and which had begun immediately after her father's suicide. The
two traumatic events that occur in quick succession—the tragic death
of her childhood friend, which she witnesses personally, and her emotional breakdown during the examination—revive old fears.

In 1926, writing about *pavor nocturnus*, Klein identified its cause in a
strong sense of guilt induced by a superego which is particularly severe

because it is fuelled by intense pre-genital sadism. On the subject of mourning, she was later to add: "The pain of the real loss of a loved person, as I see it, is markedly increased by unconscious fantasies of the grieving person so that it also lost its 'good' inner objects. Then the person feels the domination of their inner 'bad objects' and their inner world is in danger of destruction" (1940, p. 336).

To avert the danger of psychic annihilation, Julia unconsciously organises a persecutory world and gradually begins to sense hostile presences around her—"they". *They* are the monstrous beings that only come when it is dark. In the film they are barely glimpsed, but when they come, you can cut the fear with a knife.

The air of ambiguity remains until the end. We learn little more about these horrible shapeless demons that seem to have jumped out, like the Furies, from a painting by Bosch or Bacon.[1]

In her fear, Julia wisely goes back to her therapist—incidentally quite believable as a character, which is rare in films. Dr Booth appeals to her sense of reality and to her knowledge in the field of psychopathology. As a diligent student, Julia gives her own diagnosis: "Subject is suffering from post-traumatic stress from witnessing the suicide of a close friend. Influenced by the erratic behaviour of two strangers [two other friends of Billy to whom weird things are happening], she allows herself to entertain the paranoid-schizophrenic delusions of her dead friend [...] She feels a sense of personal failure. And guilt that Billy ... that her friend died."

In terms of this diagnosis, the small wound that both Billy and Julia discovered on their skin, and which they thought was where their bodies had possibly been penetrated by aliens, is the symbol of a trauma that has never been overcome.

Robert Harmon's film is given an authoritative presentation by Wes Craven, an acknowledged master of the horror genre and director of *A Nightmare on Elm Street* (1984). The film's original title was in fact *Wes Craven Presents: They*. Some critics made fun of this, for example Owen Gleiberman (*Entertainment Weekly*, 4 December 2002): "The hilarious diminuendo of that title is such that the movie might as well have been called 'Wes Craven Presents: Not a Hell of a Lot.'" *They*, however, delivers much of what it promises and with an admirable economy of special effects is able to arouse in the spectators more than a few shivers of fear, even in the most technically savvy among them. The critic for the New York Times, A. O. Scott confesses—to be sure, with a touch of ambiguity—"I was relieved when the movie ended and the lights came back on" (28 December 2002).

Others, despite expressing a negative opinion, were fascinated by the closing scene. It is indeed remarkable, and alone could justify the movie. Admitted to a psychiatric ward, all of a sudden it's as if Julia has vanished. Everyone looks for her, but to no avail. Perhaps the only one who senses what has happened is Dr Booth, her former therapist. Julia is now completely segregated off in "their" world. As if from a dark cave filled with monsters, she asks for help from the other patients, but in vain. A virtual barrier separates her from everyone else and makes her invisible. She is confined behind a diaphanous immaterial wall, made up of a kind of magnetic field. She desperately thrashes against its liquid surface, drawing the outline of a reddish spider's web. But her screams are of no use. Surrounded by a multitude of monsters like "murderous fragments of super-ego" (Bion, 1992, p. 69), Julia remains imprisoned in her psychosis.

Let us look at a passage from Bion of which this scene could be the illustration: "Dread of annihilation forces an attempt at repair and, *pari passu*, an increased impulse towards destruction of the capacity for assimilation, since such increased capacity is associated with the production of material for dream-thought [...] and therefore of awareness of the super-ego" (1992, p. 164). So when things go wrong, we try to regain a more correct view of reality and, because there is a risk of being blinded, we seek to destroy it.

Among the extras on the *They* DVD is an alternative ending to the film, less ambiguous than the one that was chosen, but perhaps more disturbing. More disturbing because, if in part it refrains from playing the supernatural card, on the other hand it spares no one, not even the audience, from confronting the question of madness. We understand that in fact the whole film has sprung from the mind of Julia the patient and that she has been institutionalised in a hospital since she was sixteen years old. Through the translucent window in the door of her room in solitary confinement Julia observes the other inmates wandering around the psychiatric ward. One by one she sees all the characters of the film pass by. Among them, sucked inexorably into the film stereotype of the mad psychiatrist, is Dr Booth.

This second ending, which the director decided not to use, is particularly interesting because one can think of it as analogous to the analyst's "second look". In fact, every time he regains an internal setting, the analyst wakes up from the dream of reality and focuses on the fiction of analysis, in other words on what is happening on the unconscious level. In this case it is we the spectators who wake up from Julia's hallucinatory world that we have been sharing throughout the film. The marking point that helps us get out of this world of illusion signals instead that Julia, as Bion would put it, is no longer able to either dream or be awake.

Significantly, the passage that apparently inspired this now famous formula of his is to be found in a 1935 article by Jenny Waelder, taken up by Melitta Sperling in her 1958 essay on *pavor nocturnus*. In presenting the case of a seven-year-old child, Waelder writes: "[...] the boy would suddenly awaken, sit up in bed, cry out, scream, thrash about with his body and arms as if he were fighting. He was obviously acting out a dream, and although he was talking and moving about, he was neither completely awake nor actually asleep" (p. 81).

From dream-work-α to the α function

Sometimes, as we see in the film, dreams may be a point of entry into psychosis. Psychosis, Freud writes, reporting an observation by De Sanctis, "may come to life at a single blow with the appearance of the operative dream which brings the delusional material to light; or it may develop slowly in a series of further dreams, which have still to overcome a certain amount of doubt" (1900, p. 88). *They* effectively illustrates precisely the regressive transition from dream to nightmare, and from nightmare to hallucination. According to Klein and Bion, quoted above, the critical factor that sets off this process is the same that hinders the work of mourning, blocks Julia's α function, and renders her incapable of dreaming. According to Bion, in fact, to be able to wake up from a dream you must "be capable of (a) frustration, and hence awareness of temporality, (b) guilt and depression, and hence an ability to contemplate causality" (1992, p. 1).

The block can be due to a load of excessive and therefore indigestible raw emotions, to a relative shortage of the α function, or, of course, to both these factors. The psychotic, it was said, is incapable of dreaming and thus both of falling asleep and waking up. His psychic functioning remains glued to the paranoid-schizoid position. "It is the synthesis of the murderous superego (which takes place at the moment all other syntheses take place," writes Bion (1992, pp. 104–105), "that makes

Ps → D so hazardous." The fear of the murderous superego prevents the subject from gaining access to the dream, the only place where "the Positions are negotiated" (ibid., p. 37). Moreover, while the movement to D gives coherence to a series of scattered data, the effect of psychic integration opens up the path to new β elements, new challenges. Here the attack on the apparatus for thinking (on the link between preconception and realisation), the equivalent of oedipal jealousy, which for Freud is directed at the parents, and envy, which for Klein involves the combined parental figure, produces bizarre objects. Then the worst nightmares become reality. It is intriguing to think of the demons that haunt Julia as insect-like accumulations of β elements, and of the barrier that Julia tries in vain to pierce as the projection of an impenetrable β screen. This is clearly different from *The Cell*, where the perversion and the construction of a secret hideaway of the mind enabled Carl not to lose contact with reality altogether.

Now, to understand the meaning of Bion's statement about psychosis, perhaps widely known but not so easy to grasp, we must take a step back and recall some notions of his theory of thought and dream. Let us look at a passage from *Cogitations* that illustrates what happens when one is capable of dreaming:

> suppose I am talking to a friend who asks me where I propose to spend my holiday; as he does so, I visualize the church of a small town not far from the village in which I propose to stay. The small town is important because it possesses the railway station nearest to my village. Before he has finished speaking, a new image has formed, and so on.
>
> The image of the church has been established on a previous occasion—I cannot now tell when. Its evocation in the situation I am describing would surprise no one, but what I now wish to add may be more controversial. I suggest that the experience of this particular moment of the conversation—not simply his words but the totality of that moment of experience—is being perceived sensorially by me and converted into an image of that particular village church.
>
> I do not know what else may be going on, though I am sure that much more takes place than I am aware of. But the transformation of my sense impressions into this visual image is part of a process of mental assimilation. The impressions of the event are being

re-shaped as a visual image of that particular church, and so are being made into a form suitable for storage in my mind.

By contrast, the patient might have the same experience, the same sense impressions, and yet be unable to transform the experience so that he can store it mentally. But instead, the experience (and his sense impressions of it) remains a foreign body; it is felt as a "thing" lacking any of the quality we usually attribute to thought or its verbal expression.

To the first of these products, that of dream-work-α, I propose to give the name, "α-element"; to the second, the unassimilated sense impression, "β-element". (1992, pp. 180–181)

A banal everyday scene. Two friends are talking about their holiday plans. In their minds, however, sophisticated processes are taking place that continually transform the experience into images, and in this way make it assimilable. A specific function of the mind ensures the success of the operation. Originally, Bion called this dream-work α.

Dream-work α transforms the non-mental into the mental, it de-materialises or "de-sensitises" [*de-sense-fy*] (Sandler, 2005, p. 242) the real, and converts into memory traces or psychic qualities the raw data (β elements) or (non-assimilated) impressions that the senses imprint on the translucent sheet of Freud's mystic writing pad. It is a kind of pre-digestion of proto-emotions and proto-sensations, akin to what happens in the mouth before digestion takes place in the stomach (analysis). This semi-processing produces α elements, that is, visual images (but also auditory, tactile, olfactory, etc., patterns.). The α elements then combine with each other in more complex narrations and produce dream-thoughts ($\alpha + \alpha + \alpha + \ldots \alpha n$) that can be stored and used for both night dreams and waking dreams (synthesis).

Initially, Bion uses the concept of dream-work α to extend to waking dream work the dream work as described by Freud in *The Interpretation of Dreams*. This is the original alphabetisation of perception. The ability to "dream" comes to mean the ability to gather up, give coherence to and assimilate sensory impressions and raw emotions. Later, however, he maintains the distinction and breaks down dream work into two stages, one more basic and generic and the other more sophisticated and specific, as if we were dealing first with the axis of words and then with that of sentences or, by analogy, with the two different forms of memory, short-term and long-term, or with the two forms of consciousness, primary and secondary or nuclear and extended, to use the terminology of, respectively, Edelman (1992, 2004)[2] and Damasio (1999).

The ability to dream and to think, or to dream while awake, to "dream" the events one is experiencing, to translate sensory impressions into α elements, comes from the integrity of the dream-work α and from the production of α elements. It is something midway between the inscription of a trace still void of meaning and an early form of narrative.[3] We can perhaps get an idea of this "something in between" by thinking of the effect of estrangement that is produced when you say the same word aloud several times. The word is reduced to the pure substance of the signifier. It is still an expression that has a meaning, but the meaning becomes more and more evanescent. Another idea comes from Bion (1992), who when talking of this system of notation mentions the points and lines that make up animated cartoons as parts of a basic geometry of the mind.

When this first stage fails to progress, there is also a breakdown in the ability to dream in the proper sense (during sleep) and dreaming while awake, or constructing thoughts made up of sequences of α elements. For this reason, because they are necessary to dream work, but are still to some extent already its product, if the α function is regarded as the zero degree of dream work, the α-elements are already elementary narrative forms for some particles of experience. In fact, α elements stand between the perception and the notation/memory, even prior to the visual image. Bion (1992, p. 325): "There is similarly something between 'visual image' and the 'thing-in-itself'—what I have called by the meaningless term 'α-element'." Perhaps it would be useful to distinguish between proto-α-elements and α-elements, reserving the second term for already alphabetised pictograms that have entered via the symbolic language that characterises the self-awareness of human beings.

Perception can already be considered a text, a micro-dream. But because the perception of a stimulus and its inscription as a signifier on the wax tablet of memory is almost immediate, the two moments can become confused. Another source of confusion comes from equating dream and thought, if at the same time one maintains the distinction between night dream and waking dream. To avoid such misunderstandings, Bion began to use the term "function" for what he had originally called dream-work α.

To sum up: the α function, previously called dream-work α, is the oneiric processing of fragments of experience of the real that produces minimal units of meaning or images-as-microdreams: α-elements. Dream-work, which takes place according to the mechanisms described by Freud, combines α-elements and gives rise to night dreams and unconscious (oneiric) waking thought. Unlike β-elements, which cannot establish bonds between themselves, or at most only weak bonds, α-elements can form agglomerations or can be ordered sequentially, as a narrative or in a logical or geometric manner. As ideograms or bits of meaning, they clump together and form the contact barrier that dynamically, in the sense that it is an ongoing process, differentiates unconscious from conscious, dream from waking. The contact barrier is a film of meaning extracted from the sense-less state of "O", in other words, a "parallel reality without categories" (Grotstein, 2000, p. 282). Conversely, if this fluid differentiation is hampered, the distinction between conscious and unconscious, between wakefulness and sleep, and between dream and thought is lost.

When the α-function is deficient, and consequently the α barrier or contact barrier is replaced by the β-screen, when awake, or when attention is focused, the individual finds himself in the condition of Funes, the character of the famous story by Borges. His memories cannot become unconscious and consequently he is condemned to a painful wakefulness that is not a true waking state ("It was very difficult for him to sleep [...] I suspect, however, that he was not very capable of thought. To think is to forget differences, generalize, make abstractions. In the teeming world of Funes, there were only details, almost immediate in their presence"; Borges, 1964, p. 66).

Or there is the painful awareness of Zeno Cosini, the protagonist of Svevo's *Confessions of Zeno*, who begins to limp when he cannot rid himself of the thought of how many muscles have to contract simultaneously to advance even a single step. Bion helps us to understand the symptom Cosini suffers from: "A child learning to walk is engaged in attempting to make conscious material unconscious; only when this is done can it walk. The same is true of any piece of learning ever done— its success depends on the central operations by which dream-work-α is able to transform conscious material into unconscious material suitable for unconscious waking thinking" (Bion, 1992, p. 71). For Bion, the unconscious is the product of the capacity to learn from experience. In other words, it is constantly being created by the dream.

This means that one can stay awake or asleep only if a series of stimuli—which, depending on the situation, can be either mainly external or internal—can be recorded and processed unconsciously, and thus bracketed off for consciousness, which remains free to think other thoughts, but only if one is able to categorise (to abstract), that is, to overlook differences and emphasise similarities. Concepts are maps of perceptual maps (Edelman, 1992) and, as such, orientated towards reality, but they are not the things themselves. They represent a small finite area of the infinite and impersonal "O" that is in constant evolution. Bion writes: "If a man has an emotional experience when asleep or awake and is able to convert it into alpha-elements he can either remain unconscious of that emotional experience or become conscious of it. The sleeping man has an emotional experience, converts it into alpha-elements and so becomes capable of dream thoughts. Thus he is free to become conscious (that is wake up) and describe the emotional experience by a narrative usually known as a dream" (1962, p. 15).

This passage and Bion's whole theory show that the fact of waking up is central to the definition of the dream, as sleeping is to being awake. The psychotic does not wake up because he does not dream or he does not dream because he does not wake up. And his dreams are not real dreams because they have a concrete quality and function as a discharge. They are hallucinated dreams that are remarkably devoid of associations, "mutilated dreams—lacking a dimension like a solid body that casts no shadow in light" (Bion, 1991, p. 91).

Two essential points still need to be clarified: what is the difference between night dreams and waking dreams (thought)? And how do they differ in the normal person from the psychotic? I would venture to answer these questions by saying that the former is a quantitative difference that involves the function of attention (from zero to its highest point of concentration), while the latter is qualitative and has to do with the integrity of the contact barrier. In dreams, in essence, there may be a "dispersal of the ego, common sense" (Bion, 1992, p. 38), which in the psychotic leaves the id exposed. As Sandler noted (2005, p. 27), "a permanent underlying layer of psychosis permeates the so-called 'normal' personality".

By theorising the dream as a kind of poetic function of the mind, Bion deconstructs the opposition between pleasure principle and reality principle and between primary process and secondary process (Civitarese, 2008a, 2011b): the primary process is not set in opposition to the real but rather transforms it so that it is assimilable. When things work, there is a kind of antagonistic cooperation. Conversely, perfect adherence to reality can come from a function in excess of what Bion describes as the process of transformation in hallucinosis.

If the α function is active, what separates the waking state from dreaming is only attention,[4] which is focused or hyper-focused in the former state and not at all focused in the latter. Attention creates a frame that adjusts the amplitude of the space of consciousness and thus the number of elements which it processes from moment to moment. The primary process, which is prevalent in dreams, differs from the secondary process, which characterises the waking dream, because the frame of consciousness is much wider in the dream. Focused attention, which we can change while in states of waking consciousness by exercising our will, but which is also affected by several other factors, is inversely proportional to the extension of consciousness. From this point of view, logical-rational thought would be nothing but a spatially very small and highly focused dream.

This schematisation implies a basic continuity between primary and secondary process. Both nocturnal dreams and wakefulness, or day-dreams, use devices known in rhetoric as "figures of speech". Essentially the mind becomes acquainted with the real by means of the same mechanisms. It intersects with it in the same way both in waking life and in sleep. In both cases, metonymy and metaphor are the tropes that correspond to the basic cognitive mechanisms of thought. It may indeed be that the latter is only a derivative of the former, and that the key cognitive principle of psychic functioning is what rhetoric calls metonymy.

Also in mathematics, says Nietzsche, by operating a transference man equates unequal to equal, because in nature no two things are exactly alike.

> Knowledge, taken in the strict sense, has only the form of tautology and is empty. All knowledge that makes us progress is identifying what is not the same, alike: that is, it is essentially illogical. It is only in this way that we acquire a concept, and then we act as if the concept "man" was something real, while in fact it has only been constructed by us, by leaving aside all the individual characters. (1992, p. 105)

The first term in this operation is always the self. A primordial and unconscious "anthropomorphism" is the ground zero of symbolisation, the basis of the rhetorical transpositions from which the symbol is born. This is echoed by Bion:

> some kind of *objective reality* is attributed to the coherent system of facts, whereas there is no evidence to suppose that such a system, say physics, is anything more than *an appearance artificially produced by the limitations of the human mind unable to do more than see a tiny fraction of the totality of facts* and prone to attribute to that fraction of facts a relationship intrinsic to itself, while the supposed relationship between the facts is only a relationship that each fact has to the capacities of the human observer. (Bion, 1992, pp. 26–27, my italics)

Attention is what makes the difference between the primary and the secondary process. Although not identical, attention is closely related to consciousness, and it focuses and frames mental contents. Logical-rational thought is a dream with a frame, for example, the product of the function of selecting stimuli. Here we find one of the many paradoxes Bion has accustomed us to. If it corresponds to maximum focus, it means that, paradoxically, what could be called the "β function" is also present in the highest degree, that is, the possibility of forgetting (repressing) all the rest, everything that falls outside the field. Attention is a function of the contact barrier. Indeed, it follows it immediately on the Grid. It determines (in part, voluntarily) its permeability, and vice versa. The contact barrier is a symbol of the symbol, which is the thin film which, like a semi-permeable membrane, regulates the flow of identification-substitution-exchange between inside and outside.

An "absolute" waking state would be the symptom of the inability to fall asleep; an "absolute" dream, however, would be the inability to wake up. To avoid misunderstandings, it would be better not to say "inability to dream" but inability to create symbols. However, once again faithful to his method of transcending the caesura, Bion inverts the terms of the problem, wrong-foots the reader and prompts him to think precisely because of the desired methodical effect of ambiguity. He is not interested in passing on presumed truths. What does interest him, however, is urging—in fact, forcing—people to think. For this reason he reverses the perspective: we do not know the real through logical and rational protocols, but reality is the portion of the real that we are able to dream, in other words, to represent, to *pretend*. Like waking (and the feeling of material reality), so also the dream (and the feeling of psychic reality) is defined at the moment of transition from one state to the other. Consciousness, therefore, is identified with the possibility of amphibiously inhabiting the intermediate area that lies between these worlds.

The figure in the narrative theory of Genette that describes this shock crossing of boundaries between logically non-communicating universes is metalepsis (Civitarese, 2007; Genette, 2004). Whenever it passes across the border dividing the two worlds, the subject frames a theory of the mind, it gains a new awareness of its own subjective states and those of others. In short, it sees things from different points of view (and not from the absolute point of view of psychosis), as only dreams can do when they present several worlds simultaneously. It is for this reason that dreaming can be considered as the most profound form of thought we have, if thought is understood to mean the conscious and unconscious psychological work that creates a personal symbolic meaning for emotional experience. Dreaming becomes "the most free, most inclusive, and most deeply penetrating form of psychological work of which human beings are capable" (Ogden, 2009, p. 104).

Using the concrete metaphor of the impenetrable membrane that conceals Julia from the other patients and doctors, *They* shows what happens when the contact barrier loses its essential function of uniting and only retains its power to separate. Although he remains in a deristic state, the psychotic can perceive things precisely and acutely. He does not differ from the non-psychotic person according to the degree of focus of consciousness. What differentiates the two is how permeable the contact barrier is, both at minimum and maximum focus, in allowing the inscriptions already impressed on the memory to interact and make sense of the new traces.

In other words, it is important that the contact barrier is permeable enough to allow the data of experience to interact and modify the text of memory, and if necessary also the small number of ultra-clear and fixed inscriptions that produce delusion.

During wakefulness, many more β elements flood in from the outside world through the senses. During sleep, on the other hand, the work of the α function mostly transforms the β elements that emanate from a real that in this state is represented almost exclusively by the internal world of the subject, since the external stimuli are reduced to a minimum. The dream springs from an almost exclusive concentration on the inner world. In sleep the real to be transformed into dream consists primarily of the fabric of memories, of the "psychic mechanism [...] found ready in the normal structure of the psychic apparatus [*bereits fertiger Gebilde des psychischen Lebens*]" (Freud, 1900, p. 589).

The dream, Freud writes, "appears to be a reaction to everything which is simultaneously present as actual in the sleeping mind" (ibid., p. 228). This is a brilliant insight, and one which anticipates recent developments in the theory of dreams. In the dream, the individual re-reads the notes taken on the notebook of memory during the day and arranges them in sentences and paragraphs. In the waking state attention makes it possible to focus on content clearly and distinctly. Perhaps dreaming and waking are not different qualitatively, but only in terms of the different degree of attention that they pay to the inside and the outside. During sleep you work on the archives; they are the mnestic traces that provide the "words" for constructing the text of the dream, even if the doors of the senses are never completely closed. The dream works with materials that are already refined, with proto-emotions that have already met their shape and have now become transformed into sensitive ideas, and only minimally with primitive sensations coming directly from the body and the outside world.

Scattered through Freud's work are other remarks that seem to foreshadow Bion's idea. For example, in *The Interpretation of Dreams*, when discussing the problem of the difference between daydreams and dreams, and between wakefulness and dream, he already casts doubt on it: "the mind seems to behave like the sleeper in the anecdote. When someone asked him if he was asleep, he replied 'No'. But when his questioner went on to say: 'Then lend me ten florins', he took refuge in a subterfuge and replied: 'I'm asleep'" (1900, p. 224).

Bion's theory of dreams

With Bion, the theory of dreams changes radically. The dream is no longer, as it was for Freud, a by-and-large spurious psychic production whose sole function is to intercept the stimuli that might disrupt sleep and whose main value lies in offering an extraordinary window on the unconscious (Meltzer, 1984). Dream work is not driven invariably by the prime motive force of a childhood wish, which through the intervention of censorship is disguised in the manifest text. For Bion, the dream is the way in which the mind thinks the real, "O", so it even thinks itself and constructs itself. This is why Grotstein places it in column two of the Grid, which is the column of the falsification-fabrication-construction of the real (and of course can extend to include the lie). If K is falsehood—and here it is as if knowledge itself joined the current of tradition that denies *a priori* that the dream has any meaning—the only truth attainable consists in evolving into "O" or becoming "O", in the "being" at one that evokes the idea of the ecstasy of love and mysticism.

Bion warns us that knowing "O", the real, the ultimate reality, the thing-in-itself, is impossible, and can only occur in a dimension of "as if", that is, fiction or, as Nietzsche would of course say (meaning it in the theoretical and not moral sense), a lie.[5] The falsification of experience is a fact, or rather it is a prerequisite for the construction of the subject as such, even if it needs to stay in a relationship of balance with moments of truth understood as unison, fusion, *at-one-ment* with the real, moments when we acquire truth by plunging into the formless and infinite real, but at the price of an albeit fleeting return to indistinctiveness.[6] Knowing the real, not reality, which is already a fictional construct, means falsifying it. It is in fact a lie, which from another angle we would call truth. For Lacan absence does not exist in the real, and therefore neither does subject nor thought. This is why Bion sets up an opposition between knowledge of "O", that is, K (for Knowledge), and becoming "O", and in the clinical situation distinguishes between asserting something about another person's lived reality and allowing oneself to be pervaded by emotions conveyed via projective identifications to an extent that is sufficiently significant to become the other.

Bion addresses this problem in terms strikingly similar to those used by Hegel. The real apprehended by the intellect alone, that is, by science, is intrinsically false because it presupposes the ontological category of identity, which is completely abstract and upon which only a tautologous discourse can be constructed. If it is true, however, it is only because of a partial aspect of Being; it is a relative truth, because, while identity is indeed a characteristic of Being, it is not its sole characteristic. Scientific knowledge is based on assuming a subject isolated from the real, completely detached from the object of knowledge. What I know is not the true real. The true real, everything that exists, exists as a denial or cancellation of that which is other than oneself, of the fact that, although denied, is preserved. The world can only be conceived and perceived from a dialectical perspective: "Negativity and Identity [not identity alone] are [the] two primordial and universal ontological categories" (Kojève, 1947, p. 199). It is the play of these two categories which gives rise to the transformation of human beings and makes man a being endowed with the feeling of existing.

Dream work, known as dream-work α and subsequently α function, is active both in sleep and in waking. Ultimately, dreaming amounts to constructing more and more sophisticated symbols, in other words, thinking. The α function transforms β elements, proto-sensorial or proto-emotional data, into α elements or into dream-thoughts which can be stored in memory and used to dream or to think. It can be assumed that this transformation activity uses materials of different origin. Nocturnal dreams, for example, to a large extent start from semi-finished materials that have already been processed and stored in memory, unlike concurrent somatic sensory and perceptual internal or external stimuli. This involves thinking about symbolism as a gradient that goes from the symbolic equation to the symbol and, paradoxically, to the "symbolic equation" of the absolute—and, in the concrete reality of the world, impossible—identity between algebraic terms, without any real break in continuity. They range from the proto-symbol of projective identification with the object to the concept. The α function is to be seen as originating in autistic forms (Ogden, 1989); it emerges from the body, and must be distinguished from dreaming and thinking. It only provides the Lego building blocks for the dream and thought. The dream is closer to the real of common sense; it is seen as an epistemological function of the mind and essentially as the royal road to reality (Sandler, 2005).

For Bion, the α-dream creates the contact barrier, the semi-permeable threshold separating the conscious from the unconscious. For this reason, only if one is capable of transforming emotions and raw feelings into α elements can one be either awake or asleep and dreaming. It is the dream that creates a mental space in which the contact barrier, composed of sequences of α elements, distinguishes the conscious from the unconscious and makes for balanced mental functioning.

The ability to symbolise, to carry out the operations of language we describe in manuals of rhetoric, is acquired through another mind—Bion's theory is fundamentally social or intersubjective (Grotstein, 2007)—and like a filter it shields the bodily homeostasis from the flood of emotions and remains within parameters compatible with life.

The dream theories of Freud and Bion support different conceptions of therapeutic action, which in practice do not necessarily exclude each other. For Freud, treatment means removing the veil of repression and translating the productions of the unconscious into something conscious; for Bion, it means passing on to the other the method for symbolising through receptivity to the projective identifications and the capacity for reverie. In short, there is a shift of focus from the contained—the quantities in an algebraic operation—to the container; in other words, on to the functions of the operation: addition, subtraction, multiplication, division. Although, of course, in terms of the mind the two objectives cannot be clearly separated, no more than form and content can be separated in art.

What links the two different models of how analysis works is Klein's idea that it is essential to modulate the expression of anxiety in the here and now of the session.

Dream images are no longer something to be deciphered but are rather already the more or less successful product of the symbol-poietic operations of the individual. If an ogre, and not the father, appears in the dream of an eight-year-old child, this does not make me think so much of masking, but of the creative work—in the sense of connecting and transforming emotions—carried out by dreaming. I focus on the *quid* of meaning that the image adds, and from there possibly I start again, proposing, as in a game of scribbles, another symbolic form or other story lines. I make available a relatively empty form, which can propitiate new thoughts or, to put it in the language of Bion, realisations. No longer the translation of ogre into father but the poetic transfiguration from father to ogre. The latter is also a translation but it is open-ended, unsaturated. More than hiding, the dream reveals. It opens up a multiplicity of points of view and interpretations.

Carla tells me a dream in which she imagines she is recounting a nightmare to some friends, and thinks she must keep it in mind to tell me too (so it is a dream within a dream). She is in an underground train carriage. The train has stopped. Next to her there is only one other passenger. She is worried. She realises that her feet are being licked by a layer of lava and she starts to feel a burning sensation. The other passenger reassures her that the train will soon start moving again, but she is anxious and she wakes up.

At this point in her life she is facing numerous problems at work and with her boyfriend, although they are more or less repressed. What is more, this is the last session before the holiday break. I associate the dream with the scene from the *Iliad* in which the opposing armies of the

Trojans and the Greeks face each other. To give an idea of the speed and violence of the clash, the text describes how the soldiers run towards each other as if the earth were burning under their feet. When I first read this image, it had excited me and impressed itself on my memory, and now it gives me a measure of the degree of violence of the conflicts Carla is going through and which are depicted in the dream, which might have something to do with something incandescent and violent, something like lava, eruptive, beta in nature, which regards the analysis.

In my daydream it is as if I had absorbed her pain—as a mother suffers the pain of her child because she loves it—and I had been charged with dreaming it for her and carrying on her dream. I could react in various ways: I could say nothing (which in itself would change the analytic field), mention to her something of my dream, or more generally tell her something starting from my dream and the additional meaning that it has produced (e.g., that it is a warning that something bad is going to happen and that it seems to her that strangely enough the others don't notice anything). My memory of the *Iliad* is not so much an association, a product of the left hemisphere, as another dream, a product of the right hemisphere.

A non-dream about Carla's dream could have been an interpretation, as it were, by the book. It could have been something like: in a few days we will have to stop seeing each other and this worries you. In short, I would only be using the rational part of the mind. The difference is quite clear. The descriptions in the *Iliad* of the bloodiest clashes between soldiers in battle are far more expressive than the images of *Saving Private Ryan*. If, however, in terms of separation, I had thought of the meeting on the city walls between Hector and Andromache, that could have brought tears to my eyes, thinking back to when she begs him not to clash with Achilles: "Hector, thou art to me father and queenly mother, thou art brother, and thou art my stalwart husband. Come now, have pity" (Homer, 1991). Here, too, a cerebral understanding would have been much less significant.

The technique of interpretation aims at maximum possible contextualisation. It takes to the extreme an important Freudian principle, since it includes the derivatives of waking dream thought and the reverie of the analyst. The interpreter's contribution to the dream recounted by the patient is already embryonically present in Freud's instruction to the analyst to maintain evenly suspended attention. This is the next step after Klein's extension of the dream to include play as a space in which experience can be shared.

Not everyone orientates himself in this way. In clinical practice, some of the analysand's communications are not read as signs, that is, as real *and* constructed or "fictitious", but only as referential, and therefore they have nothing to say about the transference relationship. They are *in-significant*, in a sense inert. Taken literally, these emissaries from the world of facts and what "really happened" induce a paralysing effect of reality. It is the situation of immersion in which the ludic space or the dream-space of the setting is erased. Reality is experienced as imprisoned mankind's dream without awakening in *The Matrix*, a perfect allegory of the operative functioning of the mind.

When a person is unable to dream, they can neither sleep nor stay awake. For Bion, the night dream is only a small part of a much larger and continuous process which takes place both during wakefulness and during sleep. In order to be able to dream, the dialectic of the positions must be active. It is in dreams, he writes, that positions are negotiated; in other words, the intervention of a selected fact marks the point of crisis that enables the passage from the paranoid and schizoid levels of the mind to the depressive ones and vice versa.

In the eyes of Bion, Freud considered above all the negative aspects of the dream, the processes of concealment and distortion of content that otherwise would be immediately understood. What Bion emphasises are the positive aspects of processing and synthesis of experience. For it to enter consciousness, there is no perception that should not first be "dreamt". Bion is interested in "the way in which the *necessary* dream is *constructed*" (1992, p. 33). The dreams we see in *Dark City, The Matrix* (which was partly made by re-using some of the sets from *Dark City*) (Proyas, 1998), *The Truman Show* (Weir, 1998), and *The Island* (Bay, 2005) are hyperrealistic, delusional, paranoid. They effectively illustrate what Bion called transformation in hallucinosis, that is, not the perception of non-existent objects, but of false relations between objects.

The story of the dream itself has less to do with the experience of the dream and more with the absorption-digestion of the data from the current context of the experience, of which, of course, the various forms of memory are also an integral part.

It is the constructive activity of the α function that produces the α elements, units that come together to form the contact barrier, the semi-permeable membrane that separates the unconscious from the conscious and at each moment adjusts the expression of the relevant psychic product. If excessive pressure from one of the two sides of the contact barrier (the slash in the formula Inc/Cs), coming either from the inner world or factual reality, assumes a traumatic quality, it prevents the proper functioning of the α function and of thoughts and dreams. The contact barrier is replaced by the β screen, a non-permeable membrane of β elements that surgically separates the unconscious from the conscious. This will then lead to different types of psychic suffering, from the all-unconscious of psychosis and hallucination to the all-reality of people who are cut off from their inner self and the lifeblood of their emotions—a more egosyntonic but in some respects not less malignant form of "psychosis". Dreams that yield no associations and reality which is freeze-dried, sucked dry of dreams, are alike: "they are similar to hallucinatory gratification" (Bion, 1992, p. 112).

The β screen cannot function as a frame, as a joining point between two worlds, because all it sees is the clear choice between inside and outside. It is disjunctive logic: either identity or difference. The secret passages between worlds watched over by the guardian of attention are blocked or seriously obstructed. This is why the psychotic, lacking the filter function of the contact barrier, can neither dream nor be awake. His universe is structured according to a symbolic equation rather than symbolisation (Segal, 1957). Words are treated as things. Symbols, however, presuppose the distance of words from things, a rupture that is equivalent to the punctiform but sustainable void of the absence of the object, the perception of the presence of a non-breast or a non-thing. This is why Julia Kristeva (2003) is able to assert that imaginary matricide is the origin of the symbol. Nonetheless, the defensive purpose of the β screen is clear: it protects against the risk that the mind be flooded with uncontrollable and potentially destructive emotions. It is here that the other, or in clinical situations the analyst, can step in with his ability to make sense of experience and to function as an auxiliary ego.

In summary, the concept of waking-dream thought deconstructs the binary opposition between dream and wakefulness. The dream does not close off all the sensory paths of external perception, just as the waking dream is infiltrated by dreams. Delusion contains a kernel of truth, just as any truth contains an element of *seeing-as* (Wittgenstein), of lies (that is, etymologically, of the images/fictions of the mind). The dream also becomes such only because of the difference that emerges at the moment of waking up. Paraphrasing Winnicott, one might say that there is no such thing as a dream if it is not accompanied by awakening. Not only that; what we have is always a mixture of dream and wakefulness in different proportions—evidently consciousness has multiple modes of operation. Both delusion and dream are expressed according to the rules of rhetoric, the metonymic law of the part substituting for the whole or the consequence for the antecedent and vice versa. What changes is the value expressed by the dream/wakefulness ratio, which is equal to the degree of awareness of the dream itself and depends on attention. Total adhesion to the real leads to hallucinosis. The use of the symbol (the dream) implies the knowledge that the word is not the thing, and that the sign is arbitrarily connected to it.[7] The psychotic's inability to dream does not mean that he does not dream at night but that he does not wake up (at all) from the dream. He cannot live simultaneously in the two worlds of sleep and wakefulness. He does not distinguish hallucination from perception.

Again, Bion's statement can only be understood if by dream we mean dream plus wakefulness, in other words the understanding that the dream also comprises the moment of awakening. Similarly, a musical note also includes the silence that follows it and film is also made up of the black strips that separate the exposed frames. Wakefulnesss without dream is a state of hallucinosis. A dream without waking is a state of hallucination. "Normality" is a measure of the ability to move between waking and dreaming. Therefore, the inability to dream is to be understood as the inability to wake up from the dream or to dream knowing that you are dreaming. It would be like using symbols without knowing that they are fictions or indices of reality and not reality itself. In Damasio's term (1999) the inability to dream should be construed as the inability to move from "nuclear" consciousness, made up of images that translate the objects present in the present time of the perceptual field, to "extended" consciousness, that which allows us to articulate these images with a sense of self.

The space of the dream

Masud Khan also talks about the inability to dream in two important papers: *Dream psychology and the evolution of the psychoanalytic situation* (1962) and *The use and abuse of dream in psychic experience* (1972) (the latter published in a revised version in *The Privacy of the Self* in

1974 and in Sarah Flanders' anthology *The Dream Discourse Today* in 1993).

A good dream, according to Khan, is a dream that successfully carries out the dream work of metabolising an unconscious desire (and thus preserves sleep), and which is available upon waking as a mental experience for the ego of the dreamer. A successful dream both reflects and enhances the strength of the ego.

Basing himself on two published contributions by Winnicott in *Playing and Reality* (1971), Khan distinguishes between the dream as a neuro-physiological phenomenon (dream-process) and the ability to make use of the dream (the mechanisms of symbolisation of the dream work) and to enter into dream space.

This concept also mirrors Winnicott's idea of transitional space and takes inspiration from the squiggle game.

Unlike dreaming as an innate psychic process, dream space belongs to the field of the symbolic and as a result is acquired over time and only if the individual receives proper care. If this care is inadequate, the subject is not really able to use the dream in a lively and creative way. In essence Khan distinguishes between the script of a dream and the ability to contain it or to incorporate it into a scene in an internal theatre. To understand this point, one need only think of the difference between reading a play and seeing it performed. Reading a play often leaves us indifferent, while the performance of that same text at the theatre moves us. Clearly, theatrical writing is, so to speak, disembodied; it is regarded as an aid to the body of the actors and the materiality of the set. If this inner space has not been developed, the dream tends to be externalised or acted out in reality. Possible symptoms of this are fantasising or dreaming compulsively and the recounting in analysis of hybrid and bizarre dreams. In such cases, Khan suggests interpreting the dream as little as possible so as not to cover the lack of dream-space.

In one of the two vignettes recounted in his article, Khan describes the case of a young male analysand with a seriously traumatic history behind him, who up until puberty had suffered from nightmares which then turned into long dreams full of strange details. These (not really dreamt) dreams, since they are a form of possession, or something the subject does not know how to use (Winnicott speaks of a person's ability to *use* the object once he has realised its external existence), have a clear defensive purpose against painful recollections and anger. They are the sign of a certain dissociation within the subject's personality. In the second vignette Kahn shows the gradual conquest of a dream space by a young man who constantly fantasises as a coerced way of isolating himself from the world and the vitality of experience.

What defines the dream then, is once again the framework of awakening, the contact barrier that acts as a boundary and transition zone between dream and waking. The dream as an innate neuro-physiological process is not enough if it is not re-dreamed in column two of Bion's grid, which is the column of lies, falsification, the "as-if" of the real, the impersonal and formless "O".

The dream nourishes the mind only if it can be actualised in dream space. Only in this second phase, which follows the first as day follows night, can the subject have access to his own psychic reality through the dream instead of acting out his undreamt dream in the world. The capacity to dream is not to be equated automatically with the brain activity inherent to dreaming at night. The dream space is not given but acquired. What is undreamt remains as a foreign body, a flaw in the warp of the symbolic, and can cause nightmares, recurrent dreams, but also rich daydreams that cut the individual off from reality—or portions of it. However, if the dream is contained in the dream space, it can become, as in Winnicott's game of squiggles, a space in which we learn from experience.

It must be said that we are unlikely to find in Bion advice as to how to analyse dreams. In general it is not easy to translate his brilliant ideas into technical principles. Maybe we need to think of his style as an analyst as being similar to the way he conducted his seminars. At least, this is how he answered the question asked of him by a colleague at a seminar held in Los Angeles (Bion, 1978). It is true that his writings, and especially his radical critique of the binary conceptual oppositions that shape meaning in the theories of psychoanalysis, can give us valuable information. It is as if he had laid the foundation for a whole new way of looking at dreams, especially with his concept of waking dream thought, and then left to others the task of building the rest of the edifice. The others who have taken up this task include Meltzer, Grotstein, Ogden, and Ferro.

Dark City

"What goes on in the city at night," asks Pontalis (2003, p. 13), "in the city where the unexpected can happen at any moment? […] How can the *same* city, busy and almost domesticated by day, be transformed at night, when it is (whether reality or imagination is of little importance) delivered to the 'shadow people', vagrants, prostitutes, when it becomes a place of lawlessness, wandering, of crime, filth, as if the underground, the slums, rose back up to the surface? I believe that Freud never stopped referring to psychoanalysis as 'depth psychology'."

Giulio is tormented by the same question. I can't believe my ears when I hear him say he is having an absurd, exaggerated, "visceral" dream. At night he feels that aliens are carrying out experiments on him. And I've just seen a film where something similar happens for real (that is to say, a pretence, as in a dream!): *Dark City*, directed by Alex Proyas, who was also responsible for the successful film *The Crow* (1994).

Dark City takes the opposite tack from *They* and recounts not the loss but the gradual (though not definitive) recovery of the α function and the ability to dream. At the beginning, the protagonist, John Murdoch (Rufus Sewell), is incapable of either really waking up or really sleeping and lives in a kind of eternal night. He finds himself in a hotel room that is unfamiliar to him. He does not even remember what it is called and has to be told by the hotel receptionist. He then gleans some more information from a wallet that has been mysteriously returned to him. Moreover, like one of Kafka's unconscious and humiliated characters, he finds himself being blamed for a series of murders of prostitutes he knows nothing about. The latest victim lies dead in the room next to his. At the beginning of the film he says, "I feel like I'm living someone else's nightmare"—hardly an original remark but nonetheless a good description of the situation. For the rest of the film, Sewell will serve as eyes for the spectator, who in fact never knows much more than he does about what's going on.

Of course, being accused of crimes he did not commit, starting from the prostitute found dead in the hotel room next to his at the beginning of the film, can be seen as representing his unconscious feeling of guilt about the sadistic attacks on the body of the mother, which are in fact psychically very real. And the Strangers can be seen as an inhuman and ruthless superego. The search for individuality (*narcissism*), on the other hand, comes to stand for the impulse to escape from a fusional, nocturnal, uterine climate, where time is suspended, and to fight against *socialism*—understood in the Bionian sense as belonging to the group and as one of two poles of all the instincts—in order to construct one's own identity, ultimately with a view to psychic (re-)birth.

Other possible allegorical readings are moral (the sleep of consciousness or of the individual), political (totalitarianism, historical revisionism, negationism, individualism *vs.* the conformism of the masses), psychological (the *après-coup* effect of memory and the unconscious lie as the necessary falsification of reality), and so on. But here I would like to focus on another perspective.

If *They* describes how a delusional idea in the dream can develop into a full-blown delusion, in *Dark City* the grey area of the nightmare is traversed in the opposite direction. The nightmare signals that the mind is struggling to perform its digestive function, but that it nevertheless still strives to remove the obstacle. It remains to be seen with what success.

One can imagine a gradient that goes from the perfectly successful dream (which is therefore forgotten) → remembered dream → to the recounted dream (a kind of proto-nightmare) → to the nightmare → to hallucinosis → to hallucination, reflecting mounting dysfunctions of the ability to dream-think. We do not remember a successful dream in the same way as we are not aware of the process of digestion when it proceeds without any problems. A remembered dream is an unfinished product that requires the supplement of psychic work. The symptom of a difficulty, however, is turned into an invaluable opportunity—as is the case with so many other crisis situations—if we do this work and go back several times to the images of the dream in the same way as we go back and re-read lines of poetry we find moving. Accordingly, it would not be contradictory to say that if dreams are forgotten when they are successful, being able to dream and recall dreams is an important incentive to seek psychic integration (Ogden, 2001a).

In a climate typical of film noir from the forties ("I mean I was really trying to do kind of a Raymond Chandler story but with a science fiction twist," the director admitted in an interview with Rob Blackwelder,[8] 1998), it is gradually revealed—by the psychiatrist, Dr Daniel Schreber[9] (Kiefer Sutherland), a character no less disturbing than the strange masters he is forced to serve—that the whole city and its inhabitants have ended up in an experiment devised by alien beings (pre- or post-human?), the Strangers. Threatened with extinction in their world, they have taken refuge on Earth, where they hide in the bowels of a city reminiscent of New York. They have strange powers that come from their extraordinary tuning ability (attunement/harmonisation), in other words their ability to identify en masse and absolutely with the orders of their leader. They use this faculty to set up spectacular experiments to help them discover the essence of humanity and thus succeed in surviving in an environment otherwise hostile to them. Unlike humans, who are individuals, the Strangers all share the same memories.

The crucial question is: how does one become a human being?

Every night at the stroke of midnight, the Strangers put all the inhabitants to sleep and pour into their minds (or maybe only the minds of a few) other people's memories, false memories, just to see how they react on awakening. The scene in which they rearrange the layout of the city to make it consistent with the new memories forcibly installed in the minds of the inhabitants is utterly fascinating.

Undoubtedly this is the sequence that is etched most clearly in the minds of the spectator—the architecture is reminiscent of neo-expressionism, the paintings of Escher, and some of the urban landscapes of Feininger: an evocative way of depicting the work of re-arranging the dream-thoughts of the dream. Equally remarkable is the scene in which the psychiatrist prepares test tubes containing the memories to be installed.

In the city nobody can resist the sleep-inducing spell of the Strangers, except for Murdoch-Sewell, who precisely because he has preserved, or is regaining, this glimmer of consciousness, represents a serious threat to them. After reformatting his memory, the psychiatrist is unable to inject new memories. Murdoch wakes up, but at this point what remains are only residual fragments of old memories. At some point he discovers that he has acquired some of the Strangers' telekinetic ("moving") powers, that is, the ability to reshape physical environments, and gradually as he becomes aware of this fiction-falsification—it is as if all of a sudden he realised he was walking around Cinecittà or a Hollywood studio set—he is able, with the help of other human beings (the detective, the "wife", the psychiatrist) to wake up for real. At this point—by now we are at the end of the film—day breaks.

Murdoch thus ceases to function psychically on the basis of the symbolic equation, rediscovers the fiction of reality, in other words, the gap that exists between the symbol and the symbolised, and begins to think. Sensing the fiction into which psychic reality forces things in order to get to know them means being able to wake up and at the same time realise that we also dream when we are awake.

Of course, the nightmare is not the ultimate frontier of psycho-physical dissolution. It still represents an attempt to give meaning to experience.

If we think about it for a moment, we realise that, like any "symptom", it has a double meaning: on the one hand, it signals the failure of the dream, on the other it forces us to wake up from the dream—and awakening is one of the two essential features of the dream—and makes it in some way necessary to continue the dream when we are awake. We feel a more forceful drive to recount a nightmare than a dream. There is a greater sense of urgency.

All dressed in black and apparently afflicted with a contagious conjunctivitis which must give them an annoying photophobia, the Strangers have the appearance of fanatical priests and bear a vague resemblance to Murnau's *Nosferatu* (1922)—or indeed Herzog's remake (1978). Mr Book (played by the talented Ian Richardson) is their head and the hotel room where John Murdoch finds himself has the number 614. The reference to the Bible is clear. John 6:14 reads: "This is of a truth that prophet that should come into the world". Similar quotations and allusions are perhaps designed to suggest that the cause of the Strangers' loss of humanity lies in their being the degeneration of an institution. They are deaf to what Bion meant by the concept of the Messianic idea, deaf to new and unknown ideas. Murdoch, on the other hand, is the individual able to bear the truth and to fight for it.

At all events, what is interesting for our purposes is to see them as expressions of the emotions or unformulated experience (Stern, 2009) that trigger dream work, disassemble and re-assemble its sets, reshuffle memories; as something that arises from unresolved tensions, from an imbalance, the feeling of having lost something vital. This is why they are still "O", the real which is not yet humanised/personalised.

The Strangers can be seen as unsublimated instincts, clouds of β elements, psychotic nuclei, internal persecutory objects, drives to fragment experience, slippages into paranoid-schizoid states of mind.

They are also "strange" in that they are alienated and unknown aspects of the self, in other words, that which has not yet been assimilated or symbolised and thus not yet dreamt, or that which has been dreamt but not in a dream, or, lastly, in that they are defences against more mature forms of thought which deny access to a sense of responsibility.

This is why Murdoch is their quarry, because he represents the awakening of consciousness. The Strangers are bearers of symbiotic or fusional values on a par with groups in (Bion's) "basic assumptions", or of Bleger's "agglutinated"/"viscous" nuclei (Civitarese, 2004); but the reason is that in this way they are always seeking to stand up to what threatens the ego. In other words, it would be wrong to identify them too absolutely with something negative and see them solely in opposition to Murdoch.

Murdoch and the Strangers, in reality, are two sides of the same person, like Julia and her persecutors, or like Carl Stargher the child and the serial killer he has become. They are bound together by antagonistic solidarity, like parties opposed in ideology but not in conflict. The only real conflict is ultimately with the annihilating forces of infinity, impersonal "O".

What saves Murdoch is the very power of *tuning* (harmony/unison?) that the Strangers have—the ability to go to sleep in order to try to dream. It is important that Murdoch shares this faculty with the Strangers, and moreover—as in a real dream—is also able to wake up. The film seems to suggest that his mental health depends on α and β, the symbiotic bond and the frustration of separation and the absence of the other, the sense of self and common sense, narcissism and socialism. It is in essence the oscillation between the paranoid guilt induced by the Strangers and depressive guilt (Cp $\leftrightarrow$ Cd), against which the alien beings represent a defence between the polarities of confusion and depression, including negative capability and selected fact (Cn $\leftrightarrow$ Fs).

There are quite a few gaps and inconsistencies in the film's plot, duly pointed out by critics. However, the question is whether they might not be an effective—perhaps unintentional—way of giving the spectator a sense of the anguished perplexity that John Murdoch experiences at the beginning, and whether they might not in fact serve to immerse him in a dream-like atmosphere.

The film never actually grabs the spectator, in the sense of moving him (or if so, only intermittently), and may strike many as inconclusive. Nonetheless it is a fascinating effort whose tremendous pace and spectacular images have won it legions of loyal fans. The *Chicago Sun-Times* numbered it among its top ten films of the year. The depiction of a dark-tinged, unhealthy, paranoid paranoid world has made *Dark City* a memorable representation of a modern *nekyia*, a journey through the most inhospitable and obscure regions of the soul.

But what marks the difference between the fates of Julia and Murdoch? Could it be the sense of guilt, denied in the former, worked through in the latter? After driving out Mr Book, and significantly only through the power of his mind, John fights and defeats him, his own fanatic and murderous superego. The only time Julia mentions guilt, during her meeting with Dr Booth, she does so in an abstract and artificial way. Unlike her, Murdoch manages to authentically pass from persecution to responsibility, from paranoid guilt to depressive guilt. Does this mean that at the start Murdoch has greater resources than Julia for interpreting reality? Or that he has found them in the street, for example, symbolically, when he falls in love for real with his (fake) wife?

Politics of the mind

Freud emphasises the negative side of the dream, whereas Bion sees it as an epistemological function of the mind, unconscious psychological activity driven by a "truth instinct or drive" (Grotstein, 2007, p. 139). He lauds its positive side as a place where the paranoid-schizoid and depressive positions (PS and D) of the mind are negotiated, allegorised in *Dark City* in the respective roles of Mr. Book and Murdoch.

First as α function and later as dream-work during the dream and during waking (and we should follow Grotstein by conceding that there are varying degrees when "cooking" α elements), the dream *fictionalises* the real and thus constructs reality. This is done by making sensory impressions unconscious at the time they are inscribed in memory—making them unconscious entails attributing meaning to them—and then selecting the derivatives that are allowed access to consciousness.

The model for how a new thought is born is how our *first* thought came into being. The child has a rudimentary consciousness that perceives without understanding/containing either in a pre-verbal or verbal way. The reverie or the un/conscious of the mother treats/digests for the child this raw data and does not simply pass on to him the final product of the transformation, but enables him to internalise the tools that will allow him to do it for himself. Contained and container structure the child's unconscious, which expands and gains a greater ability to perform a given task automatically, without burdening consciousness. The α function first transforms stimuli into traces, into initial inscriptions in memory; dream work and unconscious/waking dream thought (both of which systems work simultaneously) rework more sophisticated, less concrete, more abstract traces.

It is clear that once these skills have been acquired, in normal conditions the α function of the subject will transform β elements into α elements. The dialogue with the object becomes an intrapsychic dialogue: as Ogden writes (2009, p. 5), "This work of dreaming is achieved by means of a conversation between different aspects of the personality".

If one is faced with overly violent emotions and is not able to handle them, one again needs to turn to the mind and capacities of someone else. When situations are not particularly critical, this is what we do every day.

If they accumulate excessively, untransformed β elements that bypass being inscribed on the palimpsest of memory—not "unconscioused" in Bion's term (Bion, 1992)—can only be encapsulated and eliminated through acting out or symptoms. However, a certain suspension of β elements in equilibrium with α elements is required to escape from the psychic stagnation that would occur in the depressive position, to forget, and to communicate via projective identification. The presence of β elements also continues to bear witness to the demands of the body, as opposed to a consciousness that would otherwise become disembodied.

Ultimately, the functional state of the mind is defined at any given moment by the position that in an imaginary Cartesian chart would be expressed by the values on the abscissa regarding the degree of permeability of the contact barrier and on the ordinate by those of attention-consciousness. One defines the amplitude of the state of consciousness, which is at its maximum in the dream because that is where the focus tends towards zero, and at its minimum in waking, where attention is hyper-focused; the other expresses the ability to shift constantly between paranoid-schizoid and depressive position (PS $\leftrightarrow$ D), and between negative capability and selected fact (Cn $\leftrightarrow$ Fs).

Both mental health and knowledge need α space and β space. The negative capability that Bion recommends to the analyst is nourished by β. The β elements have the same function as the black strips between film frames: they are not one hundred per cent identical with sensory data, but they are something intermediate between these and α elements. When there is a transition from $\beta \rightarrow \alpha$, this affords relief, and you see more things, but it also implies falling from a higher level into a new state of uncertainty and persecution; in other words, every psychic synthesis presents itself immediately as a thesis for a new antithesis. The struggle between Murdoch and the Strangers never ends.

We could represent these different possibilities as follows: pure sequences of α elements ($\alpha + \alpha + \alpha \ldots + \alpha n$) produce a state of hallucinosis, sequences of only β elements ($\beta + \beta + \beta \ldots + \beta n$) a hallucinatory state; mixed α β sequences, depending on whether there is a dominance of α ($\alpha + \alpha + \alpha + \beta \ldots$) or a dominance of β ($\alpha + \beta + \beta + \beta \ldots$), correspond to a state of wakefulness or sleep/dream, respectively.

Neither α function nor dream work is directly accessible. We can only know the derivatives of waking dream thought, which means that in each current clinical situation the story of the dream tells us something of the night dream only indirectly, just as the recollection of an event only informs us subsequently about the past. The nocturnal dream is eventually taken up again (re-dreamed) in the live dream of the session, that is, the real. To paraphrase Freud, it is like recognising the marble of a Roman building reused centuries later to build a baroque palace. What is on stage is always the here and now, memories of the past and of the future included.

Dark City, then, is a film that implicitly contains a dream theory. At the origin of it all is the murder of some women, which already evokes the symbolic matricide from which the subject is born and which Kristeva refers to with the concept of abjection (1980), and then guilt. If the weight of guilt is excessive, the Inc/Cs equilibrium becomes unbalanced. The integrated functioning of the primary and secondary processes consumes too much energy, the filter of the contact barrier clogs up, the optimal ratio between dreaming and waking changes. Then exceptional defences must be deployed: special laws are passed, a curfew is imposed and the army is called upon to patrol the streets. The subject at that point is already inside the nightmare. He has become a citizen of *Dark City*.

The Strangers are those that uphold the new tyrannical regime of persecutors, who fragment the sense of self-continuity, and who defend themselves from the depression that causes their lack of vitality and their decline by plunging the ego into a paranoid climate. In aid of repression and splitting, they destroy memories, they make them evanescent, they strip the city settings of coherence. To escape from depressive guilt, they live in an inverted world of persecutory guilt.

This is the reason why early in the film Murdoch wakes up (in part) but does not remember who he is: his memory does not work. He lives in a paranoid, nightmare world, and in the nightmare he creates aliens—possibly the bizarre objects described by Bion—until he creates a fiction, or in other words again becomes able to make use of symbols. Only then does he really wake up. Only when he, just like Bion, discovers that the dream is closer to the reality of the conscious world.

At the end of the film there's a twist. We realise that we are not on Earth, but on a kind of huge spaceship, and that the people are probably there because they have been kidnapped and taken away from our planet. The ending leaves open the question of which awakening is truly Murdoch's. And this is precisely the question that *Dark City* in its role as sphinx asks us: what if all our memories were manipulated and the reality that surrounds us were an invention, a lie or a construction?

Notes

1. See, for example, Bacon's *Two Figures with a Monkey* (1973), or his *Seated Figure* (1974).
2. The transformations of the psychic elements Bion describes are the same as those which Damasio describes in his terminology as the steps from the proto-self (the stage of β elements and the absence of reflective consciousness) to the *nuclear* consciousness (the level where non-verbal descriptions or images are formed—Edelman uses the term "qualia"; these are the α elements, which give a subtle and fleeting sense of self in the here and now), and from this to the extended consciousness or autobiographical self (the ability to dream-think that implies not only the here and now but also the ability to place oneself in the broader perspective that embraces memories of the past and the future).

   The neural self or proto-self "is a collection of interconnected and temporarily coherent collection of neural patterns which represent the state of the organism, moment by moment, at different levels of the brain. We are *not* conscious of the proto-self" (Damasio, 1999, p. 174). Both nuclear and extended consciousness are nothing but maps of varying complexity describing the ongoing relationships between organisms and objects ("the relationship between the changing proto-self and the sensorimotor maps of the object that causes those changes ", ibid., p. 170). Nuclear consciousness is already a minimal narrative, the content of which is given by the causal relationship between body and object, which takes place in mere fractions of seconds. It is a *story without words*, made up of sequences of images, but also of the rhythms of tactile, auditory, etc., sensations, which correspond to the activation of neural patterns. According to the nuclear consciousness we are all like the "fleeting-improvised men" Judge Schreber described in his memoirs

(1903). Like Penelope's web, nuclear consciousness is constantly being woven and coming undone. It is the dynamic representation of the moment, the only one possible at the start of life. The object of nuclear consciousness, even just a memory, emerges from a process of exaltation. The image comes from the intensified map of the object. At the dawn of the image, then, the organism "wakes up", attention is concentrated, the object is in focus.

Extended consciousness necessarily presupposes nuclear consciousness and may be present at various levels of intensity, according to varying degrees of attention. *It is weak in dreams, strong in waking.* Because, unlike nuclear consciousness, it is expressed on a time scale of seconds and minutes, it needs considerable resources of working memory. Extended consciousness involves the ability to predict future events and to plan responses and then to implement behaviours that do not necessarily have to make sense now but may acquire it later. In this model (which, just to get an idea of how things work also in more "scientific" domains than psychoanalysis, we would struggle to translate into Edelman's terms), the α function corresponds to the transition from the proto-emotions and proto-sensations of the proto-self to visual or other types of pictograms of nuclear consciousness and then on to a first level of the alphabetisation of emotions. The apparatus for dreaming/thinking would instead be delegated the task of taking the narrative of elementary nuclear consciousness to the full self-awareness of expanded consciousness, thus making it the third order of organisation of the psyche. Obviously there are no exact matches between these concepts, the definitions are ambiguous and involve margins of conventionality. The question as to what is meant by self-consciousness, whether or not it embraces language, changes perspective depending on one's assumptions. Also, preverbal does not mean pre-cultural.

3. See Grotstein (2007, p. 92): "the infant is born with the rudiments of α function and generates α elements, albeit primitive, immature and non-lexical ones."

4. Although his book is entitled *Attention and Interpretation*, Bion actually says little or nothing about attention as a psychological function.

5. See Grotstein (2007, p. 124): "We are O and are terrified of it—thus the need for inward-directed 'sunglasses' that allow diminished illumination and disguise. O *is* the Real. What we believe we experience is a 'virtual reality'—a Reality that has become 'virtued' ('laundered') by the refractions of phantasy, imagination, illusion and symbolization, leaving us with a 'cooked' 'Real' (O) suitable for our timid digestion."

6. See Merleau-Ponty (1969, p. xii): "Before our undivided existence the world is true; it exists. The unity, the articulations of both are

intermingled. We experience in it a truth which shows through and envelops us rather than being held and circumscribed by our mind."

7. For Merleau-Ponty the word is linguistic gesture, "verbal gesticulation" (1945, p. 258). Vanzago (2012) points out that the bond is arbitrary if we think of its conceptual meaning, but stops being so if we think of the emotional meaning. The style of the speaker is expressed in the body of the word—that is to say, his own body and the story of his life.

8. www.splicedwire.com/features/proyas.html.

9. In the film there are several allusions to *Memoirs of My Nervous Illness* by Daniel Paul Schreber ([1903] 1974); hence the name of the character played by Kiefer Sutherland.

CHAPTER FIVE

The dream as an aesthetic object

Rashomon

It is not easy now to appreciate the impact that Meltzer's *Dream-Life* had when it first came out in 1984, since more recent literature on dreams has tended rather to ignore it. Bion's theory of thought, Meltzer's discussion of which is perhaps the best that his book has to offer, has since become more widely known and acclaimed. Read again today, *Dream-Life* can prove rather disappointing. One should, however, be fair to Meltzer. It should be acknowledged that he strove with dedication, passion, and creativity to popularise Bion, to saturate with clinical applications Bion's "empty" conceptual forms and to develop others in an original way—for example, the "Negative Grid", the inversion of the α function, waking-dream flashes, etc.

The author's intentions were ambitious: he wanted to formulate a new dream theory and, more precisely, an aesthetic theory of the dream. But later, after authors such as Grotstein, Ogden, and Ferro had interpreted Bion in such an inspired and original way, the book's defects became very evident. Although Meltzer places the emotions at the heart of the oneiric experience, his illustrations are rather dull, and smack of some of the residual and most controversial aspects of Kleinian technique.

97

In the book, Meltzer cites as an example of his ideas Akira Kurosawa's film *Rashomon*, an acknowledged masterpiece, which came out in 1950 and won the Golden Lion in Venice the following year. Let us take a look at it.

"I have never heard a story as horrible as this … Yes. So horrible … This time, I may lose my faith in the human soul." This is how *Rashomon* begins. Among the greatest films of all time, it has arguably become a category of the mind. People use the title of this film in a manner comparable to the way names such as Kafka and Pirandello have become adjectivised. The Kurosawa film has become a standard reference when pointing to the coexistence of a multiplicity of points of view and the ambiguity that pervades human relationships. In some ways *Rashomon* is a kind of cinematic equivalent of the poetic world of Pirandello.

The film is based on two stories by Ryūnosuke Akutagawa published in 1916 and 1922, respectively: *Rashomon* provides the setting and *In a Grove* the details of the story. The plot is well known. While passing through the forest, a couple—a samurai (Masayuki Mori) and his wife (Machiko Kyô)—is attacked by a notorious bandit, Tajomaru (Toshirô Mifune). The samurai is killed and the woman raped. However, these are the only certain facts. In a court of justice, before a judge who remains silent and invisible throughout the film, each of the protagonists gives his or her version of events. Alternating at the witness stand are the woman, the bandit, a woodsman who observed the scene, and the samurai, who speaks through a medium. The characters are the same, as are many details of the story but, as in a Rorschach test, each time it is told, the witnesses give a different view of what happened. The bandit admits to the crime of murder but denies rape, since he maintains that the woman was consenting. The woman accuses the bandit of rape, but confesses that she was the one who killed her husband. The samurai recounts the rape but reveals that he committed suicide, because at that point he could not bear the dishonour and the shame. Then finally the woodsman tells a different story from all the others.

Kurosawa catches us off balance. In *Rashomon* reality is unknowable, the things of the world are uncertain, judgement is fallible, truth elusive, perception treacherous and subjective, evil banal, men prey to the passions, the human soul ambiguous and contradictory. His purpose is not so much to relate the story of the investigation of a crime as to show that the real crime is the murder of the truth. However, he does not point to guilty parties. In virtual form, each character has in himself or herself the best and the worst of all the others. As in the dizzying changes of perspective Dostoevsky has accustomed us to, here too the samurai is both valiant and cowardly, the woman lascivious and chaste, the bandit despicable and brave. For this reason, asking how things really went is a question that leads nowhere. The answer gradually loses importance, because the real point is, rather, that everybody is both guilty and innocent.

Rashomon is a dream film. What else is the samurai's version of the facts obtained through a medium other than a dream? The whole film rests on the structure of flashbacks. Not for nothing Genette (1972) explicitly mentions it in his famous book on rhetoric in Proust. The actors, Toshiro Mifune (the bandit), Takashi Shumura (the woodcutter), Machiko Kyo (the woman), Fumiko Honma (the medium) are all excellent and are given the opportunity to prove their versatility as they are called upon to play opposite characters in the same role, an approach that has an inherently deconstructive value.

Congruent with Meltzer's choice of *Rashomon* is the idea that from the point of view of therapeutic action, historical reconstruction in analysis has little importance and is only a secondary product. The story makes sense only if it is illuminated by the transference, by the emotional experience in the here and now, by the dream of the session. As in *Rashomon*, in Meltzer's dream theory what matters is that it contains an aesthetic or dramaturgical theory of points of view. For Meltzer dreams are dramas of the patient's internal world that seek to solve an emotional problem. And as in a drama performed on stage in a theatre, also in the theatre of analysis there are actors, roles, sets, scripts, spectators, and critics.

Theatre criticism

Meltzer takes an aesthetic, but not yet intersubjective view of dreams. The analyst is the theatre critic—so he spends most of his time in the auditorium—of the drama acted out in the mind of the patient. He is a critic attentive to the most successful, and hence most truthful, moments of the performance. Above all, he knows that the interpretation of a dream, just like that of any work of art, does not so much enrich meaning as impoverish it.

In the analysis of dreams, this way of seeing things is translated into a principle of technique that Meltzer sums up as follows: "While listening to your dream I had a dream which in my emotional life would mean the following, which I will impart to you in the hope that it will throw some light on the meaning that the dream has for you" (1984, p. 90). The analyst's dream about the patient's dream, he notes, comes close to the accuracy and richness which only poetic language can aspire to in communicating the significance of intimate emotional life. The game of interpretation is played out in the interaction with a small child in therapy when the analyst responds intuitively to his expressions by trying to share the emotional experience of the moment rather than explaining the meaning of what is happening. This is precisely what a mother does when she puts her α function at the disposal of the child to help him transform his most disturbing experiences and make them more bearable, to help him move each time from a situation of confusion to one of greater differentiation.

On no other occasion, adds Meltzer, even in analysis, does one reach the level of intimacy that is experienced when two people are working on a dream. No other content gives such authentic access to a person's mental state. Conversely, those who never recount dreams unconsciously deny having a mental life and distrust the analyst.

Dreams have a narrative continuity of varying lengths of time, which is what makes them comparable to the drawings that children make in therapy. Analysts may forget the facts of a patient's life, but not his dreams; indeed these are what give him clues that help him understand how the previous session was experienced. Dreams help him listen more easily "without memory or desire", as Bion suggested, and not get lost in the mists of the presumed objectivity of the patient's biography. The historical reconstruction is no more than an interesting by-product, in itself devoid of therapeutic value. The movement of the analysis should always be clockwise and not vice versa, from transference to history, or rather from transference to the reconstruction of the "mythology" of development (ibid., p. 145).

For all these reasons, the dream is "radioactive material" (ibid., p. 199). It releases energy which is as potentially destructive as it is productive and transformative if properly channelled, and on a par with aesthetic experience.[1]

Unfortunately, Meltzer the clinician is not always on a par with Meltzer the theorist. He comes across as distant. In spite of himself, he tends to x-ray the patient. He hardly ever enters the scene in a warm, authentic, "aesthetic" way, and gives highly saturated interpretations.

He is to some extent aware of this, and refers to a certain "rawness of expression", justifying himself by saying that it is the best he can do. When one writes, he explains by way of apology, it is impossible to reproduce the special atmosphere that characterises analytic work on dreams, an atmosphere that each time changes surprisingly from confusion to intuition: "The most vivid impression," he notes, "is one of struggling out of the rather dozy confusion [...] I deal with the clarified image of the patient's dream as my own dream" (ibid., p. 137).

The fact is that in his clinical vignettes Meltzer is dull, wordy, and abstract, and they are hardly ever illuminated by flashes of emotion. If dreams have their own poetry, little of it is visible in these pages. Meltzer is unable to show vividly how he responds to the poetry-dream of the patient with his own "poetry". It is odd to think that the "poetry" of the dream is, however, to be found throughout Freud's *Interpretation of Dreams*, and that even the dramatic world described by Klein has a much greater emotional impact on the reader, despite an idiosyncratic expressive style she seems to have borrowed from the horror genre.

Meltzer knows that there are always any number of interpretations, yet he maintains the detached attitude of an essentialist critic.

The same difference exists between Freud's concept of overdetermination, the plurality of causes that produces the same formation of the unconscious, which allows multiple readings, all of which, however, are potentially exhaustible, and a more intersubjective view of interpretation, where the meaning, seized and lost at the same moment, is always a question of deferral.

Meltzer knows that the transformation of the visual images of dreams into words—an inter-semiotic translation such as that made by an art critic discussing a painting (this would be the task assigned to the analyst)—is already provided by the patient when he recounts the dream. The idea of being able to know the dream of the other in an objective sense, like watching the same film together, is problematic. It is impossible even to be reliably informed about it, since the dreamer-and-critic of his own dream does not simply translate it into a language, but first and foremost into a discourse that also has nonverbal components. In itself, the story is a complex object, ambiguous, not unlike a second dream. It is illusory to think of a direct, non-mediated rendering of the dream experience, or of a dream that is not continuously re-dreamt. The patient is in the same situation as the art critic seeking to evoke the perceptible aspects of a painting: colours, shapes, materials. Describing them is already interpreting them and one is forced to resort to meta-discourse (Segre, 2003).

In the analyst's associations Meltzer sees only interference that creates confusion. He admits, however, that the traces of personal ideas are not completely unrelated to the patient's dream. This is a theme that we find fully developed in Ogden and Ferro. The fact is that he has a very Kleinian theory of transference, but unlike Ogden and Ferro does not have an intersubjective theory (however, he does use dreams to monitor his own "errors of comprehension, of presentation, of modulating the setting, or of breaches of technique"; Meltzer, 1984, p. 134).

A patient who recounts no dreams for long periods of time would be a problem for Meltzer. He feels relief and a sense of gratitude when the patient has a dream to relate. In supervision he listens to dreams with his eyes closed and only at the end responds with one of his very free "dreams" (Horovitz, 2008). He does not interpret the dream but reformulates it. Clearly, here he is inspired by the passage in "Constructions in Analysis" (1937) where Freud writes that he does not like the word "interpretation". Keeping his eyes closed, Meltzer writes, helps him above all to reconstruct the set of the dream, which the patient usually recounts more in terms of the narration—a detail of technique that makes me think of the active way of exploring the dream described by Bromberg (2006).

Meltzer then asks what a "correct" interpretation might be, whether it is "valid" or a useful "point of view" or a "sustainable hypothesis" or just "interesting" or "satisfactory". At all events, there is no *sole* interpretation or formulation but simply *one* among many that are possible.

Plurality of vertices means plurality of readings, more truth. It means that there is not just one reality alone. Not only that, but it is the dream that gives meaning to the world. The theatre where meaning is generated is dream life. Before being put on in this theatre, the things of the world lack meaning. The common sense perspective is thus reversed: the image, the eidolon, the *phántasma* (Aristotle) does not give us reality as it is, but constructs it.

Meltzer's theory of dreams can, I think, be illustrated by other films besides *Rashomon* where aesthetically successful dreams appear: the dream designed by Dalì for Hitchcock's *Spellbound* (1945); the dream with a hearse and a clock with no hands (as in the nightmare recounted by Borges in *The Cypress Leaves*) and also the exam dream in

Bergman's *Wild Strawberries* (1957); the dream in which the mother of the narrator looks in the mirror and then dips her hair into a bowl of water in Tarkovsky's *The Mirror* (1974); or images in *Solaris* (1972), by the same director, in which the Ocean brings to life, before the eyes of the protagonist, the memories of his dead wife; the first two episodes of Kurosawa's *Dreams* (1990), and so on. They are dreams that move us. They are memorable for their beauty and because they do not lend themselves to symbolic translations.

Meltzer's attention to aesthetics in the ordinary sense of the word is present from his first contributions, for example, the dialogue with the author reproduced in Adrian Stokes' *Painting and the Inner World* (1963), reprinted in *The Apprehension of Beauty* (Meltzer & Williams, 1988). In *The Psycho-Analytical Process* (1967), he compares the analyst's activity to that of a musician, and emphasises the game of immersion and interactivity that is typical of the aesthetic experience. From the outset he also demonstrates an acute awareness of the untranslatability of language, in other words, its poetic (unconscious and performative) dimension. This is the dimension of form and the signifier; it implies an extended view of what it means to act out in the session. For example, he puts emphasis on the beauty of expression and the rhythmic aspects of the setting and analytic work. In *Sexual States of Mind* (1973), finally, he differentiates between the "pornographic" point of view and the perspective of creative artistic activity. The close link between beauty and ambiguity anticipates what he later calls "aesthetic conflict", which is perhaps the most fascinating and modern of his original concepts.

For Meltzer, in short, unlike Freud and in agreement with Bion, the dream does not hide meaning but creates it; it does not censor but rather expresses something new. Dreaming is the function of the mind entrusted with managing the aesthetic experience of the world, where, according to Keats's famous formula also quoted by Bion, "Beauty is truth, truth beauty".

The Science of Sleep

"Hi, and welcome back to another episode of Television Educative! Tonight I will show you how dreams are prepared. People think it's a very simple and easy process, but it's a bit more complicated than that. As you can see, a very delicate combination of complex ingredients is the key. First, we put in some random thoughts. And then we add a little bit of reminiscences of the day mixed with some memories from the past. That's for two people. Love, friendships, relationships, and all those '.ships', together with songs you heard during the day, things you saw and also … personal. Okay. Okay, I think there's one. There it goes. Yes. Yes. Okay, we have to run. I'm talking quietly so as not to wake myself up. I'm with my dad."

The person speaking is Stéphane (Gael García Bernal). We see him in a kind of homemade television studio, and the channel is, of course, called STÉPHANE TV. The walls are covered with egg boxes by way of soundproofing. There is a fake camera, also made of cardboard, and a set that looks like it was designed for a cooking programme such as *Ready Steady Cook* or *Chefs Without Borders*. Here, however, the viewers do not learn about sophisticated recipes, but about dreams! Stéphane spends his nights dreaming of being the host of a TV show, *The Science of Sleep*. He does all his own musical accompaniment and his own interviews (the guest of honour is his mother). But mostly he invites the public to be present, live, at the preparation of his dream visions, which thus appear like dreams in a dream.

The Science of Sleep (Gondry, 2006) is a film that seems specially designed to illustrate the aspect of Freud's theory that deals with how the physical stimuli that may disrupt sleep are incorporated and transformed through dreams. For example, Stéphane wants to dream about going skiing with the girl he has fallen in love with, and falls asleep with his feet in a mini-fridge. This works for a while, then he has a nightmare where his feet are trapped in sheets of ice and he wakes up with a start.

When we read Meltzer describing the analyst listening to the story of the dream his patient tells him and observing the image that appears in his imagination, which in turn allows the patient to "evoke a dream in himself" (1984, p. 90), we almost have the impression that he too has set about dictating his recipes to us. In his case, the main ingredient is the idea that only such resonance can somehow circumvent the limits of representability, the structurally deceptive or false aspect of language.

If, as he claims, dreams are attempts to find a solution to an emotional problem, *The Science of Sleep*—interestingly, the original title, *La science des rêves*, was also the French title of some editions of *The Interpretation of Dreams*—is just right for our purposes. If, as Meltzer writes (ibid., p. 47), the poetry of the dream "catches and gives formal representation to the passions which *are* the meaning of our experience so that they may be operated on by reason", *The Science of Sleep* really gives us back something of this poetry. Meltzer's assumption that the world takes on meaning only when it is generated in the theatre, or in the "kitchen" of dreams, is illustrated here in an exemplary manner. Michel Gondry, a director already acclaimed for his music videos, has produced a tender, bizarre, and melancholic film where reality and dream constantly blend.

Stéphane, a shy and naive young man, has just arrived in Paris from Mexico after the death of his father. His mother has made a vow to help him and has also found him a job as an illustrator in a publishing house that makes promotional calendars. After moving into his new apartment, he meets his neighbour, Stéphanie (Charlotte Gainsbourg), who is equally sensitive and imaginative and who sews stuffed toys for a hobby. He falls in love with her and begins to woo her in his dreams and in his waking hours. But in love, dream and reality hardly ever coincide, especially since Stéphane has the soul of an artist and tends to want to be on his own. This is why he has created his own theatre at night. His dreams—at night and during the day—are his way of taking revenge for the frustrations of everyday life, soothing his sorrows and giving himself the satisfactions that reality denies.

The film has a surreal style in which the poetry and innocence of childhood can best come to expression. Gondry knows how to render the stuff of childhood dreams in a way of which few are capable. The special effects are hand-crafted and decidedly low-cost: he uses poor, mundane, everyday materials. However, they undergo the amazing transmutation that touches unimportant objects every time a child plays with them. Water comes from the tap and turns into cellophane; Stéphane meets Stéphanie because, as in a cartoon, her piano falls on top of him; like a prince, he dreams of taking her away on a felt horse riding on a sea of wrinkled cellophane; for her he builds improbable time machines (to go back two seconds!), mechanical puppets, thought transmitters, and other fantastic gadgets.

The Science of Sleep is a poetic film, a fairy tale; it is so full of surprising inventions it is impossible to re-tell. Its numerous animations depict the vicissitudes of the protagonist's tumultuous inner theatre. As spectators we enter into the fantasies and dreams that Stéphane, rather confused by reality itself, often changes and redesigns in his image. It is evident that for a creative mind, dreams and reality fuse constantly, to the point that it becomes difficult to tell where one ends and the other begins. *The Science of Sleep*, in short, is an original interpretation of the assumption that in the dream scene values are created that give meaning and then colour to the world. For Gondry, like Meltzer, life is but a dream.

Seeing-as

Hinshelwood wrote a meagre half page on dreams in his Kleinian dictionary; Meltzer, on the other hand, devoted an entire book to the subject. *Dream-Life* springs from a revision of Freud's theory. Meltzer criticises Freud's purely "neurophysiological" and energy-based view of the dream as the guardian of sleep[2] and as hallucinatory satisfaction of infantile desire,[3] the dichotomy between latent text/manifest text (translated back into the Bionian dichotomy of truth/lie), and the concept of censorship. For Freud, dreams are the only entry path to the unconscious; for Bion and Meltzer they are the activities that metabolise emotional experience and give meaning to the world: dreaming is equivalent to thinking. Freud does not acknowledge the meaning of dreams as ongoing processing of emotional experience, but only as reworking of the day residues, of waking thoughts that, by connecting to the repressed wishes of childhood, produce tensions that may threaten sleep. As such, the dream destroys meaning. It is the text that remains after the erasures of censorship have been carried out.

Following on from Klein and Bion, Meltzer, in contrast to Freud, configures the dream as a form of unconscious thought. Even the deletions are significant, and the meaning is on the surface, albeit ambiguous and obscure.[4] Freud would have confused darkness with the presence of an encoded text, as if the language of poetry were a text to be decrypted and reduced to its secret dimension, and not to be taken on board for its evocative potentiality. The dream does not hide meaning but produces it (as it can). What matters, rather, is whether it can solve the most pressing emotional problems of the individual and whether it works from the "aesthetic" standpoint.

Not even for Klein does dream life have this function of symbolpoeisis. More than anything else it is the revival of past relationships, although enriched by the extraordinary complexity of the inner world. Freud already saw people's lives as determined by the unconscious, but it was only Klein who constructed a mental spatiality where characters are brought to life who spring from the primitive experiences of relationality with part objects. She thus showed how transference is a continuous flow which involves the externalisation of the internal situation in its totality and in this way introduced a new concept of continuity between unconscious life and conscious experience. The main difference from Freud lies in the sociality that Klein introduces, even if it is a sociality so primitive and mythological that it finally comes to resemble a kind of innatism. Klein, however, paves the way to Bion. The subject is no longer driven only by abstract impulses or by the transference of a more or less unchanged past, but apprehends reality through the lens of an inner world which is dynamic, animated, dramatic, and in a state of constant formation.

It is clear then that if the aesthetic conflict is at the heart of the relationship, at the forefront stands emotion. If, that is, the relationships make sense on the basis of their emotional colouring, emotion *is* the meaning. For Meltzer, the models of the dream life constructed by Freud and Klein are still too closely tied up with the archaeological metaphor. His vision of dream life is expressed rather in the metaphor of the theatre and the plurality of points of view that the theatre promotes. Klein highlights the continuous dream life of the mind, but it is still a life somewhere between past and present. The aspect of creativity is still secondary. According to Meltzer, dreams create new meaning. He endorses Bion's idea that emotions play a key role in psychic life: they give meaning to the things of the world, a meaning that is not summed up in an abstract and rational formula, but that is an aesthetic and inherently ambiguous truth. Accordingly, the dream looks more to the present than the past.

Given these premises, interpretation that aims to reconstruct historical reality gives way to play, as in the setting of child psychoanalysis, to a creative interaction between the minds of analyst and patient. The analyst helps the patient to create his aesthetic object. The line between dream and reality, and the caesura between dream and interpretation, become progressively more blurred.

For Meltzer, the Freudian model is too entrenched in the mind/brain equation to accommodate a theory of meaning. But Freud was both the theoretician whom he criticised for the static conception of the unconscious—in contrast to the dynamic vision of memory based on his own notion of "deferred action" (*Nachträglichkeit*)—and the clinician whose brilliant insights he admired. For all these reasons, what is most valuable about *The Interpretation of Dreams* is to be found in Chapter VI, the chapter about dream work. Meltzer feels no discomfort in the face of this chapter. He criticises, however, the affect theory expounded in Section H, stating that Freud does not have a true theory of emotions and that for him the dream is only the manipulation of thoughts taken from wakefulness. For Freud, the thought comes first and then the emotion, for Meltzer the opposite is true: representational content translates emotion as the prime meaning of the experience. Freud "considers affects as *manifestations* of meaning and not as *containers* of meaning" (ibid., p. 17). In this he was following Darwin and his idea of emotions as archaic forms of communication. The emotions only have a function of discharge. They are merely derivatives of representations.

To win back the cognitive, epistemological, and aesthetic value of dreams and emotions, Meltzer emphasises the role of the signifier in relation to the signified—and their indissoluble unity. The rhythm of sentences and the physical elements of language convey meaning as do concepts. Meaning is always embodied in a personal style that is also a cognitive style. Words are music; language dreams and comes into being primarily as song and dance, as emotion, or rather, as a way of communicating emotions. The aesthetic dimension thus serves Meltzer to account for the complexity of language and its lexical and prosodic features.

Essentially, Meltzer's dream theory reflects the passage from Freud's psychosexual theory, according to which the development of the mind is driven by a biological thrust, to Klein's structural theory, where the function of the mother is described in more complex terms but still within the same framework of development (from non-integration to integration), and on to that of Bion, who saw the mind developing as it acquires knowledge of itself and its internal and external objects. For Freud, the mother allows the child to discharge instinctual energy; for Klein, her main function is to modulate mental pain; for Bion, she performs mental functions for the child which he is not yet able to perform. Unless and until he discovers meaning, never before experienced emotion is "unbearably *new* experience" (ibid., p. 69). If meaning is to be found, there must be an adequate psychic container.

Carried along by his revisionist momentum, and in some ways "unfair" to Freud, at least in terms of tone—perhaps as a kind of hyper-reaction to the dogmatism with which many approach the founder of psychoanalysis—Meltzer wastes no time considering whether these concepts of Freud's might not also be seen from other points of view.

It is obvious, for example, that the two functions—relieving unbearable tensions and simultaneously creating what we call meaning—can go together.[5] Why then reproach Freud for having used a Darwinian framework for his theory? What other general point of view should he have used? And surely Meltzer does the same thing when, in essence, he links the aesthetic experience to the aesthetic conflict, in other words, to the vicissitudes of the first object relationship with the mother.

Sometimes Meltzer gives the impression of seeing everything from a naive teleological perspective: dreaming is seen as unconscious thinking that has the goal of creating symbols, and not as a form of mental activity that meets the needs of the organism to survive, that is structured in a way that no one could have predicted, and that just happens according to the logic of adaptation. What meaning do we give to the word "meaning"? Art, to stick with the aesthetic model, is a truth-time, a felicitous rhythm; and aesthetic pleasure is the experience of seeing one's tensions ease in the presence of an aesthetic object. If certain emotional tensions of the organism are represented in the psyche as desire, then surely dreams are also the fulfilment of desire.

Regarding the distinction between the manifest and the hidden level of the dream, nothing prevents us from thinking that one of the solutions prepared by the dream might be the active inhibition of certain representations of the self perceived as dangerous or egodystonic, and that these intervene in the field of tension from whence come the transformations that alphabetise β elements into α elements. Nor is it clear why the Freudian concept of the continuity of dreams should be in contradiction with the idea that the dream is, albeit only indirectly, the guardian of sleep.

Now, leaving aside other differences, the two approaches may not be as far apart as they seem, but may reflect two distinct critical attitudes: the traditional attitude, according to which the text has a definite and by and large knowable meaning, and, on the other hand, the view that sees the text as open and subject to multiple interpretations. Meltzer takes the latter view, but he is still lacking the tools to give the role of the reader all the weight it deserves in the construction of the text. In short, Freud is less Freudian than commonly thought, and Meltzer is more so than he claims to be.

In the second chapter of *Dream-Life* Meltzer discusses some philosophical trends concerning problems of knowledge and contrasts the neo-positivist Wittgenstein of the *Tractatus* with the very different Wittgenstein of the *Philosophical Investigations*. By constructing this kind of framework to deal with the question of dream theory in Freud and in post-Freudian psychoanalysis, it is almost as if Meltzer were drawing a parallel between Freud and early Wittgenstein, on the one hand, and post-Freudian psychoanalysis (and himself) and later Wittgenstein, on the other:

> It is not coincidental that Wittgenstein found so much in Freud that accorded with his basic attitudes when one considers Freud's readiness to think of dreaming as devoid of thought, judgment and intrinsic language functions. The key to this area of agreement lies not only in the attitude towards dreams but in the view that emotions are merely symptomatic of states of mind rather than the meaningful core of the experience which requires transformation into symbolic form in order for it to be thought about and communicated to fellow creatures. (1984, p. 27)

Meltzer thus outlines an opposition between a correspondentist and a constructivist approach to knowledge, and consequently to the (interpreted) truth of the dream. It is in this context that he appreciates the later Wittgenstein, the one who talked about "seeing as" (Borutti, 2006). Meltzer is in fact well aware of the limits of the representability of language: "The trouble lies with language itself [...] no language can perfectly capture the meaning of the inchoate thoughts it seeks to ensnare" (1984, p. 89).

In the second approach, emotions, also traditionally belittled by Freud, and now no longer seen only as "symptomatic mental states", play a key role. Dreams can produce knowledge. Here we come close to the point Grotstein emphasises about Bion, namely, his belief that psychoanalysis needs to be "mystical", to take on the language and figures of mysticism to develop a suitable model for its own (obviously scientific) purposes.[6] For Meltzer, Freud aligned himself with the former by identifying consciousness with rationality (ibid., p. 49), and because of his basic model he struggles to regard emotions as something that lies at the heart of mental life.

Notes

1. On the question of the aesthetics of dream, see Bollas (1987), Petrella (2000), Grotstein (2007) and collective volumes edited by Mazzarella and Risset (2003) and Campra and Amaya (2005). Curiously, Freud (1923a,

THE DREAM AS AN AESTHETIC OBJECT 111

pp. 110–111) establishes a link between particularly successful dreams in terms of aesthetics and their untranslatability: "A number of dreams which occur during analyses are untranslatable even though they do not actually make much show of the resistance that is there. They represent free renderings of the latent dream-thoughts behind them and are comparable to successful creative writings which have been artistically worked over and in which the basic themes are still recognizable though they have been subjected to any amount of re-arrangement and transformation. Dreams of this kind serve in the treatment as an introduction to thoughts and memories of the dreamer without their own actual content coming into account." Freud's point anticipates Ferro's conviction that the dream is the richest and most profound material we have available in analysis and that for this reason it has less need of interpretation.

2. But see also (ibid., p. 88): "And of course there is some truth in the idea that the dream is the guardian of sleep in so far as the excesses of anxiety may indeed disturb the sleeper, just as undue stimulation from inside the body or from the environment may do. But we will not wish to assign to this trivial function more than a subsidiary position in our theory." It is not easy to understand the gap between the indirect importance Freud gives to dreams (which represents a veritable revolution), and the spurious and secondary role as mere guardian of sleep he attributes to them in his theory of psychic life.

3. Possibly we never reflect sufficiently on the fact that "hallucinatory satisfaction" is a contradiction in terms; it is non-satisfaction. What is, however, definitely produced is an effect of meaning, albeit fixed: that is where the "satisfaction" lies. Even hallucinations give meaning to reality. Dreams, therefore, are neither pure satisfaction of a repressed desire nor an automatic response to a traumatic stimulus, but are the more or less successful attempt (depending on the individual situation) to give meaning to the real, to give order to chaos. The theories of Freud and Garma are true and false at the same time. True because they describe an important aspect of dreams, but false because they are partial. We must also distinguish the stimulus that is directly trauma from that which is only indirectly so—which is the case with a desire which is overly frustrated.

4. For Aristotle, the good interpreter of dreams is the person who knows how to reconstruct the continuity of the broken stick immersed in water. The image is extremely interesting because it contains the idea of both illusion and transparency.

5. See Freud (1950 [1895], p. 318): "At first, the human organism is incapable of bringing about the specific action. It takes place by *extraneous help*,

when the attention of an experienced person is drawn to the child's state by discharge along the path of internal change. In this way this path of discharge acquires a secondary function of the highest importance, that of *communication* [*Verständigung*], and the initial helplessness of human beings is the *primal source* of all *moral motives*", and further (ibid., p. 366): "This path acquires a secondary function from the fact that it draws the attention of the helpful person (usually the wished-for object itself) to the child's longing and distressful state; and thereafter it serves for *communication* and is thus drawn into specific action." Sixteen years later, in *Formulations on the Two Principles of Mental Functioning*, Freud himself (1911, p. 219, footnote) authoritatively explains: "It will rightly be objected that an organization that was a slave to the pleasure principle and neglected the reality of the external world could not maintain itself alive for the shortest time, so that it could not have come into existence at all. The employment of a fiction like this is, however, justified when one considers that the infant—provided one includes with it the care it receives from its mother—does almost realize a psychical system of this kind." The objection is often made that intersubjectivist models are in danger of causing the disappearance of the subject. This overlooks the fact that they are simply models: both the isolated subject and the subject seen in close relation to the other are concepts that follow from adopting fictions that express the viewpoints we carve out from the chaos of infinite and unknowable reality.

6. See Bion (1970, p. 87): "All psycho-analytic progress exposes a need for further investigation. There is a 'thing-in-itself', which can never be known; by contrast, the religious mystic claims direct access to the deity with whom he aspires to be at one. Since this experience is often expressed in terms that I find it useful to borrow, I shall do so, but with a difference that brings them closer to my purpose. The penumbra of associations is intended to help those who look for my meaning."

CHAPTER SIX

Losing your mind, finding your mind

Losing your mind

When a patient enters analysis, Ogden writes (1997, p. 141), "he in a sense 'loses his mind' (in the process of creating a mind of his own)". If there were no quotation marks around "loses his mind" to guide the reader, and if there were no insert in brackets immediately afterwards, there would be something to worry about. The quotation marks tell the reader that the author is using the term idiosyncratically and so he should look behind the literal meaning. When Ogden talks about losing oneself he is actually talking about finding oneself. The mind is inherently, constitutively, intersubjective. Starting from birth, one finds one's mind only by "getting lost" in the other. The phenomenon that Ogden is describing, namely the fact that analysis constructs a shared dream space, goes much wider. Even when one is alone with oneself, one communicates with internal voices, assimilated presences, objects that have their origin in internalised relations. From this point of view a mind on its own cannot actually exist. Depending on how you look at it, the concept of an isolated subject is essentially an approximation, a myth, a useful fiction.

It is as if, by changing position, each individual entered into a plurality of wireless areas that may overlap partially or totally, switching each time from one emotional "connection" to another. At each "hookup", depending on the intensity of the signals emitted and received, the characters and the furniture that appear in the continuous dream of the conscious and unconscious mind take on the form of holograms that fuse both and become impossible to tell apart. A communication takes place from unconscious to unconscious that passes through the crossed projective identifications of both, that is, through various forms of effective mutual induction to identify with the mental contents transmitted. The psychological field is no less full than the fields of gravity or electromagnetism.

It is like, for example, the game where children pretend to be pirates and imagine that they are at battle with a ghost ship. Each assumes a different role within a shared scenario. This is what always happens, and happens automatically in an unconscious way in every relationship in a measure that is directly proportional to its emotional intensity. It becomes hard to tell what belongs to one and what to the other. It is easy to understand, then, why entering the emotionally significant relationship of analysis can be described as a process of losing your mind that it is actually a way of finding it.

The feeling of being alive that we have as human beings—what Winnicott (1965) calls "feeling real"—flows from the possibility of entering into a relationship with another person that nourishes one's mind. All analysis does is to take this kind of interpersonal experience from everyday life and channel it into a device that enables it to be used in a targeted manner. The aim is to enhance the analysand's ability to think/dream emotional experience (to carry out unconscious psychological work) and to ensure that, where it is missing or lacking, a room of the mind is constructed from the dual "network" of the relationship. Ogden uses the term "intersubjective analytic third" for this unconscious common area when it forms within the analysis. He describes it as a joint construction involving several subjects linked by an emotionally significant relationship: "does it any longer make sense to speak of the patient as the dreamer of his dream or are there always several analytic subjects (dreamers) in dialectical tension, each contributing to every analytic construction, even to a psychic event as seemingly personal (i.e., seemingly a production of the workings of the individual unconscious mind) as a dream or a set of dream associations?" (1997, pp. 140–141).

Analysis uses the processes that exist in any human relationship and simply brings them to an ideal temperature. It transforms the unconscious emotional field that forms spontaneously between two people in a process of therapy. In particular, in order to shed light on the area of exchange that comes into being between two subjects and the communication that takes place between unconscious and unconscious, analysis sets up a scene that functions according to specific rules, that is, a setting. The immediate aim is to make available both a space of communication and private spaces to enable contact between two minds and to facilitate the movement of go-betweens—to borrow from the title (*The Go-Between*) of a beautiful film by Joseph Losey, which won the *Palme d'Or* at Cannes in 1971—who constantly shuttle through this common space from one terminus to another in the form of reveries. Freud called these messengers of darkness "allusions": "the patient's associations emerged as allusions, as it were, to one particular theme, and [...] it was only necessary for the physician to go a step further in order to guess the material which was concealed from the patient himself and to be able to communicate it to him" (1923a, p. 239).

Just as Klein tends to use the adjective "concrete" to refer to the inner world, the magic word for Ogden is "dialectics". With this term, borrowed from Hegel, he expresses his original synthesis of the ideas of the classic authors of psychoanalysis—Freud, Klein, Bion, and, especially, Winnicott—to reflect the intrinsically intersubjective nature of the mind and how the subject is structured. In this way he adds a personal touch to Winnicott's idea of transitional area and Bion's idea of proto-mental system. The inspiration comes mainly from the brilliant interpretation of Hegel made by Alexandre Kojève, a Russian exile living in Paris, who held frequent seminars at the *École pratique des hautes études* in the period 1933–1939 (among the analysts present was, for example, Lacan), which were annotated, and later published, by Raymond Queneau.

At this point it is worth making a short digression to understand why Ogden picks up this key concept of philosophical thinking.

Aufhebung

Harold Pinter based his screenplay for the 1963 film *The Servant* (1963), directed by Joseph Losey, on a novel by Robin Maugham. We are in 1960s London. Upper-class Tony (James Fox) has just bought a Georgian-style house in Chelsea and has taken on a working-class servant, Hugo

Barrett (Dirk Bogarde). A subtle and ruthless struggle for power plays out between them that leads gradually to a complete reversal of roles.

Two women play a key role in the process: Tony's haughty and cold girl-friend, Susan, and Vera (Sarah Miles), Barrett's girl-friend, whom he introduces to Tony as his sister. Tony is seduced by Vera, but when he learns that the two are in fact lovers, he sends them packing. Later, unable to do without his servant, he takes him back, but now he, the master, has become the servant of his own servant.

The film is directed with great sophistication and makes virtuoso use of mirrors and the narrative device of *mise en abyme* in scenes that recall celebrated paintings by, among others, Velasquez and Vermeer. This enables Losey to highlight the moments when there are twists in the plot as the relationship between the two protagonists gradually collapses.

Taking this key stylistic element as a basis, the female figures can be interpreted as two aspects of a maternal object incapable of modulating the distance in the relationship for lack of the internalisation of a paternal function or "third" and therefore not able to promote optimal subjectivisation.[1]

The film can thus be seen as an extraordinary exemplification of the allegory Hegel used in *Phenomenology of Spirit* (2009)—significantly the book's original title was *Science of the Experience of Consciousness*—to found a radically intersubjective or social theory of how the mind develops: the master-servant relationship. The servant engages in a struggle to gain recognition from another sufficiently worthy consciousness and thus to attain humanity. To do this he must master his anguish and negate his own given identity and his state of servitude to the natural world of the instincts. The gentleman at first takes possession of the other as an object entirely identified with the self. When the object, however, resists identification, the relationship is reversed and he takes the position that belonged to the other, and so on.

For Hegel, then, self-consciousness (*Selbst-bewusstsein*) is a goal which can be achieved through a dialectical process whereby one satisfies the specifically human desire for recognition: in Bion's terms we would say a kind of mutual relationship between container and contained ($\male \female$). It is not given *a priori* but develops in the course of a historical process, involving an exchange with the other, another consciousness, another self. Knowing the world in terms of one's physical or mental condition means wanting to transform it so as to assimilate it to the self, and therefore to deny it. If the other recognises me, my attempt is not entirely unsuccessful; in part, I was able to transform it, and vice versa. To be able to differentiate myself from the other as subject, I must pass through a certain negation of myself, "[…] in reality, self-consciousness is reflection out of the bare being that belongs to the world of sense and perception, and is essentially the return out of otherness" (Hegel, 2009, p. 82). It is thus the desire for the desire for the other, that is to say, "something that does not really exist (the Desire being the 'manifest presence of the absence of a reality')" (Bodei, 1991, p. xi).

The pulse of being comes from the continuous oscillation between inner world and outer world, between emotion and perception, between the negation and the affirmation of the other-than-self, between projection and identification, between assimilation and accommodation. When two subjects face each other, each thinks of the other in terms of itself, that is, the other is denied in its very being. But if the other reflects the subject only by introducing a minimal difference, that is, by recognising it and desiring to be recognised itself, behold, it sees itself reflected, that is, both denied and transformed in turn and identified as subject. It is only difference, a *certain* difference, that enables it to be constituted as a subject. The process never ends. Recognition by the other, that is, reciprocal recognition lays the foundation for the emotional sharing/consensuality which we usually give the name of truth.

So we can understand why Bion regards truth as nourishment for the mind: because it is nothing other than consensuality (incidentally, the English word *truth* comes from truce, meaning armistice or mediation). The dialectical synthesis of thesis and antithesis is the first degree of consensuality/unison/*at-one-ment*/reconciliation between two subjects. Each acts as a mirror for the other, just like when you put two mirrors facing each other and immediately on their surfaces a theory of images is formed *en abyme*, two infinite sequences that bind them together in a reciprocal relationship of inclusion.

The term that describes this dialectic is *Aufhebung*. Mills[2] (2000) sees *Aufhebung* as very close to the idea of projective identification. The German word is almost untranslatable: in English it is rendered as *sublation*, in French as *relève*, and in Italian it is often translated as *superamento* or sometimes *sublimazione*. Understood in its most abstract sense, the concept of *Aufhebung* helps us understand how the subject emerges from pure sensoriality. *Aufhebung* is the movement by which, in a kind of transference by promotion, a datum is denied-and-preserved, removed-and-elevated,   deleted-and-maintained,   suppressed-and-positioned-higher-up. Inscribed in the concept, in short, is a twofold, contradictory dynamics of stability and change, which is the dynamics underlying subjectivity. Human existence emerges from undifferentiated nature as discontinuity "through a dialectical process that is not teleologically predetermined" (Vanzago, 2012, p. 13). Visually, some Futurist paintings depict, as well as one can, the laborious birth of consciousness within nature, for example, *Railway Station in Milan* by Carlo Carrà (1910–1911). There is an interpenetration between body and environment, a continuous osmotic exchange of energy. The boundaries of the self carve out dynamic states from a background made up of electromagnetic fields. The subject is a "field of relations" (Civitarese, 2012b, 2014; Merleau-Ponty, 1945) which comes into being by differentiating itself from the real from which it will never be able to free itself altogether.

More precisely, at the beginning of life the subject—which in reality cannot be defined fully as such—knows the world according to its own corporeality, that is, with a primitively anthropomorphic or unconsciously self-centred view. The elementary sensations are the letters of the alphabet with which it begins through contiguity and contact (through transference) to read the world. The world as such, its objects, and its things are therefore initially denied in their intrinsic qualities, but as a reflex they deny those who identified them by alienating them from themselves. Of course, so do things that "resist" desires, though not always. Humans, however, need to meet other human beings because only they can accept being denied ("subjugated" says Ogden (1994), a verb that derives from "subject") in their qualities, but also being invested, and resonating with the projections of others, confirming them and giving them back transformed. It is a never-ending game of identity and difference, or rather, when things go well, sufficient identity and tolerable difference, that generates a field of interaction in which nothing belongs to only one or only the other, but in which any psychic element is located inside the framework of the relationship, is influenced by all the other elements, and is denied to the extent that it is created.

The subject is thus born by confronting the non-self, which is initially known through the projection on to it of its own experiences in the form of sensations that are initially elementary and then gradually become more complex. Thus is established a master-slave dialectic, in other words, a dialectic of mutual adaptation-recognition initially only with things. The inert non-self of matter at times lends itself to being recognised and recognising—for example, the food that you absorb and assimilate because it "recognised" the need that gave rise to the search— but most of the time this does not happen: reality resists and causes friction. This would still not be sufficient for the development of the mind and for survival, were it not for the encounter with another human being, usually the mother. Only this *other* has the special ability to take on the role of caregiver, to adapt to the needs of the child, to be denied in her isolated identity and to give back to the sender a negated and transformed version of sensations—emotions that the latter has sent by express post through projective identifications. Micro-experiences of recognition progressively build an area of the self whose frontiers are in a state of constant expansion.

The developing mind (nascent subjectivity) is the product of these energy flows, a concrete and mutual interpersonal pressure—really the world of atoms described by Lucretius, since, ultimately, Bion[3] himself uses the metaphor of the β elements as subatomic particles as compared to atoms, which are the α elements. In the same way as a word makes sense only in the differential game it plays with the other words in a language, a psychical element is not contained only in the mind of A or only in the mind of B, but is in each and in the intersubjective third which the two create in this immediate and obligatory reciprocal process of losing and finding, resisting and getting involved. It is merely illusory to see the mind as isolated. In actual fact it is the outcome of tensions that originate from an ever-changing field of forces. It is never divorced from the broader context of sociality, not even when, already formed, it engages in dialogue with its own objects (as in a dream, almost totally) or with elements of nature.

Ogden's theoretical borrowing from Hegel of dialectics and the connected concept of *Aufhebung*, which, however, accepting Derrida's critique of Hegel, I would interpret in terms of *difference* and not as an albeit upside down way of restoring a concept of *presence*, expresses the idea, which is also integral to linguistics and deconstruction, that there is no such thing as a pure original event-term-sign. Such only exist in constant reference to other terms, in an incessant play of mutual definition. A exists only in relation to non-A. What Ogden terms intersubjective third is something that in itself is elusive and cannot be grasped on the basis of the abstract logic of ontological categories and intellectual identity. Bion's so-called mysticism obeys the same necessity, and is nothing more than a way of circumventing the limits of this logic, which is the logic of scientific knowledge in its strictest sense, and of making disciplined, rational use of the mental processes we refer to by the term intuition. It is the very idea of separateness that falls into crisis, whether it regards elementary sensations, the global sense of self, or the individual elements of a text or a language.

In his famous book Hegel highlights the falsification necessary so that a person is able to know an object as separate. There is no absolute truth and all knowledge can be neither entirely true nor entirely false. Each finite object, that is, each part of reality, cannot exist in isolation, but only within a network of relationships. The dialectic that comes into force at the moment when the subject opposes an object does not imply only negation-suppression but also affirmation-creation. The only definitive negation regards the apparent fixity and separateness of the object seen as outside the network of reciprocal interactions and determinations. In *Aufhebung*, the synthesis is what results from this integration of opposites and itself becomes a new thesis. What presents itself as unitary actually reveals inside it an internal tension of opposing forces.

Today, this critique of the subject/object dichotomy and the idea of the separateness of the subject is more relevant than ever. We find it in all areas of research, from neurobiology to psychology, which seek to re-evaluate the role of emotions in cognitive processes and to give the body back to the mind. Indeed, emotion, or rather *Affekt*, which, like the drive stands between the body and the mind, expresses the resonance of this encounter at the border between I and the Other (Badoni, 2011).

In the wake of Hegel, we have an understanding of the concept of container/contained (♂♀), which Ogden takes over from Bion and successfully clarifies. It is not a static concept. Rather it indicates a force field, the interaction of energy flows of particles that collide and create ever-changing forms. It is a dialectical interaction of mutual negation/creation. When you activate a process of sustainable identity (identification) and difference (differentiation), that is, when recognition takes place, the area of the intersubjective third (or the field) evolves. That is to say, the container stretches—which is neither the individual mind as a container nor the sum of two minds, but at one and the same time the one and the other. It is as in art: we can distinguish form from content, but at the same time the content is the form and the form the content, and we do not really know how to keep the two apart; all we can do is locate two polarities in tension, two points of the concentration of forces in a common field.

The subject, according to Ogden, springs solely from the recognition of the other. This is not painless; it involves *struggle* and *work*. For self-consciousness to develop, the capacity for self-reflection, which is the distinctive characteristic of the ego, must be recognised by the other. "If they are to be *human*, they must be at least *two* in number" (Kojève, 1947, p. 43). Not even the intrapsychic dimension of the mind corresponds to an isolated entity because it always reproduces within itself the master-slave dialectic. Reflective consciousness comes from the dialectical relationship between a consciousness that is *opposed* to itself, and thus thinks its own existence, of an ego that struggles with itself, reciprocally creating and denying itself in order to differentiate itself from the real.

The fine-grained mechanism of this dialectic is the interplay of projective identification-reveries and communication between unconsciouses that is expressed in effective interpersonal interaction. On the one hand, Hegel's concept emphasises the essential element of negation in this process; on the other, it returns it to a more general mode of being and reality that also relates to phases of the constitution of the ego for which Kristeva uses the term abjection.

Each person has an experience of the intersubjective third which is personal and different from that of the other—and yet continually and reciprocally defined by this other-than-self. This is why it does not belong entirely to either oneself or another, but rather to neither and both (or several) at the same time. This *extended* mind is always being created, both in inner dialogue (i.e., with the internal objects of the mind, always assuming that it has had the opportunity to be formed), and in dialogue with each other. But without a first *real* contribution, without the concrete interaction of caregiving, which is the recognition of one's own desire by the other's desire, as happens at the beginning of life, it could not be structured. It follows from this premise that every claim to know the world as separate subjects leads to truths that are inevitable falsifications of the undivided real or what Hegel called the absolute.

Now, the current term "mirroring", which is also a valuable metaphor, fails to capture the nuance of violence that is intrinsic to this dynamic, which the Hegelian allegory of the master-servant relationship succeeds in doing. The exception is Lacan who, inspired by Kojève even before Ogden, makes the mirrors the very symbol of the fundamental alienation of the subject and the matrix of narcissistic identification.

The process of becoming a subject corresponds to this process of mutual recognition, a "co-feeling" which, however, constitutively integrates a negating demand that leads to the construction of a con-sensuality of ways of having experiences of reality (Bion's "common sense"). The objects that populate both the outer and the inner world thus acquire sufficiently stable characteristics and enable the operations of the consciousness to function effectively. This tuning work, which is founded on and made possible by difference, regards both percep-tions and emotions. From the continual confrontation with that which was experienced as "external" when the boundary of self was erected, we get a consensus view, an intimate consonance with (and which also becomes) the real/"O". Perceptions are the "emotions" of the senses, just as emotions are the perceptions of the inner world (and both can sometimes give rise to illusions and delusions). Let us take a look at a passage from Bion:

> We may now consider further the relationship of rudimentary con-sciousness to psychic quality. The emotions fulfil a similar function for the psyche to that of the senses in relation to objects in space and time. That is to say the counterpart of the commonsense view in private knowledge is the common emotional view; a sense of truth is experienced if the view of the object which is hated can be conjoined to a view of the same object when it is loved and the con-junction confirms that the object experienced by different emotions is the same object. A correlation is established. (1967, p. 182)

The dialectic that establishes subjectivity—which could be formulated in terms of the binary pair narcissism/socialism in Bion's sense of the term—is an ongoing process. It is what Winnicott seeks to encapsu-late in his famous gerunds: *coming-into-being, a going concern, holding, handling, object-presenting, realising, indwelling etc.* With these expres-sions, according to Ogden (1994, pp. 50–51), Winnicott "captures some-thing of the experience of the paradoxical simultaneity of at-one-ment and separateness. (A related conception of intersubjectivity was sug-gested by Bion's [...] notion of the container-contained dialectic. How-ever, Winnicott was the first to place the state of the mother on an equal footing with that of the infant in the constitution of the mother–infant.

This is fully articulated in Winnicott's statement, 'There is no such thing as an infant [apart from the maternal provision]'".

This is also why it can be misleading, when defining the characteristics of the intersubjective third, to use the classical concepts of transference and countertransference. Ogden explains this in another passage: "I believe that the use of the term *countertransference* to refer to everything the analyst thinks and feels and experiences sensorially obscures the simultaneity of the dialectic of oneness and twoness, of individual subjectivity and intersubjectivity that is the foundation of the psychoanalytic relationship" (1994, p. 74, footnote). The concept of countertransference is not in the real sense intersubjective, although in some meanings it comes close to being so, since rather than giving an account of the subjectivity of the analyst it only indicates his willingness to make room for and to resonate with the patient's transference-as-misunderstanding.

It goes without saying that the development of a mind, a sense of self, serves to liberate the subject from the contingencies of the immediate context of experience, to create an interior space that is untainted by the all too compelling need for constant contact with the object and thus an essential basis for mental health. Dialogue with the other becomes an inner dialogue. Moreover, the individual establishes his own hierarchy of what is meaningful to him, and in doing so moves from being a largely passive element responding to environmental stimuli to becoming a subject/agent. Proust vividly expresses one of the effects of the construction of an inner space: "those who have made for themselves an environing interior life have little regard for the importance of events. What profoundly modifies the pattern of their thoughts is much more likely to be something that seems quite unimportant in itself but which reverses their experience of the order of time by making them contemporaneous with another period of their life" ([1927] 2003, pp. 34–35).

Let us now look at the importance that the concept of the subject can have for a theory of dreams.

Finding the mind

Freud decentres the subject of consciousness from the classic locus where it held sway and declares that the ego is not the master in its own house.

Klein emphasises the weight of psychic reality.

Bion dethrones the subject from itself, from its own unconscious, from the dwelling place in which it continues to reside even though it is no longer the undisputed master, and relocates it to a proto-mental area common to the group.

Ogden and Ferro bring to an end the second Copernican revolution initiated by Bion. They pass from the Cartesian dualism, which even Freud essentially endorses, to a radically intersubjective, that is, social, experiential self. It needs to be borne in mind that not all intersubjective theories make this step in the same way. Some in fact maintain an I/you or subject/object dichotomy because they lack a notion similar to that of the analytic intersubjective third or of the analytic field.

Ogden's idea of the subject, on the other hand, is something that emerges from a duality which, with Merleau-Ponty, we might call "syncretic intercorporeality", above all as a pre-reflective and pre-linguistic bodily ego. His psychology, from this point of view, is neither uni- nor bipersonal, if by bipersonal one means the interaction between two isolated subjects and not their mutual co-determination as such. Reis (1999) argues that if Ogden's ideas are avowedly Hegelian, with his theory of the autistic-contiguous position and by radicalising some ideas of Winnicott, he expresses a way of thinking that is entirely congruent with Merleau-Ponty's phenomenological theory. For Hegel, the subject is still equivalent to the conscious ego; there is still a mind-body dualism. For Merleau-Ponty, on the other hand, the original relationship with the world is constructed through the body, which is prior to and irreducible to the subject/object and consciousness/world opposition. It is in this sense that Merleau-Ponty is able to affirm that the subject is actually a field of relations.

Can one talk about intersubjectivity before there is a subject? Yes, provided one thinks of a (pre-symbolic, pre-discursive or semiotic) ground zero of perception of the other-than-self in the form of elementary sensations of continuity/discontinuity which are, nonetheless, organised in meaningful rhythms; as long as one thinks of consciousness not in absolute terms but as something that evolves from a minimal point to a notional point of full and maximum extension. When we are close to this second pole, reflexive consciousness can only be understood as a matter of language. It is also not a good idea, however, to have too abstract a conception of language, because language is not only meaning but body, matter, flesh, music, rhythm. The word is body and action. Pre-symbolic aspects still continue to be an integral part of language—and often, as expressions of affective states, play the main role in the construction of meaning—just as at birth the culture deposited in the mother tongue passes to the baby through the music of gestures and words and helps it to find a meaning for the experience that it is not able to assimilate alone. Ogden writes: "the breast is not experienced as part of the mother's body that has a particular (visually perceived) shape [...] the breast as autistic shape is the experience of being a place (an area of sensations of a soothing sort) that is created (for example) as the infant's cheek rests against the mother's breast. The contiguity of skin surfaces creates an idiosyncratic shape *that is the infant at that moment*. In other words, the infant's being is in this way given sensory definition and a sense of locale"[4] (1994, p. 174).

The unconscious dimension of experience that is expressed in dreams is closer than conscious experience to these primitive forms of "coming into being". The unconscious is closer to the indivisibility of the real, consciousness to its falsifications. The concept of relationship based on the game of transference-countertransference is not to be equated with that of the intersubjective third, because it only suggests the reciprocal attribution of psychic contents between patient and analyst, which are, so to speak, more or less fixed and not the creation of something shared and new. According to this model, the patient sees the analyst mistakenly against an ideal parameter of objectivity; he distorts and misunderstands things.

For Ogden the analytic encounter is a dialectical game of reverie that helps develop the intersubjective analytic third. This unconscious common area is the premise for creating predominantly verbal symbols for "heretofore unspeakable and unthinkable aspects of the analysand's internal object world" (1997, p. 112).

No nightmares, please![5]

In line with this model of the analytic relationship, Ogden proposes some significant modifications in technique. He does so, however, only after making it clear that technique is of no value in itself but only as it serves to advance the psychoanalytic process. Firstly, he uses the couch for low-frequency therapy. The couch provides a private space in which the analyst can "render himself as unconsciously receptive as possible to the patient's unconscious and [...] attempt to avoid becoming mired in conscious (secondary process) efforts at organizing his experience" (ibid., p. 113). The reverie is the royal road to understanding the unconscious allusions coming from the analytic third and a clue to the ongoing dynamics of transference and counter-transference. It is not clear why, when a patient cannot attend analysis with the standard frequency of sessions, one should have to give up a tool that in its simplicity proves to be optimal for analytic work. Having a private space makes it possible to enter into a dialectic of privacy and communication, to activate an authentic analytical process and to be more readily open to reverie. Reveries are the most sensitive probes we have to help us explore the analytic field, the transpersonal emotional area that is created when two minds meet. For Ferro (2011) they put us in direct contact with the pictograms of waking dream thought.

Freud recommends listening in a state of evenly suspended attention. He advises the analyst against taking notes or trying to keep everything in mind so that he can attune himself to the patient's unconscious. Bion expresses the same idea when he suggests giving oneself up to one's reverie, that is, to a psychological state characterised by the absence of "memory and desire". According to Ogden, reveries can be ruminations, daydreams, fantasies, and bodily sensations, fleeting perceptions, images that emerge from states of half-sleep, moods, phrases that cross one's mind, but also memories. The only thing is that, while the analyst's listening is directed mainly outwards when his attention is free-floating, in reverie it is also directed at the mind of the analyst. The arc of interest is 180° in the first case and 360° in the second. "[R]everies are not simply reflections of inattentiveness, narcissistic self-involvement, unresolved emotional conflict, and the like. Rather, this psychological activity represents symbolic and protosymbolic (sensation-based) forms given to the unarticulated (and often not yet felt) experience of the analysand as they are taking form in the intersubjectivity of the analytic pair (i.e., in the analytic third)" (Ogden, 1994, p. 82).

A second variation in technique concerns the so-called fundamental rule. The classic formula whereby the analyst suggests the patient should say everything that comes into his mind is a rather paradoxical injunction that is often difficult to heed. What the analysand actually also needs, however, is to be able to pause in a private space. If he does not want to or cannot do so, he should feel free to remain silent, not to communicate, to turn temporarily to forms of sense-based experience, to live through a situation of personal isolation, to enjoy a room

LOSING YOUR MIND, FINDING YOUR MIND

of the mind to which no one else has access. Starting from the very first meeting, Ogden introduces the patient to the new dimension, different from normal conversation, which characterises the analytic dialogue. And he is careful not to present the whole thing as a bodying forth of technique, but rather as a way of giving the patient to understand that in the therapeutic space he is free to speak or not to speak, and that the analyst will behave likewise.

The third variation in technique concerns the analysis of dreams. Ogden does not think it essential to engage in the methodical work of free association with elements of dreams, as recommended by Freud. He allows the patient a certain amount of space to reflect and, if he wants, to associate with the dream, but freely uses his own associations, memories, reveries as if they were connected to the patient's dream. What he does is to look at them from the point of view of the inter-subjective analytic third and the shared dream of the session. A dream dreamt in the course of an analysis, he writes, represents "a manifes-tation of the analytic intersubjective third [...] therefore, the dream is no longer to be considered simply 'the patient's dream'" (Ogden, 1997, pp. 139–140).

As is clear, personal psychological space, including dream space, and analytic space begin to converge more and more until they over-lap: "This is a 'felt place' that is by no means restricted to the analyst's consulting room. It is a mind (more accurately, a psychesoma) that is in a sense the creation of two people, and yet is the mind/body of an individual" (ibid., p. 142).

Before Ogden, no one had ever pointed out so radically the intersub-jective or dialectical dimension of dreams (perhaps something analo-gous can only be found in the ancient idea that dreams are messages the gods send to mortals). The dream no longer belongs to the analysand or the analyst, nor the analytic third, but the "the three must be held in an unresolved tension with one other" (ibid., p. 142). Ogden's observa-tion, as always brilliant in its simplicity, can be extended to any fact of the analysis, and is the best reply one can give to those who blame relational psychoanalysis (in the broad sense of the term) for the disap-pearance of the notion of a subject. As it is outside this conception, clas-sic technique easily becomes a routine practice of translating dream material and can become cold, mechanical, and uninspired. Not so the analyst who sees a continuity between the patient's dream and his own (even sense-based) states of reverie, produced by the interpsychic dialectic, which in this case involves all positions and modes of the mind in generating experience (autistic-contiguous, paranoid-schizoid and depressive).

I began this chapter with Ogden's paradoxical statement about entering analysis and losing one's mind. I would like to take this further: the final section of his article on the three aspects of technique holds yet another surprise in store for us. I am referring to the part where he talks about the importance of not understanding dreams (rationally). Dreams and reveries are the true markers of the unconscious work of understanding that really contribute to psychological growth and which belong more to the order of "becoming O" than to knowledge (K).

Ogden's style resists paraphrase, stripped as it is of superfluous elements. Extraordinarily communicative, it is both extremely precise and poetically ambiguous (Civitarese, 2010b). What he says about Winnicott concerning the indissoluble intertwining of ideas and style also applies to him. What is more important, it is a way of writing that pursues the ambition of giving back something of the effectiveness that words should have in analysis. On this point, we should, therefore, listen again to the musicality of his prose:

> Dreaming (or "dream life") is a specific form of human experience that cannot be translated into a linear, verbally symbolized narrative, without losing touch with the *effect* created by the dream experience itself, the experience of dreaming as opposed to the meaning of the dream [...]. For this reason it seems to me particularly apt that the reveries (of analyst and analysand) serve as a principal psychological (and psychosomatic) means through which dream experience is processed in the analytic setting. In the reveries of analyst and analysand, unconscious receptivity that sometimes involves "feats of association" [...] might take place in relation to a dream as opposed to thought processes through which a dream is deconstructed, "translated" (Freud, 1913), understood or even interpreted. "Dreaming itself is beyond interpretation" (Kahn, 1976, p. 47). In utilizing reverie as a principal form or shape in which dream experience is "carried" in the analytic setting, the analyst and the analysand allow primary process, the "drift" of the unconscious (as opposed to its decoded message), to serve as a medium in which dream-life is experienced in the analytic space and an

important component of the context in which dream analysis is conducted. (Ogden, 1997, p. 153)

And further: "I do not conceive of the analytic interaction in terms of the analyst bringing pre-existing sensitivities to the analytic relationship that are called 'into play' (like keys on a piano being struck) by the patient's projections or projective identifications. Rather, I conceive of the analytic process as involving the creation of new unconscious intersubjective events that have never previously existed before in the affective life of either analyst or analysand" (ibid., p. 190).

Although Bion makes dialectical all binary oppositions between concepts that organise the theoretical-practical field of psychoanalysis, for example by asking what in the session really belongs to the patient and what to the analyst, in his writings the idea of a shared dream space is not expressed clearly. This is more like the Winnicott of the transitional area, and also the Kahn of dream space. However, there is the idea that we communicate through crossed projective identifications and that dreaming is an ongoing activity at night and when awake.

Basically, Ogden complements Bion with Winnicott and both with the Hegelian dialectics. Thanks to the contribution of narratology, Ferro takes a further step and potentially extends the role Ogden reserves for reverie and dreams to include the whole text of the session, without making any distinction between the communications of a patient—if they have to do with dreams, stories, childhood memories, anecdotes, etc.—and only trying to get in contact with the α element, or with the narrative sequence of α elements, or narrative derivatives of the α element (Ferro, 1999).

The analytic third or the intersubjective analytic third, already "extracted" from the philosophy of Hegel, now located in the psychoanalytic and no longer philosophical field, is understood as an area made up of overlapping states of reverie, which each of the parties involved in its formation experiences differently, but which is defined only in relation to the contribution made by the other and reciprocally in a differentiated and dialectical way. So the visual images of the one (α) complement elements provided by the other and vice versa. Depending on the individual patient, the same event in the life of the analyst takes on different meanings; in other words, each time it is re-contextualised. Reveries can suggest transference and countertransference feelings active at an unconscious level in the relationship and still inaccessible to reflective thinking and verbal symbolisation.

"On not being able to dream" (2005b) is a dazzlingly good essay in which Ogden gives an extraordinary interpretation of Bion's theory of dreams and in particular his assertion of the psychotic's inability to dream and, as a result, to sleep and to wake up. Via a reinterpretation of the already mentioned Borges' fiction *Funes the memoroius*, he illustrates Bion's assumption with a brilliant vignette. It is the most original part of the work, because it shows what happens when the analyst himself becomes unable to dream and falls for longer or shorter periods into states of countertransference micro-psychosis. The analyst realises he is not able to use his own reverie to gain access to the subconscious level of the analytic relationship and the experience. He feels temporarily disorientated with respect to time and has the feeling of being overwhelmed by masses of words without any real meaning. In other cases, he experiences difficulty staying awake and falls into a state of half-sleep in which fleeting dreams appear which reassure him about his ability to dream, or unsuccessful dreams of dreaming the dream that the patient is unable to dream at that time, pseudo-dreams. The analysis is eventually composed of dispersed elements, unconnected by any emotional thread, and thus insignificant, and stagnates in a semi-hallucinatory condition.

Ideally, however, the analyst must participate in dreaming undreamt dreams or dreams interrupted by the patient. In this way he comes to know the analysand in depth and can try to say something that he feels "to be true to the emotional situation that is occurring" and which *"must be utilizable by the patient for purposes of conscious or unconscious work, i.e., for dreaming his own experience, thereby dreaming himself more fully into existence"* (2005b, p. 10).

Undreamt dreams are like night terrors, and correspond to areas of the psychotic mind (from which come psychosomatic disorders, severe perversions, pockets of autism, "de-affectivised" states, schizophrenia). Interrupted dreams are nightmares and correspond to non-psychotic areas of the personality. Night terrors and nightmares are metaphors for varyingly severe states of being unable to dream. Dreams, thus, are not all equal. There are "night terrors" or undreamt dreams, "nightmares" or interrupted dreams, emotional states without images, dream hallucinations, recurring post-traumatic dreams, and so on.

All patients who are in analysis either suffer from night terrors or nightmares. The analyst must have the ability to enter and maintain a particular psychological state of receptivity (reverie) to their undreamt or interrupted dreams as they are expressed in the transference and countertransference (if we see things from a classic perspective), or in the intersubjective third (if we use a two-person model). This is how he helps them to dream their undreamt or interrupted dreams. This pre-supposes an asymmetrical working relationship, which however sees the communication between the unconscious minds as symmetric. Ogden listens to the effect his words have on the other and the effect the other's words have on him. He listens to the way he listens. He believes that in analysis too, truth is dialectical and cannot be generated by the mind of one person. Something becomes incontrovertible only if it is felt emotionally. Moreover, the very moment it takes shape, it will inevitably change (be falsified).

In using the term dreaming in place of thinking or symbolising, Ogden preserves the richness of the Freudian concept of dream work. In a less flashy way than in the dream, dream work (*Traumarbeit*) continuously creates, without any real interruption, the metaphorical-metonymic loom upon which concepts are woven. Dreaming (psychological work) is the most essential element of the psychoanalytic function of the personality. When dreaming, the subject "treats" emotional experience, creates linkages between α elements and erases the differences sufficiently to be able to abstract. If this is successful, the mind grows.

Ogden explains what it means to resume one's interrupted dreams by reference to a film.

Raising Arizona

A pair of likeable, energetic, wacky newlyweds discover they cannot fulfil their dream of becoming parents. Biology and the prejudices of others have conspired to keep them childless. The wife, Edwina McDunnough, abbreviated to Ed (Holly Hunter), is an ex-cop who has been pronounced sterile after undergoing tests ordered by the doctor. The husband, H. I. McDunnough (Nicolas Cage), abbreviated to "Hi", was once a compulsive robber of 24-hour convenience stores. On his robberies he uses an unloaded gun, so he is not a real villain. As Rita Kempley, the *Washington Post* film critic wittily remarks, Hi "is a deep thinker but without the IQ to support his habit" (20 March 1987). In any case, with his criminal record, adoption is out of the question.

Ed and Hi met in prison; their roles were different, but as we can see, reversible. They fell for each other and decided to set up home in the Arizona desert, a place which is in itself an allegory of infertility. When they discover that Nathan Arizona (Trey Wilson) and his wife, Florence, who have undergone specialist medical treatment to cure their infertility—have just had quintuplets, Ed and Hi think that if they steal one nobody will notice. After all, five is more than they can handle, says Edwina. And so they go through with the robbery. The family gains a new member, Arizona Junior. Hi now has the problem of how to cope with his new responsibilities as a father. In order to procure food and nappies, he is forced to resume his criminal career. Back on the job as a robber, he tells the incredulous cashier: "I'll be taking these Huggies and whatever cash you've got."

This is briefly the plot of the 1987 film by the Coen brothers. In Italian it was given the title of the unconscious protagonist *Arizona Junior*. The original title, however, was *Raising Arizona*. The whole cast, both the main characters and the supporting actors, is extraordinary. The film was co-written by the two brothers, Joel and Ethan, with Joel directing and Ethan co-producing (together with Mark Silverman). Their second film, after their debut effort, the superb *Blood Simple* (1984), *Raising Arizona* was further proof of their talent, even in the choice of actors alone. Cartoon-like comedy and high-brow sophistication, post-modern trash and sentimentality, innocence and cruelty are blended together in a moving, alienated, and hilarious comedy.

Two dreams, the first interrupted, the second successful, provide the backdrop to the story. Hi is a criminal out of a sense of guilt who cannot stay out of jail for long, and in a recurring nightmare he is haunted by a sinister biker called Leonard Smalls, the ex-boxer Randall "Tex" Cobb, who stalks him constantly, appearing to him as a figure of the Apocalypse ("The Lone Biker of the Apocalypse") or a messenger from hell. Randall wears a tattoo that shouts as loud as a prison sentence: "Mama didn't love me". In the second dream, Hi sees himself instead with Ed, now both old and surrounded by their loved ones. Between the two dreams come the flight, the fight with Randall, and his unexpected but definitive victory. Hi is at last able to silence the guilt that never lets him breathe.

The cast includes William Forsythe and John Goodman in the roles of Hi's former cellmates. In one memorable scene, after escaping from prison, they emerge from the bowels of the muddy earth, as in a difficult delivery. The cheerful convicts become comically involved in the new McDunnough family ménage. For example, they warn Edwina about the harmful effects of not breastfeeding ("That's why we wound up in prison"—not a bad insight for two jailbirds, as Ed calls them). But then they have unhealthy ideas about the fate of Arizona Jr., at least from the point of view of Hi, imagining that they could kidnap him again in order to return him to his rightful parents and pocket the ransom.

Central to the film is the figure of the bounty hunter, Leonard Smalls, named after a character in Steinbeck's *Of Mice and Men*. We see him appear before Hi's nightmare and then materialise as a mercenary hired by the authorities to capture the fugitives. At one point Smalls offers his services to Nathan Arizona, who, however, declines. Then he devises a plan to get the child back and sell it on the black market. Astride a roaring Harley Davidson, with two rifles sticking out from his shoulders like wings, Leonard Smalls has the menacing and violent look of a Hell's Angel. He is so ruthless that he almost seems the precursor of Chigurh, the killer in *No Country for Old Men* (Joel and Ethan Coen, 2007), the Coen brothers' film based on a novel by Cormac McCarthy. As good as Chigurh at hunting down his prey, Smalls destroys everything that comes in his way and, in the words of the narrator, turns day to night.

The whole film runs hectically from one brilliant gag to another in an atmosphere that is in itself already dream-like. The main themes are birth and recognition. It is the story of the remarkable path Hi takes from crime to punishment, from persecutory guilt to chastisement, the fate that is already laid out for him and the chance to redeem himself, being forced to constantly relive his nightmare and finally managing to dream himself into existence. It goes without saying that the spark that gives him hope that he will be able to break free from his repetition compulsion is his love at first sight for Edwina. It is a rebirth that is immediately followed by the difficulty in having a child. Like Pinocchio's fox and cat, the two false friends appear, and then the biker of the apocalypse materialises in his nightmare. Hi struggles with his nature, with "Mama didn't love me" tattooed on Smalls' arm, but also on his heart, because Smalls is but a figment of his psyche. Eventually, after a series of extremely risky tests, he manages to defeat the bounty hunter (his guilt) and the metamorphosis takes place. At that point Hi finds his mind. At last he can dream. We see him as an old man together with Ed and surrounded by a large happy family with children and grandchildren. The final scene of the film, showing him in bed with his wife, suggests that everything may only have been a dream dreamt by Hi.

The same dream of getting rid of evil (momentarily identified also with me as his analyst!) is what a patient describes while recounting a recurring nightmare. "I go up and down ramps and stairways, and run away and someone pursues me, I keep running, but he is always there, and sometimes it really is the monster—UGH!—the ogre. Other times it's not. Why don't I face up to him, turn and look to see who it is? For me, the cure would be to kill him, then I would stop being afraid."

Ogden writes about *Raising Arizona* in a wonderful article in the *International Journal of Psychoanalysis* entitled "On talking-as-dreaming" (2007). In certain circumstances and with certain patients who are not able to dream in sessions by freely associating, the difficulty can be overcome if the conversation is allowed to turn to movies, books, sports etc., without the game of analysis being interrupted by too many interpretations. Sometimes in a more relaxed atmosphere the analysand will for the first time find his own voice and a way of dreaming himself into existence, that is, becoming human and alive. At moments like this, patient and analyst sometimes feel a special sense of intimacy—and there is no need to explain the symbolic meaning of the movie or the book in question.

In the clinical vignette in Ogden's article, the patient identifies with the character played by Nicolas Cage and his repeated failures. More than anything else, he is struck by the tone and content of the final dream, where it seems that there might be a ray of hope for him in the future. These apparently non-analytic conversations, talking without following a particular direction, are thus revealed as moments of encounter, game-changing reveries, exit routes from repetitive dreams and nightmares. The asymmetry of the analytic setting and the maintenance of the internal setting by the analyst then ensure that even if the analyst participates, the dream that is finally dreamt—that is, the hitherto unthinkable experience—is ultimately the patient's dream.

Notes

1. For a more detailed analysis of this film, I refer to Civitarese (2012a). It is also worth noting that Bion introduced the characters of Roland, Rosemary, Alice, and Tom at the beginning of *The Dream*, the first volume of *Memoir of the Future*, following the same narrative schema of the relationship between master and slave, as outlined by Hegel.

2. Hegel anticipated many concepts of psychoanalysis and developed a first theory of the unconscious. For example, the concept of desire (*Begierde*) is very close to that of drive (*Trieb*).

3. See Bion (1992, p. 182): "The function of dream-work-α is to produce something that bears a relationship to an idea that is analogous to the relationship an elementary particle bears to an atom in physics."

4. One can read the statement by Ogden (and Bion's *Transformations*) in the light of a passage in which Derrida (1972, pp. 73–74) deals with the concept of the Hegelian dialectic structure of reality and, albeit at a more speculative level, describes the birth of the psyche: "[...] how do space, how do nature, in their undifferentiated immediacy, receive difference, determination, quality? Differentiation, determination, qualification can only overtake pure space as the negation of this original purity and of this initial state of abstract indifferentiation which is properly the spatiality of space. Pure spatiality is determined by negating properly the indetermination that constitutes it, that is, by itself negating itself. By itself negating itself: this negation has to be a determined negation, a negation *of* space *by* space. The first spatial negation of space is the POINT [...] The point is the space that does not take up space, the place that does not take place; it suppresses and replaces the place, it takes the place of the space that it negates and conserves. It spatially negates space. It is the first negation of space, the point spatializes or *spaces* itself. It negates itself by itself in its relation to itself, that is, to another point. The negation of negation, the spatial negation of the point is the LINE. The point negates and retains itself, extends and sustains itself, lifts itself (by *Aufhebung*) into the line, which thus constitutes the truth of the point. But secondarily this negation is a negation of *space*, that is, itself is spatial; to the extent that essentially it is this relationship, that is, to the extent that it retains itself by suppressing itself [...] the point is the *line*, the first Being-other, that is, the Being-spatial of the point. [...] According to the same process, by *Aufhebung* and negation of negation, the truth of the line is the PLANE [...] is it still to be asked how time appears on the basis of this genesis of space? In a certain way it is always too late to ask the question of time. The latter has already appeared. The Being-no-longer and the Being-still which related the line to the point, and the plane to the line—this negativity in the structure of the *Aufhebung* already was time. At each stage of the negation, each time that the *Aufhebung* produced the truth of the previous determination, time was requisite."

5. So reads the dedication Bion wrote on the copy of *Memoir of the Future* he gave to Green (Green, 2000).

CHAPTER SEVEN

Reverie, or how to capture a killer (-content)

Godzilla

"I was part of a children's patrol," Matteo tells me. "We were trying to defend ourselves from Godzilla, who was wreaking havoc across the country. We used to take a minibus and make our way up some narrow winding mountain roads to look for it. I didn't think we would ever manage to catch it and I told the others this several times, but they reassured me. We managed to get to the top and they saw it, but I didn't. So they told me to look harder, it was right there. But I didn't see anything. Maybe because it was too big. Then, I don't remember what happened, but I found myself with a woman with Oriental features. I felt happy being there with her and I told her that she was beautiful. In fact, she was so beautiful that when I re-awoke I was disappointed to be back in reality."

The dream makes us think of the East as a possible rebirth, the desire for another place untouched by persecution. Matteo wishes for an existence free from Godzilla, from that which prevents him from getting a clear vision of his inner reality and practice. He wishes to extricate himself from the quicksands of a devastating conflict with his parents in order to project himself into his life, to give a personal meaning to his

137

experience. Talking about the dream, he explains that it was a gang of children-adults, as in *Peter Pan* (Hogan, 2003) or *The Lord of the Flies* (Brooks, 1963). The association suggests various hypotheses about a past catastrophe that he has already been through, but which is ongoing and projected into the future.

Knowing that Godzilla is there without actually being able to see it ("Maybe because it was too big," he muses), Matteo relives the anguish that he had previously placated with heroin and which he now treats through his dependency on analysis. When he meets the woman in the dream, there is a sudden transformation because he sees himself touched, loved, and recognised—at all events the dream also reflects the perception in the other/analyst of a new openness. The woman is an exotic figure, perhaps the inhabitant of a country which for him is not so much to be found as to be discovered for the first time, the antithesis of a catastrophe. One might think of the body of the mother as the world and "the first lodging" (Freud, 1930, p. 91), and the setting as a womb (Winnicott, 1947). Finally Matteo notices Godzilla, thanks to the group of other children; in the analysis, thanks to the person who sees things he cannot yet see.

A few days later, he describes another nightmare: "I was in a room and I knew that Bob from *Twin Peaks* was on his way. I told myself that I would beat him up. In fact, he arrived shortly afterwards, but I was terribly afraid and I ran away."

Who is Bob? A character from the highly successful television series created by David Lynch and Mark Frost, Bob is a less sophisticated version of Zero, the villain of Shinya Tsukamoto's *Nightmare Detective* (Civitarese, 2010c). He is the embodiment of the evil that corrupts the moral principles, and the inhabitants, of a peaceful village on the border between the United States and Canada. But how can he be captured?

Harry, our job is simple: crack the code,
and you have the key to the crime!

To comment in a few lines on these two dreams, I have of course used certain codes of interpretation. My thoughts went back to the movie *Godzilla* (Emmerich, 1998), featuring a monster who, if possible, was even more threatening than King Kong, but also the gigantic Anita Ekberg in Fellini's *The Temptation of Dr Antonio* (1962), then the episode of *Twin Peaks* in which Bob, the character dreamed by Matteo, appears. In particular I thought of one scene. Not being able to show actual images, let me try to evoke them by means of an excerpt from the script:

COOPER: Let me tell you about the dream I had last night.

TRUMAN: Tibet?

COOPER: No. You were there. Lucy, so were you. Harry, my dream is a code waiting to be broken. Break the code, solve the crime.

LUCY: (Writing, whispering) Break the code, solve the crime.

COOPER: In my dream, Sarah Palmer has a vision of her daughter's killer. Deputy Hawk sketched his picture. I got a phone call from a one-armed man named Mike. The killer's name was Bob.

TRUMAN: Mike and Bobby?

COOPER: No, it's a different Mike and a different Bob. They lived above a convenience store. They had a tattoo, "Fire, walk with me." Mike couldn't stand the killing any more, so he cut off his arm. Bob vowed to kill again, so Mike shot him. Do you know where dreams come from?

TRUMAN: Not specifically.

COOPER: Acetylcholine neurons fire high voltage impulses into the forebrain. These impulses become pictures, the pictures become dreams, but no one knows why we choose these particular pictures.

TRUMAN: So what was the end of this dream?

COOPER: Suddenly, it was twenty-five years later. I was old, sitting in a red room. There was a midget in a red suit and a beautiful woman. The little man told me my favourite gum was coming back into style, and didn't his cousin look exactly like Laura Palmer, which she did?

TRUMAN: Which cousin?

COOPER: The beautiful woman. She's filled with secrets. Sometimes her arms bend back. Where she's from birds sing a pretty song and there's always music in the air. Then the midget did a dance. Laura kissed me and she whispered the name of the killer in my ear.

TRUMAN: Who was it?

COOPER: I don't remember.
TRUMAN: Damn!
LUCY: Damn!
COOPER: Harry, our job is simple: break the code, solve the crime.

In this scene taken from the third episode of the first series, the FBI detective Dale Cooper (played by Kyle McLachlan) recounts to the astonished sheriff and his secretary the dream that will help solve the murder of Laura Palmer (Sheryl Lee), and which at a deeper level will also help investigate the nature of evil, embodied by Bob, the demon who has created the criminal. Dreams, says Cooper, are created by impulses coming from cholinergic neurons that become images, but we do not know why they take the form of certain images and not others. Some have seen this as almost a declaration by Lynch of a dream poetics. However, the important thing is to understand the dream's meaning. In Cooper's statement there is not even the shadow of Freud's idea of the dream as wish fulfilment but more that of the dream as a way of being able to read reality. Even though he uses the term 'code' ('Crack the code, and you have the key to the crime'), Cooper is not referring to a general meaning system valid for all dreams but rather to the specific rules of a given text.

The world of *Twin Peaks* (1990–1991), like the pages of Kafka or Ishiguro, is made up of details and precise descriptions, but still a bit off-centre. Despite its apparent clarity, it always remains somewhat weird. *Twin Peaks*, like *Lost Highway* (Lynch, 1997) and *Mulholland Drive* (Lynch, 2001), reveals the dream dimension that always pervades reality precisely because, by refraining from strong caesuras, it shows almost imperceptible fluctuations and curvatures.

At times it is also a world of surreal comedy. The Icelandic delegation who have come to Twin Peaks to close a major import–export timber deal—the forest here symbolises the unconscious—leave in a hurry, frightened by the vices of this latter-day Sodom and Gomorrah. Andy, the naive and sentimental cop, bursts into tears every time he faces evil. Lucy, the sheriff's secretary, is over the top and childish—but on several occasions both she and Andy will play a decisive role in advancing both the investigation and the plot. Above all, Special Agent Cooper, surreal and hyperreal at the same time, dresses like a positive version of Mr Smith from *The Matrix*.

The dream-like quality is particularly suited to depicting an underground life of turbid passions that contrasts with the gilded surface of a quaint town nestled in a natural paradise. As the episodes unfold, *Twin Peaks* is increasingly revealed as a kind of televisual descent into hell.

A valuable contribution to the dream-like atmosphere of dream is made by the music of Angelo Badalamenti. The extraordinary effects of the dilation of time and the feeling of stepping into another dimension of reality owe much to the effective mix of music and images, equalled perhaps only in the films of the truly great directors and in the results achieved by other famous partnerships, such as Morricone and Leone or Rota and Fellini. The result is unique. Few filmmakers would be able to sustain such a difficult register of expression over an entire movie.

Agent Cooper, an enlightened man endowed with a Tibetan spirituality, knows how to make good use of the insights that come to him in dreams and daydreams, and seeks to extract from them a method for his work as a solver of riddles. In an experiment that has an air of Zen wisdom, he summons all the detectives who are working on the Palmer case to a clearing at the edge of the forest. He then writes on a blackboard a list of the names of some suspects, asks Lucy to read them aloud in turn, and at every name throws a pebble at a bottle a short distance away. Cooper calls this bizarre investigation technique "The technique of throwing the stone". He is convinced that dark, unconscious knowledge of things directs their aim and may reveal some clues. He explains to Lucy that when two events unconnected to each other but both relating to the same investigation occur simultaneously, one must always examine them with the utmost care. It is no coincidence that the title of this (second) episode is "Zen, or The Skill to Catch a Killer."

Strange, indeed, but there's nothing extrasensory. Cooper uses intuition but then, when he examines the insights they have drawn from it he applies a stringent logic. In comparison with other detectives, he is not suspicious and *faux naïf* like Columbo, he is not a brain box like Dupin or Poirot, nor a disenchanted romantic like Marlowe, and has none of the realistic traits of Montalbano. Cooper inspires sympathy because he knows pain and passion, and is sincerely troubled by evil; however, the attitude he takes is balanced and positive, not moralistic or cynical. In addition, with almost childlike candour he is acquainted with rapture at the small pleasures of life. He loves, for example, the famous Twin Peaks cherry pie.

Cooper has an enviable inner balance. Truman, the sheriff, and he form the classic male couple to be found in numerous detective stories. In the first episode, Truman jokingly tells him that he had wanted to study medicine because he had always felt a bit like Dr Watson.

Cooper proves to have a highly developed capacity for thought, an α function that he puts at the service of the interrupted dream/ nightmare of the community. That is his role. His capacity for reverie must serve to stop Laura Palmer's murderer, that is, to transform the killer contents into images and thoughts. In Twin Peaks it is not the sleep of reason that generates monsters, but the inability to dream that causes the criminal instincts—in other words, the undigested accumulations of proto-emotions or hyper-β contents—to emerge from the recesses of the mind. The town has stopped dreaming: the mill where timber is processed—the symbol of the collective function, the device for transforming everything that grows in the forest—has come to a standstill.

While The Cell shows the reality of the inner world, Twin Peaks depicts the dreamlike side of material reality, as in The Science of Sleep, but in a more subtle and effective way. Lynch's surrealism is natural and "innocent", not artificial. In his films every image is steeped in dreams. One is always aware of something that rips the veil from the effect of reality. One feels the same systematic bewilderment whenever in analysis one acquires an angle of vision from which to look at the facts of the session as determined by the analytic field. Here the same magic is produced; one is transported into a dream space. It's like when you look at certain paintings by Monet and the images of things are transfigured into abstract stains of colour.

Lynch's cinema is painting with film. Blackness and darkness have a hypnotic effect and represent the access road to go beyond the visible. In an interview (Rodley, 1997, p. 20), Lynch has said that it is the darkest things that appear to him to be most beautiful: "Black has depth. It's like a little egress; you can go into it, and because it keeps on continuing to be dark, the mind kicks in, and a lot of things that are going on in there become manifest. And you start seeing what you're afraid of. You start seeing what you love, and it becomes like a dream."

We are not very far from the poetics of Bacon, a painter Lynch has always been deeply fond of, an artist who captures reality and its complex layers only by subjecting it to deforming tensions, showing what is unfamiliar in the familiar, the hallucinatory and the dreamlike in the perception of everyday life.

Just like Bacon, Lynch mocks narrative conventions and adopts a rhetoric of excess to de-realise material reality and to demonstrate the superiority of looking inwards over looking outwards. His at times parodistic deconstruction of various kinds of film language coincides with his deconstruction of common sense. The paradigm of this poetics can only be the dark background of the dream. Thus, in Lynch's films the explicit dreams—at the end of the first episode Cooper dreams that he is told the name of the killer by a woman who has the face of Laura Palmer—are only at one remove from the dream-movie that provides the frame. This is also what happens in analysis.

Reverie and dreams have the same apparent randomness and the same unconscious needs as the trajectory of the stones Cooper throws at the bottle. Both represent the point where the outside of the Möbius strip of reality twists while remaining in continuity with the inside of the phantasy. Lynch's cinema is made up of these secret passages, these openings through which one can cross the threshold between worlds. The mind is born out of recognition—in other words, the satisfied, though never completely satisfied, desire for the desire of the other. This amounts to saying that it arises in an immaterial space, not from simply possessing the object or being possessed by the object. The mind is born and develops in crossing borders.

The analytic field

Central to the theory of the analytic field as developed by Ferro are the Bionian concepts of α function and waking dream thought. For Bion, the α function[1]—which transforms ("transduces and 'translates'" [Grotstein, 2007, p. 69]; "exorcistic dreaming", ibid., p. 45); β elements, proto-sensations and proto-emotions (raw, as such, indigestible emotions which cannot be assimilated as food for thought, in other words unthinkable; "the most vague and inarticulate registrations of emotional states such as anxiety, fear, terror and dread" [Ogden, 2005a, p. X], "the emotional-sense *impression* of O, the ghost of O" [Grotstein, 2007, p. 59]; "somatic and inchoate emotional sense expressions"; ibid., p. 68) into α elements or (generally, but not only) visual images (or emotional pictograms or visual photograms[2])—is active both at night, during sleep, and when we are awake. The sequences of α elements,

elements of experience "that may be linked in the process of dreaming, thinking and remembering" (Ogden, 2005b, p. 101), instead of a first level of aggregation, are composed to form dream-thoughts, clips that can be stored in memory and used to produce scenes of the dream or to generate waking dream thought, and hence the conscious components of thought or narrative derivatives on which are based self-awareness and other operations of abstract thought. It is the process whereby the mind gives meaning to experience. Thanks to the α function, the chaos of the real takes on some kind of order and becomes a world.

The β elements, on the other hand, cannot engage with each other to produce thoughts or to be stored in memory. Scattered particles of experience, "disparate bits of psychic stimulation" (Meltzer, 1984, p. 114), "crazy pixels" waiting to form patterns of images, "Unthought-like thoughts that are the souls of thought" (Ogden, 2005b, p. 101, quoting Poe), they cannot be assimilated and woven into more or less coherent patterns, that is, they can only be structured within a connective tissue made up of thin fibres of emotion and only after passing through the α function. The same differentiation between conscious and unconscious is the result of the work of the α function since the α elements are aligned to form the contact barrier, the dynamic and semi-permeable membrane that separates the two domains of the mind.

At birth, we have only an inchoate consciousness. For there to be differentiation between unconscious and conscious what is required is the mother's reverie (the un/conscious). This is how the child makes its entry into the world of symbols. In psychoanalysis the unconscious is therefore not the neural unconscious but it belongs to language and sociality. It is to be equated with the very possibility of interpreting reality. Extending *this* unconscious means increasing the effectiveness and the amplitude of the cognitive operations that occur automatically, freeing up spaces in consciousness for new learning.

In coining the concept of α function, Bion acknowledges that he cannot explain the passage from body to mind. However, he does establish a close link between corporeality, proto-emotions, emotional pictograms (i.e., emotions already embodied in images), dream scenes, reveries, and more abstract forms of thought. The new theory anticipates the rediscovery of emotions by neuroscience. Both Edelman (1992, 2004) and Damasio (1999), for example, are engaged in "restoring the body to the mind" (Barile, 2007) and extracting theories of the workings of the mind from the quagmire of their traditional logocentrism. Both these authors also make reference to the work of Lakoff and Johnson (1980) and their concept of metaphor as an elementary cognitive structure through which we make non-arbitrary connections (because each derives from the other) between different areas of the body and the mind.

If analysed in depth, the concepts turn out to be interwoven into a subtle though inapparent metaphorical fabric. In turn, the metaphor (which Eco, 1980, sees as a complex figure based on a double metonymic device), like a karst river of sensory-motor excitations combined in recurrent patterns, brings water from the concrete world to the mill of abstract thought. They are, for example, the experiential patterns that correspond to the representations in space of up/down, left/right, forwards/backwards, in/out, etc. The concepts are shaped by how the body is made, how it moves, and how it lives in the environment that surrounds it. Ultimately it is a logic based on the aesthetics of being.

The significance this theory holds for psychoanalysis is obvious because it restores the body to the mind, overcomes the mind-body dualism, and frames a convincing model of how emotions record, almost like the sensitive tips of a seismograph, the slightest vibration of the body immersed in its natural medium. Finally, also the equivalence between dream and thought appears far more understandable. The body is the fundamental and foundational level beneath all other levels of higher complexity. Even the more abstract images and concepts then become metaphorical projections of sensory-motor, pre-linguistic and pre-conceptual schemes. In short, metaphors are at the heart of what Johnson (1987) calls the faculty of the imagination. Intermediate between the one and the other are *image schemata*:

> Image schemata can be intuitively conceived, then, as stylized images, while distinguishing both from these and from propositional representations. The difference between *schemata* and images, already pointed out by Kant, consists in the fact that, compared to the single non-propositional images (precise, albeit analogue representations, which contain details and relate to concrete, single individuals) schemata, on the other hand (which emerge at the body level, through perception and movement) consist of *parts and relations* between the parts (which are few in number). They are *organizational structures* at a more abstract and general level of image, which only later become elaborations. The schemata, therefore, represent the set of *structural* features of an object, an activity,

>an event, etc. Consequently, they are more malleable and flexible
>than the images themselves. (Barile, 2007, p. 133)

The conceptual equivalent of what, at least on the functional level, are image schemata, in Damasio are at the neural level, what he calls *dispositions* or *dispositional representations* (analogue proto-representations in image format). These are still, in fact, neural and not mental (schemata), that is to say, they "give order to other neural patterns, giving rise to neural activity *elsewhere*, in places connected to them [...] *potential* patterns, inactive but which can be activated if necessary [...] they do not constitute deposits of knowledge, in the form of images, but rather a means to rebuild it, activating *elsewhere* circuits that can do it" (ibid., p. 137).

These terms and the transformations they describe could be roughly equated to the terms used by Bion (e.g., "faculty of imagination" to α function, β elements to proto-emotions, α elements to "dispositional representations", dream-thoughts to images etc.). The fit is not exact, since all these concepts, even those used by neuroscientists and philosophers, have an ineluctable aura of ambiguity. However, there is a striking number of points of contact between the two theories: the centrality of emotions (conscious or unconscious, punctiform or lasting) and corporeality in even the most differentiated psychic life, since they are "considered *external* manifestations associated with motivations [actually, the emotions would be] the other side of the *same* process" (ibid., p. 7); the design of a continuous line of responses by the body to environmental stimuli, which start from emotions and arrive at concepts, and the biologistic and evolutionary framework of the theory of the mind in opposition to theories that offer computational representations and which consequently end up underestimating the significance of the emotions; an integrated view of the living organism in which body and mind are one; a conception of emotions as part of the basic systems of regulating the organism that determine survival and well-being; a theory of consciousness as an evolutionary achievement, because it makes it possible to discriminate between emotions in a more sophisticated way, and if required, to be in conflict with what would be automatic responses to stimuli from the environment to react in a creative and non-stereotypical way; the role assigned to metaphor as a cognitive structure (here it is impossible not to think of the mechanisms of dream work pointed out by Freud and implicitly picked up again by Bion in his original formulation of the α function as dream work α); and, finally, the importance of taking into account the philosophical reflections on the nature of the mind that have accumulated over the centuries.

There are similarities and convergences. Even neuroscience still manages to give an account of how we pass from the body to the mind. Something new could come from the theory of mirror neurons, which some identify as the neuro-physiological basis of intersubjectivity and empathy (Gallese, 2006). What is unique, however, is the ability of psychoanalysis, and of Bion in particular, to theorise how the mind is formed from sociality.

We have no direct access to dream-thought, unless through *dreams* in sleep and through waking *dream flashes* or *reveries*. For Ferro the only other way to get an idea of the intense activity of transformation into shapeless sensory images that occurs incessantly through the channels of the senses is indirect: from the sequences of α elements, which, like the individual frames of a film, are invisible if taken one by one, and, alternating with black strips,[3] film in real time the emotional experience of a given moment, and produce other images, which are a pale copy, an abstraction of them. This is the concept of "dream spectrum".

The same emotional content can then be narrated using different narrative genres or different idioms, for example, historical, intrapsychic, relational. The narrative derivatives of the α elements are the product of the narrative ability of the waking mind (the apparatus for thinking thoughts)—"sets and scripts in continuous transformation". They correspond to characters or situations in life that somehow have a relationship with the α element that has formed upstream and involves an inevitable degree of distortion (Ferro, 1998). Another way is to see them is as "free association under duress", a bit like the story or the review of a film or the soundtrack of a film for the blind, like a painting covered with a cloth of which it is impossible to imagine anything through a narrative (Ferro, 1999), and, finally, almost like *dream photograms* (Ferro, 1992).

Once again, between waking dream thought and narrative derivatives we find the link that connects the direct experience of the dream to its story, in other words, the link between the dreamt dream and the transformation of dream images into discourse. A narrative derivative is a bit like the story of the unconscious waking dream, and likewise it is already organised (revised and edited) by the dreamer, made consistent and self-interpreted. The characters of the analytic dialogue, the actions they perform, the experiences they go through, give the point of view of the analysand's unconscious (of the analyst, of both: i.e., the field!) on the ongoing relationship. Narrative derivatives can then be used for the purpose of thinking and self-consciousness, and to carry out conscious and unconscious psychological work (Ogden, 2005b).

It is still not clear why some patients develop one symptom and others a different symptom. Several explanations suggest themselves: fragility that is constitutional or generated by emotional or physical trauma; particular sequences of alpha elements (Ferro, 1999); the variable distance at which it is necessary to project the β elements (Bion, 1992). These may be risky hypotheses but they are not reckless. Basically we do not know, but from the point of view of psychoanalysis as a field of transformations, the question of the psychopathological specificity of a certain clinical picture is only of relative importance and essentially clashes with the refusal to objectify the other.

Night dreams trigger a sort of "α *metafunction*" or narrative ability of the mind in the dream (Ferro, 1999) and correspond to the work of re-dreaming images already stored in memory while awake. As Freud observed at an early stage (1900, p. 590), by virtue of their "hypermnesia", dreams readily draw both on the most recent representative contents and on older contents (from childhood), and thus can concentrate rich dream material "into the briefest moment of time [because they capture the] ready-made structures already present in the mind."

We thus have two levels of transformation—the α function and the equipment for thinking/dreaming (whose operating mechanism Bion saw as PS ↔ D oscillations, and those between container and contained (♂ ♀), to which Ferro adds CN ↔ FS). Corresponding to these are two different loci of the disease, depending on whether the formation of α elements is hindered or their weaving into more complex narratives. In the first case (inadequate function) we have evacuation and undigested β elements (hallucinations, psychosomatic disorders, character defects, etc.); in the second (poor functioning of the tools for dreaming/thinking), thoughts are treated as if they were α elements.

Even night dreams in the session are just stories, and from this point of view have the same status as any other fact of the analysis. It may be a free association, on a par with any other association, or a reverie. The analyst can play the dream interpretation game, as I do with Matteo in the vignette, but he will see it also (and primarily so, but still remaining within the game of immersion/interactivity; Civitarese, 2008b) as a precise description, albeit hypothetical and seen from his point of view, of what is happening in the present situation.

To understand the dream—but here we have to be careful, because, as we have seen, for Ogden it is equally essential *not* to understand it—the dreamer's associations are no longer indispensable because the dream is no longer seen as something that belongs only to him, but as a product of the transpersonal emotion field. Associations with the dream become what the patient said before, or after, recounting the dream, or what occurs to the analyst.

> the visual image used by the analyst—provided, of course, that it results from his reverie in the session—is the most meaningful and transformational contribution he can make to the construction of the session, operating along row "C" of the grid and fully achieving not only the extension in the field of meaning and passion but also the "extension in the domain of myth" referred to by Bion in *Elements of Psychoanalysis* (1963) [...] [The image] becomes the selected fact, the organizer whereby a new *Gestalt* can be defined and the field can be newly configured and thus "extended" to encompass the permanent possibility of assignment of new meaning. (Ferro, 1996, p. 141)

The story of the dream becomes a narrative derivative of the waking dream at that very moment, even if it draws on the memory of the night dream. The night dream, however, differs "from α elements because the former result from a sorting and filtering (re-dreaming) function applied to what has been 'filmed' continuously, alphabetized and stored constantly during waking life" (Ferro, 2002, p. 52). The closest analogy would be to editing a film or the function of directing a film (Ferro, 1998).

We also draw on this repertoire of images, however, during the day and in fact at night the senses are only partly occluded. Even during the day the director films the scene while always remaining in touch with his phantasies. The difference, then, between daytime and night-time dreams would seem to be largely quantitative.

This short account already gives us an idea of the key metaphors used by Ferro. In addition to the sexual metaphor (already to be found in Bion, for example, in his use of the symbols for male and female ♂ ♀ to refer to the container/contained relationship), which he extends to the coupling of minds in the session, and the gastronomic metaphor, which complements Bion's metaphor of mental functioning as a digestive system, we also repeatedly find the Freudian metaphors, as pointed out first and foremost by Derrida (1967a), of the text and writing—and finally film.

While the concept of the intersubjective third in analysis has its origin in a Hegelian-Winnicottian, and only later Bionian, matrix, the general framework of Ferro's ideas is taken from Bion, the concept of field from the Barangers and from Mom, the idea of the spiral development of the analytic dialogue from Nissim Momigliano, and his first glimpse of the concept of narrative derivatives comes from Langs. He then successfully cross-breeds this theoretical apparatus with principles of narratology: the game and the function of the characters, casting, the reader's cooperation in the act of interpretation, the text as an "open work", the concept of the limits of interpretation, point of view, or internal focus, the concept of a "possible world", etc. There are some further concepts I would like to add to this list, again drawn from narratology, and to which I have personally contributed: immersion, interactivity, virtual reality, metalepsis, intermediality, mise en abyme, form of content, effect of reality, metonymy as an elementary psychological principle, the aesthetic experience as a model of transformations in analysis etc.; other "contaminations", however, I have taken from the philosophy of Derrida and Merleau-Ponty. The notion of radical "transformation in dream" (Ferro, 2009) is to be found in Ferro's writings from the outset, while Ogden only takes this over in his later articles and, remaining partially in line with the tradition, he seems to apply it only to certain forms of pathology.

The impression is that while one has a more extensive view of the nature and technical use of the analyst's reverie, the other has a more restricted view. Ogden gives ever more space to Bion's concept of waking dream thought; Ferro makes it the tool with which to expand to the utmost the dreaming paradigm of analysis. The scene of analysis becomes a field of possibilities, a place of dream. Everything that happens has to do with the virtual field and the transference.

Although each has his own very personal style, both have an extraordinary talent for writing and communication, and a rare ability to bring the reader into the intimacy of their clinical work. Both seem to assign a limited role to the concept of countertransference, because they see it as still too unipersonal and think that it is in fact "diluted" in the field.

An ideal conduit between the two authors could be Merleau-Ponty, since he inspired the Barangers in their model of the analytic field and, according to Reis (1999), inspired Ogden's phenomenological conception. The meeting between the two took place in the preface that Ogden (2005a) wrote for the American edition of *Seeds of Illness, Seeds of Recovery* (Ferro, 2002).

In Bion's theory of the analytic field as developed by Ferro, the analyst as an observer is not ousted from the field of observation, but remains part of it. He sees and is seen, or better, is seen seeing. The concept of the field refers to a totality that cannot be broken down into its individual component parts; it is a global structure, a Gestalt, made up of concrete interactions that are not purely abstract or intangible. There are more and more layers of meaning: reflective and pre-reflective (pre-logical, pre-verbal, embodied). For this reason it is not confined to the symbolic in the strict sense of language. It is made up of discontinuities and identifications, identity and difference, tensions and easings that are meaningful, even if only in the semiotic sense. The extraordinary thing is that in the analytic field physical objects have a life too. The material basis, which is inevitably part of it (its nature) and from which human beings are also made, albeit as life forms capable not only of existing but of knowing that they exist, is affected by this emergent quality of the psychic that we call the symbolic. In fact the symbolic pervades everything, in that it is also pre-reflexive and pre-representational but not for this reason *meaningless*, like a notion without a concept.

Between nature and mind lies the body. The body anchors us to matter, to the real. Mind, concept, consciousness are the points of maximum extension of the elastic band that binds us to the sensible. "Consciousness is being-towards-the-thing through the intermediary of the body" (Merleau-Ponty, 1945, pp. 159–160), the most distant point from which to observe the real, always ready to spring back on itself, an elastic band that must never snap. If it snaps, the person dies both as body and as mind. The mind can distance itself from the material body and what keeps it alive, but cannot do without it. The caesura between the interior and exterior of the subject is not clear-cut. In fact, it is an inside which is always outside and vice versa. We can know nothing about our inner parts unless we start from the exterior nature of our body and behaviour. Equally, we would know nothing about our body and the world if we had not developed the virtual world of psychic reality. The visible is the premise of the invisible and vice versa.

It is on these principles that Merleau-Ponty chooses the phenomenology of perception as the ideal perspective from which to investigate the body and the world. Even the β elements already have the (pre-)symbolic nature of a large-meshed net. The very instant they are produced they acquire this nature from the body and from its meanings embodied in the course of phylo- and ontogenesis. They immediately and literally take shape. "Besides," comments Vanzago (2012, p. 43),"without global perception there would not even be similarities and contiguity, which are the usually admitted associative links. Therefore, these associative links, contrary to what many believe in psychology, are not objective conditions".

Within the analytic field the meaning that objects take on is not given or absolute but is always dynamic and future-orientated. It can never be the result of a perception without the world, but always depends on a continuous interplay between subject and object. The subject emerges from an initial situation of syncretic intercorporeality or relational structure shared with other subjects and with which it will always continue to be in touch. Separation can never be final.

Making a film inside your own head, or the metaphor of cinema

One original aspect of Ferro's model is the both rigorous and radical way he theorises the need to set aside the dimension of the external or historical discourse of the analysand in order to focus on the facts of the session, which, according to Bion, are the only ones that can be observed and known. This does not mean neglecting the importance of the past as much as reconstructing it as carefully as possible, even as a secondary effect. To do this the outside must enter the inside, not "forced" to enter, but welcomed in. If, on the contrary, too much attention is paid to history, there is a risk of neglecting the patient's suffering, of establishing a kind of operational thinking of facts and memories-as-facts and rationalisations that involve no real emotional concern and tend more towards a defensive pietism and the subtle removal of responsibility.

It is a question of receptivity and listening, the centrality of the dream paradigm and the radical assumption of the Freudian notion of unconscious communication between minds. I would stress this formula, which involves the concepts of the internal setting of the analyst's mind and listening style, and not that of the here-and-now, which is sometimes misunderstood as if it signalled a sort of absurd and suffocating translation of the patient's words made explicit in real time, a re-inclusion that does not complement material reality with psychic reality but could prove to be quite traumatic.

That is why, to illustrate a point that I believe salient in his film work, and taking inspiration from the dreams of my patient, I think of Lynch and *Twin Peaks*—given its intrinsic qualities, it matters little that it is a TV series—but I could also think of *Mulholland Drive* (2001), or the feature-length version of *Twin Peaks* (*Fire Walk with Me*, 1992), or indeed any other of his extraordinary films. Ferro made me think of Lynch because of the hyper-inclusive character that the dream dimension has in the theory of the analytic field. In using vivid clinical vignettes that show the ambiguity of reality and, like Lynch, by systematically deconstructing the effect of reality, Ferro, like the brilliant American director, continually surprises his readers and enchants them with his vivid clinical descriptions. The locus of the analysis is the locus of the dream, as in any given film by Lynch.

Dreams are like "shorts" (i.e., short films; Fairbairn, 1952) that illustrate the situation of the inner landscape. Everyone must make their own mental YouTube videos. They express the poetics of the subject-director, his point of view, and, when they are recounted, they are addressed to the other—in a therapy session, the analyst—or, rather, they become part of a shared dream. As I said, in his books Ferro often uses the metaphor of film. For example, he equates hallucinations with a film projection that is disrupted by some mechanical failure, "so they are violently projected, along with bits of film, even pieces of the cranking mechanism, the lenses, the wheels of the projector, the effect of producing visual experiences in the viewer no longer integrated into the sequence of images that was flowing on the screen, and therefore meaningless" (Bezoari & Ferro, 1994, p . 256).

In such situations, the work of putting into images carried out by the α function is interrupted, and untransformed quotas of anguish are evacuated outwards. Less severe, but essentially similar, is the phenomenon of transformations in hallucinosis or of dream film frames (or flashes) of wakefulness. In transformations in hallucinosis there are no perceptions without an object, but the relations between them are false. It could be, for example, a kind of delusion of concreteness. In turn, "Delusion performs a self-containing, protective function, through the projection on to the outside world not of β-elements, which are by their nature unknowable, but of balpha-elements, which are projected like a film that separates, protects—and encloses—the patient inside a 'bubble'; however, although it protects him, it isolates him at the same time" (Ferro, 1999, p. 69).

Dream flashes, already theorised by Meltzer, are an intermediate phenomenon between hallucination and dream. Dream thoughts are formed, but since they still have a suitable container, they are projected outwards, as if in a cinema the urgency to begin the performance were such that one cannot wait until it gets dark in the room (or in sleep), or that the screen is set up, with the result that the film is projected outside the edge of the screen and the room itself, as can actually happen when films are screened outdoors.

And again:

> I should like to make a radical distinction between, on the one hand, the *production* of α elements and their sequential ordering in waking life (which may be likened to a film cameraman constantly recording in images everything meaningful that happens), and, on the other, the organization, composition, and re-working of this collected material, which is undertaken during sleep by the apparatus for thinking thoughts (the system for dreaming dreams)—like a film director or editor creatively selecting from thousands of frames the material of the final cut. (Ferro, 1996, p. 67)

When the α function is lacking, it is as if the actual celluloid for the film were missing, and when the thinking apparatus is lacking, it is as if the film material had been exposed but not yet developed, or as if one could not re-assemble the α frames although they are available. A third possible pathological factor is when situations are so traumatic that they cannot be transformed from β to α even when the function is in itself intact (Ferro, 2002).

The analyst should turn up to the session with a punk haircut

By making this challenging and paradoxical suggestion to a colleague who presented a case study at one of his supervision seminars in São Paulo, Ferro (1998) was, I believe, trying to say that the analyst must have the courage to face his own madness as well as that of others, that he should not stifle creativity through the conformism and institutional pressures that mortify thought and make it psychotic. To quote Nanni Moretti in *April* (Moretti, 1998), the analyst should ideally be able to say at least "one thing that is left-wing", as have the greatest authors of psychoanalytic thinking from Freud onwards. And as regards punk hairdos, Lynch knows what he is talking about!

If one wants to, one can see other similarities between Lynch and Ferro. Lynch started as a painter. In a brief autobiographical book he explains that he become a director because he wanted to lend movement to his paintings, and he regards his films as film-paintings (Rodley, 1997). Ferro is passionate about the drawings that children make in therapy and suggests seeing the analytic dialogue as a sequence of drawings made up of words or film frames. Waking dream photograms are almost a freeze frame of a videotape waiting for the movement to develop (Ferro, 1992), and the whole situation of analysis is like a "living picture" (ibid., p. 52).

In the last episode of the second series of *Twin Peaks*, when Cooper looks in the mirror, he discovers the Bob that lurks inside him. Ferro avoids using concepts such as destructive narcissism, negative therapeutic reaction, and the like; in other words, he never sees the "monsters" only in the other, but recognises them as something that in a virtual sense belongs to everyone.

It's a bit like in *Twin Peaks*, when it comes out that Truman has his secrets, or again in *The Hamiltons* (2006), a rather original horror film. Left without their parents, four siblings are living in the same house. After a while the spectator becomes uneasily aware that they are serial killers, but at the end of the film their true nature is revealed: they are vampires fighting for survival. We discover their distressing secret and come to see things from their point of view, a bit like what happens with the Strangers in *Dark City*. Similarly, Ferro writes that the criminal has no real choice, and that certain crimes are "obligatory" and that they come from negative reverie (Civitarese, 2011c). The shock throws us off balance. Lynch and Ferro also have in common a passion for psychological thrillers and *films noir* (as well as for soap operas).

For Lynch, as for Ferro, a film is like a dream, an inherently polysemic work open to a variety of interpretations. Visionary and disturbing magic, a certain black humour, and a taste for traumatic images akin to that of Lynch can also be found in *Rêveries*, a small book in which Ferro recorded his daydreams in a collection of extraordinarily evocative micro-scripts. The images are often crude, violent, and suggest crime scenes. Some readers will be amazed, unmindful of what makes up the phantasies that come alive in the human mind and in the consulting room, and which perhaps only painting and film are able to make visible. Let us take a look at one of the most compelling, entitled *Concreteness* (Ferro, 2008, pp. 71–72):

> When the fog came down it was no longer possible to carry on by car, because it was still trapped and blocked by the solidifying droplets, in a sort of vice.
>
> In the autumn, one of the greatest risks came from the marble-like leaves that fell from the trees and shattered the windscreen.
>
> When someone showed too much emotion, their soul was taken and feelings were ironed and given a flat, smooth surface from which nothing protruded.
>
> To settle a disagreement people took small sharp arrows which they threw at their adversaries. There were no words or writing, every train carriage stood for a letter, then you had to line up the carriages and take them to be shown if you wanted to talk.
>
> Only the rich could have carriages.
>
> I had entered the realm of the concrete.

Both Lynch and Ferro are masters in the art of transporting us into the parallel world of dreams, into the anti-realm of the concrete. Anyone attempting to distinguish clearly the dream level from the level of reality in Lynch's films would end up frustrated. There is only one world and, as in some stories by Borges or drawings by Escher, it shows different faces to those who inhabit or experience it. For both Lynch and Ferro everything is already there on the surface. There are no secrets to reveal. It's just a matter of looking, and, if anything, each time the mysteries are without secrets.

Functional aggregates

Ferro has a great deal of confidence in the possibility of monitoring the state of the emotional field of the analysis through the play of characters in the text that makes up the session. However, when the inevitable and even necessary magnetic storms break out (which represent the diseases of the field), using the reveries and narrative derivatives of waking dream thought as a compass for orientation and for grasping the point of view of the other gets to be difficult: diseases of the field lie along a line that goes from a situation of sterility or impasse, which is very difficult, to situations of negative therapeutic reactions and psychotic transference when they are allowed to spread and become unmanageable (Ferro, 1992). This paradox was already very well expressed by Winnicott:

> as analysts we get involved in the treatment of patients whose *actual clinical breakdowns of infancy* must be remembered by being relived in the transference [...], as analysts we repeatedly become involved in the role of failure, and it is not easy for us to accept this role unless we see its positive value. We get made into parents that fail, and only so do we succeed as therapists. This is just one more example of the multiple paradox of the parent-infant relationship. (1961, p. 75)

The analyst should not be too attentive and at the same time should cast systematic doubt on everything. He will be able to combine these two principles if he is guided by the emotional meaning that a character can convey in the analytic dialogue. This is precisely what is meant by the concept of "selected fact". Not the intentional organisation of a certain number of data in a framework that you want to make consistent at all costs, but an opening up to the unexpected, the belief that something amazing will happen. The analyst must be able to use negative capability, the ability to tolerate uncertainty and not knowing. Accordingly, and even at various levels of significance, sensing the emotional function in the field of a given character should ideally correspond to the choice of a selected fact (CN ↔ FS), to an oscillation that moves from a hitherto held back paranoid-schizoid position (PS ↔ D), and that is sustained by the sudden arrival of an emotional wave. This is why the expression is a bit misleading, because it suggests a rational act, whereas a selected fact is like a firework. It implies surprise, wonder, the casting of a certain light on things and some dismay.

In this state of not knowing, reverie, just like the memory of dream images and of the atmosphere with which were suffused, is the conscious pole of the waking dream which continually alphabetises the contents of the patient's projective identifications. The richness and fluidity of his reveries reflect the analyst's maturity and creativity, besides the characteristics of the analytic field that a particular pair creates at any given time. The interpretations that arise from reveries tend not so much to decode meaning as to expand it. The field is the locus of all possible histories.

The interpretation, but perhaps I should say the narrative transformation, must, in the Bionian sense, be imbued with myth (it must be situated in the dimension of meaning construction that depends on narration and then remain in row C of the Grid), with the senses (which comes from perceptible, observable, current realities) and with passion (it should not be cold and mechanical but should have its origin in shared suffering). Only in this way can the analyst approach the patient's emotional truth, his "O". This is why Ogden suggests replacing the concept of interpretation with "talking-as-dreaming" (2007), in other words, speaking with the utmost simplicity possible about the conversation-dream of the session. If bearable, the interpretation leads to an experience of unison, it promotes non-persecutory transformations, it enhances the ability to think. To go back to Matteo's dream, it paves the way from Godzilla to Bob, and from this to the beautiful woman with Oriental features in his dream (but beware: she could also stand for the siren of dependence on drugs or analysis!).

As Catherine Deane explains to Novak, it is a question of entering into contact with the patient's mind, and in particular with the pictograms through which he constantly orders experience. If the analyst takes into account the point of view of the other and the way in which he himself may have contributed to determining it, the interpretation is the result of two-person narrative work. Thus, the analyst sets up his specific listening vertex to match the vertex of the patient. This makes for the coupling of minds in the session.

In reality, the two points of view can never coincide completely; and so difference, in other words, an increase in meaning, can make inroads as long as it is contained within a common framework. The analyst tries at all moments to modulate the way he acts so as to enable the patient to live an experience of emotional attunement (spelling out the letters of the alphabet together), an intimate contact with the other, a recognition that reinforces his precarious sense of identity. The experience of unison then leads to the gradual acquisition of the ability to perceive psychic qualities in a sufficiently distinctive way.

Analysand and analyst are engaged in a process of negotiating meaning, in a dance of mutual recognition and mutual adaptation. The process takes place thanks to crossed projective identifications that weave the intersubjective matrix of the meeting. Both are struggling with the task of accommodating and assimilating, make transferences out of their own psychic reality. Both seek cognitive and affective agreement (expressed in terms such as unison, becoming "O", affective immediacy, intimacy). In order to avoid entering the dimension of *folie à deux*, consensuality (let us see it as a circle) is guaranteed by more areas of overlap between the real and virtual communities to which each belongs; more intersecting circles: society as a whole, the wider community of colleagues, theories, other disciplines, life experience, possible worlds, etc. Everyone, as it were, is a member of several clubs, and each club acts as a boundary to the others.

Every person is committed to modifying external and internal reality and to adapting themselves to it by modifying themselves. The screen on to which objects, worlds, characters, the stories of one's inner world are projected (everything in the analytic scene is dream, or the semioticisation of any object) is made up of both. Like holograms, the objects that inhabit the emotional field are formed from the encounter between the layer of projections of the two participants in the relationship. That's how "functional aggregates" are formed, quasi-transitional areas which correspond to the characters of the analytic text. It is impossible to establish to which of the authors/actors of the analytic scene they belong.

We have seen, however, that what matters is the ever-shifting game of perspectives and their dialectical intertwining: based on the concept of functional aggregate you can avoid attributing to one or the other member of the couple what is proposed; then you can "play" with the characters to develop the various possible stories.

That's why Ferro believes that encouraging associations with the dream can easily become a way of seeing the dream as something that already has a meaning in itself and not as something that affects the emotional and relational truth of the couple and an opportunity to expand the faculty of giving meaning to the emotions. Of course, there is always the possibility of a meta-level on which the classic game of interpreting dreams might prove to be the most successful way of establishing greater emotional intimacy with the patient. From the perspective of a dialectic of points of view, one of the most difficult conceptual problems of contemporary psychoanalytic theory is resolved: the past is the most intimate picture of the present and the present is "the most intimate picture of the past" (Benjamin, 1966, p. 136).

Catch me if you can

So how can we capture the killer contents, rehabilitate the thieves of vitality, liberate the impounded zones of the mind? Let's listen to someone who understands. Matteo is still speaking, sometime after the two dreams about Bob and Godzilla:

> I saw this crook in a Spielberg film *Catch Me If You Can* ... a genius!
> He is constantly being hounded by the police until they eventu-
> ally catch him. You see them putting him in a cell. He has been
> sentenced to a long stretch in prison. But the fact is that he is no
> ordinary guy. A policeman takes a liking to him, has him do things
> and a love–hate relationship is established between them. Then,
> because the policeman appreciates his incredible skill at recognis-
> ing false cheques, he encourages him to join the police force. They
> begin to work together. After a while, however, the crook tries to
> sneak away. There is a scene at the airport, where he is about to
> run away and the policeman, who knew him very well, stops him:
> "Where are you going?" he asks. The thief explains that he can't
> carry on, he can't help it, he can't take it any more. But the police-
> man replies: "Whatever, I know that you'll be at work tomorrow as
> usual." And the man says: "What makes you say that?" "BECAUSE
> THERE IS NO ONE HERE TO CHASE YOU!" ... Eh, makes you
> think ... doesn't it?

Matteo came to the session in a state of elation because the day before he had successfully resisted the temptation to "do drugs". There was no one to check up on him. He was alone with himself and his inner persecutor. But something must have happened, just like in the film, something that suggests he felt recognised. It is clear that he is describing what is happening between us and also within himself. Maybe he finally feels accepted, liked, "adopted" as a person, not just like anybody but as someone who is "unusual", "brilliant", "incredibly good". Together we are finding a way of arriving at our truth about the things that concern him, and in this journey dreams play an exciting role. We have managed to overcome a disastrous relapse during the summer holidays, with all the inevitable "garnish" of guilt, shame, humiliation, expectations of retaliation, etc. He no longer—or at least, not only—experiences me as Godzilla or Bob, or as the policeman I must have resembled at the beginning. This is not because (from a certain point of view) I am not that too, but because not only has he changed for me, but I too have changed for him (or rather, the field has changed). In other words, Matteo is starting to assume responsibility for his inner world.

Catch me if you can (Spielberg, 2002) is the challenge that each patient lays down before his analyst. It's what happens in an example that Ferro often cites: a scene in Victor Hugo's *Les Misérables*, when Jean Valjean is accused of stealing two precious candlesticks. When the Cardinal finds out, he tells the police that in fact he gave them to Valjean as a present, and in doing so saves him from prison.

Notes

1. See Grotstein (2007, p. 45): "I posit that the infant is born with rudimentary (inherited) α-function with which it is prepared to generate pre-lexical communications and to receive prosodic lexical communications from mother" an "emotional counterpart to, or equivalent of, Chomsky's [...] 'transformational-generative syntax'." See also ibid.,: "When O intersects our emotional frontier and makes an impression there of its presence, the initial response is the formation or appearance of an *α-element* (personal). It may either continue in its transformational course into dream elements, contact-barrier, and memory, or come to be rejected by the mind and degraded after the fact into 'β-elements' and thereby remain 'impersonal', 'unclaimed' in the 'dead post office' of the mind. May not Bion have also thought of this idea when he selected 'β,' which follows 'α' in the Greek alphabet? Moreover, α-elements are, in my opinion, continuations of their *Anlage* as 'thoughts without a thinker' which have been thought all along by 'godhead' ('godhood')!" (pp. 61–62). And (ibid., pp. 184–185): "the infant or infantile portion of the personality, under the strain of accumulating emotional distress, *induces* a symmetrical state in the vulnerable-because-willing mother (or analyst) so that the mother/analyst unconsciously surveys (self-activates) her own inventory of past actual or possible experiences with her conscious and unconscious self, selectively recruits the most pertinent of them for conscious consideration, and then *generates* thoughts and/or actions (interpretations) to address the distress in the infant or analysand [...] What the mother or analyst contains, consequently, is not really the infant's or analysand's projections but, rather, the emotional results of their corresponding unconscious recruitment of the mother's own experiences, which constitute her own subsequent reconstruction

of the infant's experience to which they resonantly correspond. They remain self-contained in the presence of the emotional induction by the infant/analysand. In other words, the mother/analyst and the infant/ analysand each contain 'shared representations'".

2. See Ogden (2005a, p. X): the β element is "transformed into a *visual pictogram* [that carries the emotional force and valence of the β elements from which they are derived, e.g., feelings of hate, envy, jealousy, terror, infantile adoration, omnipotent grandiosity, and so on]". But it is also the element from which, because it can transform into an α element, must be subtracted "the excess of emotion", which would otherwise be toxic (Bion, 1963, p. 38).

3. *Phi* effect: the effect of continuous movement, and not a series of pictures, is produced by the stream of frames at a rate of 24 frames per second repeatedly alternating with black strips (Journot, 2002). These frames symbolise black very well, the darkness that is within each brightness of the dream, film, and perception; finally, in any contemplation of the mother's face lies the darkness of what is hidden inside her (Meltzer, 1981).

CHAPTER EIGHT

Dreams of dreams

Locked up in a nightmare

A man talks about having a nightmare; all he remembers about it is that there was a garden. In the middle of the nightmare he is woken up by his only enemy, who has come to kill him. As a last wish, he asks to be allowed to take with him from his library a single volume of the works of Emerson. By the light of the moon they travel on a horse-drawn carriage to a chosen destination. The air is still, the streets deserted, the silence absolute. On the way, the man realises that the clock tower has neither numbers nor hands. Once they arrive at their destination, he is told to lie down. Above him he sees the leaves of a cypress tree hanging down. The gleam of steel is already before his eyes when he wakes up and by touch recognises the surface of the wall of his room. At this point, the text reads: "What an odd nightmare, I thought, and I wasted no time in burying myself in sleep." The next day—in this case the word "wake" does not appear—the man notices that the book of Emerson has gone. Ten days later he is told that his enemy had left the house one night and not returned. "Locked up in my nightmare," he deduces, "he will go on discovering, under the moon which I did not see, the city of

163

inexplicable clocks, of fake trees which cannot grow, and who knows what other things."

Thus ends the story by Borges (1979, pp. 1–2) entitled *Cypress Leaves*, which was also published in *The Conspirators*, his last collection of poems. The disappearance of the book by Emerson is the key piece of evidence that also makes the second part of this short text the account of a dream within a dream. Indeed, if one wants to stick to a psychological explanation, if the book is not in its place it means that the protagonist has *not* yet woken up, or rather, he has woken up, but *in* his dream, not *from* his dream. He, like his enemy (himself?) is caught within his nightmare.

In the story we have a first dream (S1), about which all we know is that the content is distressing, from which the man wakes up (fictitiously) to enter into a second dream (S2). This dream (but it is in fact another nightmare: the scene of the cypress) is not indicated as such except at the time of the second awakening (in the room), which is, on the other hand, presented as real. Immediately afterwards the man falls asleep, and we must assume that he has another dream (S3), from which he wakes up the following day. However, from what he tells us about the next day and the following days we understand that he is still entirely in the dream or nightmare (S4). The crucial detail that suggests he has not woken up is precisely the fact that the space on the shelf where the book by Emerson stood is now empty. Indeed, only in a dream can one really lose an object because it has already been lost in a dream.

The structure of the dream changes depending on how one interprets the moment of the *second* awakening. If it is understood as real, we first have a dream within a dream, and then the template is repeated again because we again have sleep (and presumably the dream, or nightmare) from which he awakens only fictitiously (S1 → S2 → S3 and S4). If we also consider the second awakening to be fictitious, the awakening *from* the execution, as it is the pattern that the author is repeating (he inserts an awakening that might be true or fictitious between two clearly fictitious awakenings), we would have a dream that serves as a frame (the nightmare in the garden) and then a sequence of three dreams in a dream, all introduced by an awakening (the one caused by the enemy, the real/fictitious one when he finds himself in the room, and finally the awakening from sleep the night before he discovers that the book has disappeared, etc.). The pattern would become: (S1) → S2 → (S3) → S4 (with the dreams-nightmares whose content we do not know between brackets).

But there is a further complication. In general, depending on whether the dreamer tells the story of having a dream S1 and then, within this frame, a second dream S2, or, on the contrary, that he (fictitiously) awakens from a dream S3 to find himself in a dream S4, according therefore to the consequential logic of the two scenes, the part of the dream dreamed in the first case would be S2, while in the second case it would be S3. The frame-dreams would then be S2 and S4. What would count is the direction of the arrow which expresses the transition from dream to wakefulness. It may also be convenient to neglect this aspect and consider only the order in which the various dream scenes are narrated. In this case we would have S2 and S4 as recessed dreams and S1 and S3 as frame-dreams. The dream within a dream would then always be the one that is told last. This would enhance the functional meaning of the scene switcher that takes the form of the word "dream" or "wake up" as opposed to the direction that it takes.

This is the premise on which I have examined the story. According to logic, however, it would also be possible to regard the first nightmare as recessed or, rather, because we do not know much about it, the execution scene. The frame-dream would then become the last of the series. From this perspective, Borges' text would represent, as we have seen, a kind of cascading succession: S1 (nightmare) → false awakening → S2 (night scene) → (sleep) → false awakening → S3 (the Emerson book missing). Since, however, we know nothing about the initial nightmare from which he falsely awakes and the sleep before the discovery of the book, the pattern could be simplified and we would only have two dreams, one embedded within the other.

Borges then switches between a nightmare without memory and a nightmare whose content we know; then a dream about which we know nothing that appears to be another nightmare, even if it is presented as a state of wakefulness. In the end, the fate of the author, the protagonist-narrator (a character) and his enemy (the character in the protagonist's dream) coincide at the same point.

Even if it has been read differently, for example from a political angle, as an allusion to the tragedy of the "desaparecidos", Cypress Leaves comes across as a baroque variation on the theme of life as dream, or rather, as anxiety dream. With its complicated architecture, the story also illustrates in an exemplary way how difficult it is to identify the transition between dream and waking and to have a precise idea of the structure of the dreams patients report in analysis. As we have seen, it is different if a patient talks about having *dreamt* in the dream or about *waking up* in a dream. In this case what would be the frame dream?

But the story is especially remarkable because, by introducing with consummate skill some illogicalities and ambiguities, Borges manages to immerse the reader in a rarefied dreamlike atmosphere, suspended somewhere between anxiety and mystery. He manages to create a sense of vertigo brought on by a multiplicity of undecidable perspectives, especially in such a short text, just by playing with the description of the protagonist's different states of dream and waking and the relative transitions between these two dimensions of the experience. The more precise the writing is, the more the reader experiences blurred vision, but precisely because of this luminous darkness, which is the characteristic of consciousness in the dream. The text is invaluable not so much, or not only, because it is possible to decipher the symbolic content of the dream, which is indeed rich and meaningful, as on account of the virtually infinite game of interpretation the reader is called upon to play and the tension, first aroused and then allayed, of the effort to find each time the right dreaming or waking frame within which to place the facts of the story in order to understand them. In other words, it is necessary to re-establish the ground rules of the game of narration, which is also the game of consciousness, meaning, and life itself.

Borges's fiction can be read as an implicit reflection on how the frame of experience (but we could also say setting instead of frame) contributes to structuring its meaning. This is because, before meaning exists, there is a need for margins that define a psychological space, an ego that can dream the dream, or, in other words, contain dream-thoughts. For the mind to take note of the experience, and here I think of Freud's wonderful metaphor of the mystic writing pad, its psychic sheets must first be differentiated (Civitarese, 2011a).

Dreamed in a dream

From the point of view of dream theory, but also within a general theory of knowledge, the dream within a dream structure—not particularly frequent but also not very rare—is intriguing. *The Interpretation of Dreams* has little to say about it, but the little it does say is significant.

Freud deals with it in a paragraph that is the result of two later additions to the text, the first in 1911 and the second (the last two sentences) in 1919. This fact alone is telling. The twice repeated insertion, once a decade, of a text into the text has an interesting performative effect in terms of content. It performs the action that it describes. The insistence on coming back to the same point is very much like the symptom of the return of the repressed. One can imagine that for Freud it must have been a problem because it was difficult to fit into his theory of dreams. Let us see what he writes:

> The interesting [...] problem, as to what is meant when some of the content of a dream is described in the dream itself as "dreamt"—the enigma of the "dream within a dream"—has been solved in a similar sense by Stekel [...], who has analysed some convincing examples. The intention is, once again, to detract from the importance of what is "dreamt" in the dream, to rob it of its reality. What is dreamt in a dream after waking from the "dream within a dream" is what the dream-wish seeks to put in the place of an obliterated reality. It is safe to suppose, therefore, that what has been "dreamt" in the dream is a representation of the reality, the true recollection, while the continuation of the dream, on the contrary, merely represents what the dreamer wishes. To include something in a "dream within a dream" is thus equivalent to wishing that the thing described as a dream had never happened. In other words, if a particular event is inserted into a dream as a dream by the dream-work itself, this implies the most decided confirmation of the reality of the event— the strongest *affirmation* of it. The dream-work makes use of dreaming as a form of repudiation, and so confirms the discovery that dreams are wish-fulfilments. (1900, p. 338)

Applying this scheme, the last dream in *The Cypress Leaves* (the dream of the dream: the enemy trapped in his nightmare) expresses the event of denied reality, the first (the frame dream: the execution that doesn't take place and the awakening), the desire of the dreamer. Could these be, respectively, the representation of an event that translates for the man a feeling of being imprisoned (an enemy aspect of self that populates his dreams) in a nightmare (life itself? its pervasive blindness?) in which each time the internal persecutor comes to take him, as happens in the frame-dream, and the desire to wake up? This is only one hypothesis among many.

For Freud, as we see, the part of the dream dreamed is the victim of a double censorship, twice devalued. It is a special container: the more real it is, the more it is de-realised. On the one hand, the dream work denies this reality by using the well-known defensive formula of "it's just a dream", which in this case has even become hyperbolic; and on the other, as in dreams where one of the protagonists is the analyst himself, it becomes a dream that arouses intense curiosity. Like the traumatic memories whose ultra-clear (*überdeutlich*) quality is emphasised by Freud (1937, p. 266), these dreams give off a special light, have an aesthetic impact which is in itself significant. It should not necessarily be so. If we think for a moment, why should there not be *other* dreams among the contents of dreams, since they take up such a large part of everyone's mental life? The fact is that dreams are inherently disturbing. As I have already pointed out, it is a *nekyia*, it is contact with the world of shadows, as Borges never fails to underline whenever one of his poems is about a dream. Maybe it confuses us to have to dive into a dream-like atmosphere that is even more disturbing than usual. For this reason we see them as inconceivable, almost unthinkable.

Freud implicitly invites us to look at these psychic phenomena with suspicion, the way a detective might focus his attention on a clue that is seemingly insignificant but that in his eyes promises to prove essential and to fit into a coherent framework. The dream within a dream brings into play a rhetoric that deserves attention. The part of the dream dreamed is what you want to obliterate, a negative event, probably traumatic, depicted in a realistic way, as it is. What is more evanescent and more unreal, the universe of dreams, undertakes to represent a maximum of reality, even if it is not necessarily true that it must be an "objective" reality. The form of expression looks after the dream-like deformation, what linguists call the "form of the content" (Dubois, 1970). But sometimes even images of the embedded dream are made enigmatic by the dream work, and should also be clarified and interpreted using the dreamer's associations.

The different reality quotient of the embedded dream compared to the frame-dream reproduces at this structural level the latent/manifest dichotomy. Compared to the first-order text, the most highly fictional text refers to the reality of the latent text of the dream. A denial of a different type characterises, according to Freud, the first-order dream, that is, the frame, which represents the desire, the event one wishes would replace the other. This container dream thus obeys the classic principle of the hallucinatory wish fulfilment and is by definition a deceptive text in that it is subject to dream censorship. As such it can only be truly understood if we proceed to undo the dream work and the veil that covers the latent text is torn off.

Between recessed dream (the part dreamt within the dream, or the part where you wake up in the dream) and frame-dream we then have the dialectic that exists between the different principles of mental events, between the reality principle and the pleasure principle, between the external and internal, between consciousness and the unconscious. It is as if, by representing an unrepresentable reality in the part of the dream dreamt, the logic of infantile wish-fulfilment is temporarily suspended (which for Freud was the ultimate key to the interpretation of the dream), and the logic of the anxiety dream intervened, the failed attempt at wish-fulfilment. At the end of its path, the dreamer who dreams he is dreaming finds reality, and it is a negative reality. The first-order dream fails to cope with it and eliminates it by saying that it is just a dream.

The dichotomy between dream and wakefulness is not so important in an absolute sense, because it can be reproduced in the dream itself (just as dreams can occur during wakefulness). What is more important is the frame, the intermediary world that separates the two universes—or, as we should now say, the multiple universes. Dreaming and wakefulness cannot be defined except as dialectical processes made possible by the proper functioning of the dividing line that regulates the reversible passage waking ↔ dream. The dream within a dream shows that the weakened but not zero consciousness that governs the dream can "wake up", even if only slightly and without restoring the fully alert consciousness of wakefulness. After all, why should we not think of the possibility of different degrees of immersion in dreams, just as we recognise that in the waking state there are various levels of consciousness and attention?

The question becomes entirely different when the dream is told. Here the conventions of fiction come into play. Or rather, one must differentiate between two levels, just as Kristeva distinguishes between two aspects of language: one which is more semiotic, closer to the primogenial sensoriality of dream images, and the other which is more discursive and symbolic; one closer to a kind of primary consciousness and the other closer to an expanded consciousness (Damasio, 1999). The former entails the transformation of emotions in the here and now, while the latter bespeaks the experience of the dream to the extent that a more highly developed consciousness allows us to throw off the tyranny of the present through memory. One can decide to privilege one or the other depending on the psychoanalytic model one chooses and the view it takes of therapeutic action. It is as if the interlocutor of classical psychoanalysis were expanded consciousness, whereas the interlocutor of relational psychoanalysis were primary consciousness.

The Matrix[1]

A young patient of mine recounts the following:

> I could hear my mother's screams and I said to her, "Mum, it's impossible ... I can't sleep!" But she carried on screaming. I saw then that I was fleeing from a building. But I was like Neo in *The Matrix*: I had superpowers, I was walking on walls and things like that. That's why I took things easy. Then, however, they take me and shoot me—with rifles. Rubber bullets entered my head and I felt that I was losing bits of my mental faculties. Then I died. In the dream I woke up, but I was immobilised. I couldn't turn my head, and I was doomed to see the same portion of the bed and the wall. I was in anguish, and I wondered: "Surely this can't be death? Being like this and not being able to move, as if paralysed?" Then, I really woke up, and I was very relieved.

The structure of this dream is that of a dream within a dream, such that, while I listen to it, it immediately comes across as frightening. Mauro describes the inability to sleep, or to dream ("the most free, most inclusive and most deeply penetrating form of psychological work of which human beings are capable," Ogden, 2009, p. 104) as entailing a serious defect in the ability to think. Mauro enacts an attempt at compensation and acquires superpowers. I think back to the film and I seem to remember that Neo fights against the mind control put into effect by robots that have overwhelmed their creators, that the Matrix universe is an illusory world, and that the reality to which human beings are reduced is a fictitious reality constructed by computers.

For Mauro, the Matrix (the word comes from *mater* and originally meant "uterus") may have represented a certain emotional climate—mechanical, impersonal, "computer-like"—in the primary object relationship. Certainly it was also the illusory, analgesic reality of his long history of drug abuse, from which, like Neo (a name that suggests a state of immaturity and impotence, a rebirth, a bug in the Matrix software), he has at some point "woken up", and now he has to tackle the many fanatic internal and external Mr Smiths that once again are trying to draw him into their perverse world. This first part of the dream is an interrupted dream: a nightmare from which Mauro awakens for the first time in the dream itself. But then immediately he enters another. It is like when the protagonists in *Cube 2: Hypercube* (Sekula, 2002), trapped in a labyrinthine building, started going from one room to another and each time the last room was worse than the one before. And indeed in the next scene of the dream Mauro sees himself in bed, paralysed, and wonders if he might even be dead.

Here the patient enacts something that could be of the type of what Bollas (1987) has called the "unthought known" and Nietzsche before him "knowledge without representation" (Gallo, 2004): the finely-woven fabric of lived experiences in stages of life one cannot preserve memory of and that, mysteriously, are relived in the images of the dream (Mancia, 2006). I wonder whether Neo (new), in relation to the past, might not stand for the new-born child (neo-*nato*) who may have suffered from the mother's lack of reverie and may have felt mortified by the β-elements-as-bullets that are ricocheted to the sender and are thus even more violent; or perhaps he stands for areas of the mind that for this reason have not been developed, that are just born, fragile dykes holding back emotions that periodically overflow and that reawaken the historical experience Winnicott's term is "primitive agony". In recounting the dream, Mauro moves from various forms of the past tense ("saw", "walked", etc.) to the historic present ("take me", "shoot me", etc.). The change of style confirms my hypothesis because it seems to be signalling the work of transference, the part of the past that has come to life in the present.

At yet another level, I note that the dream faithfully reflects Mauro's repeated account of the atmosphere that prevailed and still prevails in his family, in particular the rancorous, conflictual relationship he has with his mother. Of course, the dream can also be seen as a map of an inner world of post-nuclear apocalypse (in the film the human beings had unleashed nuclear war against the machines). The sense of death that pervades the dream has become the void that has been perceived and treated but also fuelled by the artificial excitement of drugs. In addition to *The Matrix*, other works come to mind in rapid succession: first,

Cormac McCarthy's *The Road*, and then the film *Wall-E* (Stanton, 2008). In retrospect, I think that this in itself perhaps opens up scenarios that are different from Mauro's dream in the session, from the therapeutic relationship and from his prospects in life.

Lying on the couch, Mauro says he feels "immobilised". This brings me to realise that—as if the usual transference indicator of *"lei"* in his description of the dream were not enough (the Italian word *"lei"* can mean both "she" and "you")—I should also pay attention to what's going on between us. I wake up with a start from being immersed in his story and the flow of my associations, and wonder what the dream might mean in relation to the session and to the dream of the session. According to which Matrix, schema, or code does Mauro feel trapped by the analysis or by something that I might have told him? Is it perhaps my vague sense of mistrust in his ability to succeed? Is it the touch of scepticism I feel because I know from experience that the risk of failure is high when drug-addiction is involved? Has this attitude perhaps led me to exert some involuntary pedagogical pressure? Does he feel that I want to get rid of Carl Stargher (the criminal protagonist of *The Cell*; Singh, 2000), in other words, the killer contents of his mind, without taking into account that the traumatised child I want to save lives in them?

The images that have crossed my mind—incidentally, film is a passion we both share and has become a kind of *private language* for us—might be seen as an attempt to revive an α function that is in its death throes and to open up his history to new possibilities, as we see in the endings to McCarthy's beautiful and terrible novel or to the delightful Disney movie, rather than to lock it into some coded meaning. What I have described is merely the opening phase—in fact, only the first few minutes of a session—of the largely successful work we did together starting from this dream, and I do not intend to dwell any further on this here. So I shall now turn to some theoretical reflections.

In Mauro's double dream it is not easy to find Freud's orderly schema. Which part of the dream seems to us more realistic and which part is the frame? Might it not be more appropriate always to consider the embedded dream the dreamt which in the patient's account comes afterwards? To understand Freud's precise distinction here, one would have to deconstruct what, according to his definition, is the part of the dream dreamt into two fragments: the first has the flavour of a traumatic memory (the screaming mother, etc.), while the second (Neo and his superpowers) would already seem to be the kind of hallucinatory wish-fulfilment that is the distinguishing mark of the frame-dream. In the frame-dream (or first-degree dream, when he finds himself in bed facing the wall) it is as if Mauro wanted to erase the reality of a psychological death (symbolised in the dream images by physical death) that initially must have existed, which continues to exist and is projected into the future, and which is linked to the "actual memory" of his mother's piercing screams and perhaps to the memory of an insufficiently shielded and therefore excruciatingly painful reality.

Overall, the dream—which is in part failed, in that it is a nightmare—is remarkable for the thought capacity it reveals. Mauro represents himself as projected into the psychotic world of *The Matrix*, a β-world of unmentalised experiences (Cartwright, 2005). Compared to the robot-machines of *The Matrix*, the Strangers are still at an experimental stage (just as *Dark City* itself paved the way for the films of *The Matrix* trilogy). The degree of simulation humans are immersed in is lower. They continue to live independently although each time on the basis of memories and fictional settings. By contrast, in the Wachowski brothers' films human beings are reduced to comatose beings encapsulated in special containers (in perpetual sleep), and their lives, aside from their neuro-vegetative functions—the robots need to maintain some of their vital functions in order to stock up on energy—are entirely virtual (dream-like, or rather, hallucinatory, since they never wake up).

In seeing himself as one of the larva-men cocooned by the robots, who keep them artificially alive in order to suck out all the energy necessary for their survival (which we can understand as an allegory of the inversion of the flow of projective identifications and a deficient maternal α function), using software that makes them lead a virtual, fictitious or alienated life, Mauro achieves an insight into himself which no rational explanation (or interpretation) could possibly match for depth and truth. "Virtual, fictitious or alienated life", then, can be understood here as its non-existence, that is, a kind of original alienation or lacuna in his being, presumably caused by insufficient experience of recognition/at-one-ment, the dimension of illusory life linked to his "self-therapeutic" use of heroin; or the void that for a period characterised the therapeutic relationship in the fictional context of the analysis. Obviously, the recurrence of the disease in the theatre of the analysis—where the dream could be a symptom—is a necessary prerequisite for treating it.

Having said that, I think that what is important is not only the content but also the act of passing between worlds, between past and present material reality, between the inner world and the field, or analytic third. Every time Mauro secretly passes through the customs house of the dream (following the intriguing etymology Pascal Quignard has suggested for "rêve", 1995) he adopts multiple simultaneous points of view on things.

Another patient of mine, Olga, describes a dream in which she

> opens a door and sees the members of her family who have been stabbed or battered to death, surrounded by a sea of blood. Then she watches a film in which she sees herself as the perpetrator of these murders.

When she starts pharmacological therapy, the nightmare disappears, but she is assailed by obsessive, impulsive thoughts urging her to carry out the same kind of violence against the same people. The content of the delusion was the same as in the psychotic breakdowns she suffered during the history of her illness. This very short clinical fragment is interesting for various reasons. First, because it shows that, however crude they may be, film nightmares can never rival the horror of real nightmares. Second, because it demonstrates continuity of content between various psychic productions. What changes is the degree of wakefulness, which grows in the sequence delusion → nightmare → obsession. Thirdly, because it is another amazing example of a dream within a dream.

Mauro's dream, the film of the mind, is significant primarily because it depicts his awakening or, rather, his various awakenings, the main one being perhaps the realisation that he is dreaming and that he represents himself in dreams of great richness. What I want to emphasise is the fact that even in the case of the dream within a dream there has been a paradigm shift since Freud: we no longer have the explication of latent content but rather the narrative-aesthetic construction of meaning that passes through moments of emotional attunement, moments in which the analyst's attention turns to anything that can reveal a connection between proto-emotions and representations. No longer work *on* dreams, which can also turn into the act of firing bullets of meaning, but work *with* dreams. The fact is that we wake up from the dream of reality every time we get in touch with our inner world, with emotions, with our own idiosyncrasies. The same thing happens every time we manage to see a situation from a new and surprising perspective.

The problem of reality

The literature on dreams within dreams is not extensive and, with few exceptions, mostly tends to confirm Freud's point of view. Wilder (1956) distrusts these dreams; he finds them mystificatory and thinks they are influenced by the analytic process, while also believing that they are useful for the analysis of resistance and transference. Grinstein (1983) compares the dream within a dream to the dramatic device of the play within a play. According to Freud, in the theatre, the recessed play may be more than the representation of an event one wishes had not happened, as in the famous scene with the troupe of actors in *Hamlet*, but also something you fear might happen in the future. It can be a way to prepare spectators emotionally for later dramatic developments. Grinstein does not take the next step, but one might wonder whether this aspect of the dream within a dream might not also be seen as analogous to the play within a play. It would be difficult to understand why this particular representation emerged at that precise moment in the analytic relationship and not at another. One might think, for example, that it may have something to do with the transference re-enactment of something that has happened in reality and one would like to erase. An indirect confirmation of such a hypothesis could be seen in the case reported by Silber (1983), who describes in great detail the meaning of a dream within a dream in relation to the transference neurosis.

Echoing in some respects the clinical material discussed by Silber, Berman (1985) wonders to what extent the most secret scene of the dream within a dream might be a way of depicting the primal scene. The caesura-frame of the game between inside and outside would be the hinge which opens or closes the door to the parents' bedroom. Whatever it may be—the primal scene, fear of something that has already happened or that might happen, the crucial point of the transference neurosis—more than ever the dream within a dream invites us to train our eyes on something obscure.

For Stein (1989), inserting a dream within another is one of the more subtle editing tasks that are part of the secondary elaboration (or revision, or, according to Isakower's overlooked proposal (1954), "redaction") of the dream. Secondary elaboration is at the service of resistance.

A cover story is created or a false trail laid that is logical and coherent enough to conceal repressed desires.

Mahon (2002) repeats the point that in the literature the topic has been largely neglected. He finds it curious that—starting from Freud himself (no one remembers that he only added the note to *The Interpretation of Dreams* in 1911)—so little attention has been paid to the frame dream, which he regards as association work on the first dream, compared to the recessed dream. Equally, there has been scant discussion about the way the two scenes join together. Mahon reflects that it is as if in a dream within a dream the dream work needs to acquire an additional further rhetorical device, what I have elsewhere called "the form of the content", in other words, a special formal way of treating the structure of the text, since the underlying conflict would be too intense to be "worked on" in a routine manner. Then he draws a parallel between the experience of the dream within a dream and children's play and compares it to altered states of consciousness such as the experiences of flight or depersonalisation.

Arguably, the most interesting contribution of all comes from Lipschitz (1990). In his view, the dream within a dream is too abstract, sophisticated, and complex a phenomenon to be framed within traditional parameters. He emphasises its creative and communicative aspect, and laments that no one has studied it from an interpersonal point of view. Lipschitz believes that one should ask oneself the question what this type of dream expresses in relation to the current state of the relationship with the analyst. The dream within a dream would then take on the task of making up for the absence of the other as a true interlocutor, constructing in itself a dyadic structure of mirroring or dialogue between container and content ("I view the dream within a dream as a reparative substitute for failed or nonexistent interpersonal transactions", ibid., p. 718).

On a less sophisticated level, the very setting of the analysis becomes the dream container for the second-level dream, in the same way as every dream scene in a film reflects this recessed structure. When it is said that "it is only a dream", it is as if there, on the boundary between the first and second dream, a sense of self as agency arose.

So with Lipschitz the dream within a dream ends up assuming the meaning of "a transitional state between the isolation of the non-active dreamer involved in self-experience and the awake person engaged in action and mastery. The inner dream provides an example of creative

DREAMS OF DREAMS   177

construction half way in the dream between the act of dreaming and the analysis of the dream. It is a two-person activity designed to be shared with the outer dream, and in addition, the analyst for whom both dreams were dreamed." The frame dream then works as the substitute for an insufficiently available analyst. The patient constructs for himself his own analyst-container and the external dream interprets the internal dream.

As we can see, Lipschitz relegates the Freudian topic of the repressed content of the dream within a dream to a secondary position and puts the emphasis instead on the creative aspect.

Spielraum

The analyst who listens to a dream inserted within another dream identifies with the dreamer of the frame-dream and, with a mixed feeling of curiosity and disquiet, contemplates the even darker scene of the dreamt part of the dream. This scene is highly artificial, while the first-order dream appears to be more real. A dizzying hall of mirrors is created, a dialectic made possible by the frame, the junction between the two paintings. In the story, the verbal flag of one of the terms of the dreaming/waking pair indicates, and at the same time establishes, the switching between states of consciousness. The view can only be endured if we tolerate the dizziness of ambiguity. A space of illusion is created where nothing is true or false, or more or less false, but only more or less true in relation to a term of reference that is never the same.

For Freud the baroque dream theatre of the dream within a dream has the purpose of representing unrepresentable content with normal stage design and with the usual tricks. If dreams have always also been seen in terms of divination and the appearance of the numinous, here the effect is paroxysmic. In the second place, then, as self-reflection it is theatre raised to the power of ten. In the foreground we have double structural dramatisation, as in "the play within a play", which, while it illuminates the dream scene, immediately obscures it with a second layer of narrative fiction, and the specularity of the text in the text as the "form of the content" (Dubois et al., 1970).

This scene sets off a dual and apparently contradictory movement. On the one hand, it reaches its acme, the explication of the fictional *structure* of the setting, its self-conscious dramatisation; on the other hand, according to Freud, the ultimate content conveys something of the real in a direct way. However, more than the reality of a recessed dream, the dual structure of the dream within a dream can be better interpreted as a second factor of fictionality, just as in a Chinese-box narrative structure.

Specularity is the specific shape of these dreams, as is reflected in the, by definition, "virtual" nature of the reflected image. Its function is to prolong the splitting of the initial frame story of the setting. That which cannot be represented at the zero degree of the analytic scene, where the force of gravity of the common sense of reality is felt, or even on the second level of the dream, comes back again at the third level of the dream within a dream thanks to a surplus of fiction. Some content is placed at a safe distance, marked as "other" and written down while the screen of the dream lights up with the constitutive diffractions of identity, accompanied by the more subtle fracture lines that are at the origin of mental suffering.

From a narratological-transformational point of view—or from the point of view of the field—these dreams have value primarily because they highlight the fictionality of the device of the setting, of the stories that are told, the images that are projected on to its screen. This is the source of their therapeutic potential. The therapy lies in the opportunity to play the game that unmasks the referential illusion; that is, to live through, in a sufficiently secure context, the crisis of the presence of the other which is the basis of the representation.

The transformative potential of dreams of dreams lies not so much in the indefinable something that Freud calls "true recollection"—both as a real fact of the past and as a phantasy of the patient's internal world (an important level but one that is background, secondary or epiphenomenal)—but rather in the game of mirrors that involves both patient and analyst. Mental growth depends less on rational explanation or the intelligence of the other's unconscious, and more on the dialectic of recognition and emotional attunement.

Focusing on the here-and-now meaning of the dream within a dream, as Lipschitz invites us to do, means coming closer to the place where the meaning is created in the intersubjective third, in the self-other dialectic, in the struggle and in the effort to achieve mutual recognition. It works in a more fine-grained way at the level at which mental disorders arise, which is the level of transition from the body of the emotions to the mind of dream images and dreams proper. If we hold on to the equation setting = cinema = frame dream, dreams of dreams have a value as models of the functioning of the analysis. They tell us that we do not live in a universe but in a *multi-verse*, in many possible worlds, each of which is defined dialectically in relation to the others.

Dreams of dreams are effective spatial articulations and dizzying refractions of inside/outside, internal/external, psychic reality/material reality, textual/extra-textual and the constant coming and going of the ego from one to the other term. Each of these movements reflects the passage external → internal and, in reverse, internal → external in the aesthetic conflict. Each step across the borderline that connects the different worlds, mimics *Fort/Da*, the oedipal alternation of the maternal and the paternal, the absence and re-appearance of the object. If customs control (*rêve*) is not closed, the economy of the ego benefits from these possibilities of movement. Consequently, it is more important to play than to unmask the game, more a question of "talking-as-dreaming" than remaining in silence, more talking about "talking-as-dreaming" than "making interventions" or "interpreting" (Ogden, 2009).

The frame of experience is usually a discreet presence, while it comes to the forefront in the dreams of dreams or in dreams in which the scene of the analysis is depicted, the dreams that I have called recessed or mirror dreams. To use a film image, it is what Lars von Trier (2003), the director of *Dogville*, does when he relinquishes the mimetic effect of reality as the setting for his story and emphasises instead the artifice that makes for the representation.

But the meaning is always to some extent artificial; it is always the product of a game of frames. With Khan we could say that the frames create the space of the dream, without which the dream itself would be a dissociated experience. Indeed, if the dreaming process is biologically determined, the space of the dream, by contrast, is an achievement of individual development.

Self-consciousness arises from the constant movements across the boundaries between worlds. To grow, one must become foreign and cross frontiers so as to define oneself in a differential and dialectical relationship with the other. However elementary it may be, each story is made up of frames and worlds, that is, different simultaneously active diegetic levels. If, as Lipschitz says, the dream within a dream creates a dialogical structure in which the frame-dream is an interpreter of the recessed dream, this means that each time a highly sophisticated metaleptic apparatus comes into play. The area of overlap is guaranteed by the emotional sharing made possible by the sequences of enactment (and I use this term almost as a metaphor to emphasise the performative nature of the discourse) that make up the interaction between patient and analyst, and it is registered in the reveries of analysand and analyst.

Illuminating the frame produces the effect of integration mentioned by Ogden when he writes of the importance not only of dreaming but of remembering dreams (2001b, p. 313): "It might be said that when a dream is both dreamed and remembered, the conversation between the conscious-preconscious and the unconscious aspects of mind across the repression barrier is enhanced."

Essentially, dreams, and also later recounted dreams, appear more relevant because of the rhetoric they exhibit than of the content they transmit. It would be wrong, however, to think that this function of "holding" or primitive containment is divorced from content. First, because between painting and frame there is interplay between background and figure, and second, because within the picture there is an infinite regression that involves other frames.

The function of unreality

To look now at dream theory: we can differentiate between a more traditional strand, which looks primarily at the intrapsychic and content—What does the cypress tree mean? Who is the enemy? Why Emerson? What does the quotation from Virgil mean? And what about the other characters in the story I did not mention in my summary? The Roman she-wolf? The cat Beppo? The ceramic tiger? And a more modern strand, which is relational in origin and which I like to think of as a more updated map, which is closer to the interpsychic or the container[2] and more ready to take on *this* level. The classic approach looks at the dream with the presupposition that the ego is already constituted and up and running, and hence, in Winnicott's terms, it looks at the id-needs, the expression of the drives.

The basic attitude is that of Freud, who, as we have seen, sees the dream within a dream as depicting a particular content, a reality which is doubly negated but precisely for this reason very effective, and which one wishes had not happened. The relational perspective on the dream, however, takes more account of *ego-needs*,[3] of the need for the frames of the experience to be structured in a functional way. It also emphasises the functions of holding and reverie (functions that enable the formation and the "maintenance" of the ego) as essential to first promoting psychosomatic integration (the psyche taking up residence in the body, Winnicott's concept of in-dwelling; Bonaminio, 2009) and then every subsequent repair of this basic level of personal identity.

However, we must acknowledge that Freud had already sensed this path, when, in speaking of anxiety dreams, he assigned them a task situated, as it were, this side of the pleasure principle.

The dream within a dream is paradigmatic of this second angle of vision. The work carried out in preparing the set where the performance will later take place and the vicissitudes faced in the dialectic of recognition that establish it are illustrated in an exemplary manner. If it is the occasion for moments of emotional sharing, the game of frames that the environment-mother (and not the mother-object) provides, which necessarily occurs at birth on a sensorial basis[4] (and to some extent continues to be so for life, as Ogden's concept of autistic-contiguous position indicates), discreetly constructs the background of the performance.

One may reflect on the fact that if Freud placed the recollection of a "real" reality in the part of the dream dreamt, it was to imply that the subject had failed in its capacity to represent or transform something that could be called the trauma of the real. The images of the mind, writes Bachelard (1960, p. 13), have a vital *"irreality function* which keeps the human psyche on the fringe of all the brutality of a hostile and foreign non-self." It is as if Freud himself moved in the direction of a lack in the maturation of thought located precisely at this level—more a deficit than a conflict—and which regards more the intersubjective constitution of the dream space (as Winnicott and Kahn would say) than dreaming as an innate biological process or the dream as a scene already prepared for the representation of psychic conflicts.

In some way we would have to say that Foucault (1994) is right when, in his introduction to Binswanger's *Dream and Existence*, he argues that Freud gave the dream the same status of words, something that did not go beyond semantics, without grasping its structure as language, morphology, and syntax of images within which meaning is produced. It is as if a theory of aesthetics took into account only the content and not the form. So Freud, again in Foucault's view, set up a kind of theology of meanings in which the truth precedes its formulation and constitutes it in its entirety. (But Foucault is not entirely right: he is not very fair to Freud and seems unable to give him credit for clarifying the rhetoric of dream work.)

That form and content, or the psychological space of the ego and impulses, are two different evolutionary levels, but which are then always present simultaneously, and indeed dialectically related as a way of experiencing reality, is demonstrated by the fact that there are adult patients who show real dissociation between morbid daydreaming and imagining, between the innate neuro-physiological activity of dreaming and the dream-space where this process takes place. For Khan, the former is an innate given, the latter an achievement of personal development, the internal psychic equivalent of what Winnicott called transitional space.

Let us go back one last time to dreams within dreams. There are other possible vertices from which to look at this peculiar product of the psyche. For example, one might think that the twofold performance of dreams serves to highlight a certain detail; in the same way as a spotlight on an actor removes him the shadows, or in some paintings the play of perspective focuses on a key element of the whole scene. This is the function performed by the mirrors in Losey's *The Servant* and in many works by painters such as, among others, Velasquez and Vermeer, Memling and Escher.

As in these paintings, the dream within a dream represents the essence of reflexive consciousness, the consciousness of being able to break away from direct adherence to reality and move towards the self and one's own inner world. If, as Ogden has shown so excellently (1994), self-consciousness comes from the self-other dialectic, from mutual reflection and becoming implicated, or from elevating and negating, the dream in the dream reproduces exactly the same pattern of the dynamic process of mutual definition that underlies subjectivity. Never, not even by waking, does one wake up from the dream completely.

The dream within a dream, therefore, tells us that we live in many worlds in which wakefulness and dream blend constantly in varying proportions, and these are the various worlds of the dream within a dream, the first-order dream, wakefulness, reverie, transformation in hallucinosis, the flash waking dream, hallucination—in short, the whole range of states of mind that Bion placed in the left-hand column of the grid (Civitarese, 2013).

Therefore, if we identify health with full self-consciousness, with maturity, with the ability to dream ourselves into existence, and if we believe that self-consciousness issues from mutual recognition, then every dialectical self-other movement is like a transition between worlds, the construction of a potential space. The play of reflections that the dream within a dream shows so well (and which is of value because it illuminates an aspect that is inherent in a less ostentatious way in any kind of dream) is the ever-open construction site where the ego is built, the space in which the individual acquires a theory of the mind and the attendant ability to attribute to oneself and to others subjective mental states—in a word, the ability to mentalise.

This is the reversal of perspective with respect to Freud. For Freud, once the dream is *translated*, it gives access to the unconscious; for Bion it creates the unconscious. For Freud, the dream is all in all a spurious product; for Bion it is the deepest form of thought, that which enables us to apprehend reality simultaneously from several points of view, the unconscious psychological work by means of which we give meaning to emotional experience in both sleep and wakefulness. For Ogden, who takes Bion's dream theory to the extreme, interpreting the dream in order to translate the unconscious into the conscious becomes (self-reflexive) talking about talking-as-dreaming in the conversation he has just had with the patient.

Under the right conditions, the game of interpretation can still be played in the traditional way, but the patient's ability to bear it must be taken into account and it must be seen as one narrative genre among the many that are possible. Paying attention to what the patient is able to put up with emotionally prevents interpretation from becoming the mortifying extraction of meaning or something that resembles a "break-in" into the patient's mental "setting" (Collovà, 2007). Intolerable "breaking and entering" produces unnecessary suffering and negative therapeutic reaction because it erodes the margins within which the individual gives meaning to his life. In fact, the frame of experience has the value of an institution, and like every institution is based on an intersubjective pact and settles at the deeper layers of identity—what Bleger calls the meta-ego (1967).

If one were to respect psychic "institutions", this would lead not so much to the explication of latent content as to the narrative-aesthetic construction of a meaning that depends on the exchange of states of reverie and moments of emotional attunement. Thinking back to how therapeutic actions work urges us to be careful about anything that may reveal a link between proto-emotions and proto-sensations and representations as a way of promoting the development of the ability to think. It would therefore no longer be a question of privileging the content of the dream, which risks becoming, as it were, a barrage of bullets of meaning (for example, as I could have done, with Mauro, if I had been biased in favour of a certain prognosis), or in other words, the introduction of random elements of disturbance and disorder into the rhythms that produce a feeling of the continuity of existence, but of paying more attention to dreaming as a psychoanalytic function of the mind.

Let me conclude with a question: could the intersubjective dimension of the psyche in general, and the intersubjective meaning of the dream as recounted in the here-and-now session in particular, be the elements that Freud "represses" or leaves in the shade? These elements could then come back and recur as a symptom, as something in his theory of dreams that has not been transformed (or is perhaps not even transformable), into the image of an actual reality that one wishes had not happened and the remarkable structure of his pronouncement about the part of the dream dreamt which is made up—as a mirror of the content—of the two parts added on two occasions, in 1911 and in 1919, to *The Interpretation of Dreams*. In other words, might this section betray Freud's conflicted attitude towards what he himself, in a famous passage (1911), described as the *fiction* of a child enslaved to the pleasure principle and without regard for the world outside—a fiction which, since such a psychic organisation would not be able to survive a moment, can only be maintained provided one includes maternal care? Lastly, is it still possible nowadays to maintain this fiction?

Notes

1. A shorter version of this section is to be found in Civitarese, 2011d.
2. See Ogden 2009, p. 102: "The 'container', in Bion's theory of the container-contained, is not a thing but a process: it is the unconscious psychological work of dreaming, operating in concert with preconscious dream-like thinking (reverie), and conscious secondary process thinking." In the analytical field, but also in life, there are always

multiple and reciprocal container/contained relationships—and they are potentially endless if we also consider the minimal dimensions of interaction. The child holds in its mouth the mother's nipple, which contains milk, but in the meantime it is also held by its mother's arms. Both are located in wider contexts that both support them and support others, etc.

3. See, however, the quotation from Freud given in endnote 3, Chapter One.

4. Freud (1950 [1895], p. 366): at birth *the information of one's own scream serves to characterize the object.*

CHAPTER NINE

Are dreams still the guardians of sleep?

Giving the body back to the mind

Godzilla, Bob, King Kong, Zero, Leonard Smalls (aka the Lone Biker of the Apocalypse), the Strangers, the Hamiltons, the Hulk, the monsters of *They*, Nosferatu, Chigurh—these are just some of the extraordinary characters that populate cinematic dreams and later enter our own dreams (or is it the other way round?). They give shape and form to the dark depths of the soul that we deal with as analysts. But what is ultimately the function of this colourful assortment of spectres?

In this chapter I want to attempt a concluding summary. I would be satisfied if the reader who retraces his path through the pages of the book were able to gain a sufficiently clear idea of the elements of continuity—but also the differences—between the various models. Central among these differences is Bion's introduction of the concepts of the α function and waking dream thought. I have come back to these two points on several occasions but each time from different angles, in much the same way as a *leitmotif* recurs in ever new forms in a musical score. The unsolved problem that these concepts help to frame is the shift from body to mind, from proto-sensations and proto-emotions to images.

Emotions are the body's reactions to stimuli of varying provenance (exteroceptive and proprioceptive) and are some of the devices of adjustment to the homeostasis of internal states that is necessary for life. Homeostasis does not mean a state of absolute stability, but the possibility for the chemical and physical parameters of the body to oscillate, albeit within limits. A living structure engages with the environment according to a complex process of concrete interactions interspersed with recurring shifts from states of imbalance to states of balance and vice versa. This is why an emotional connective for the higher perceptions and functions of the mind is never entirely absent, because it is linked to the expression of the basic biological values of the organism.

With this in mind, the α elements, and the very images of dreams, correspond to the emergence of new levels of organisation of the mind. During the course of evolution, our biological system has gradually acquired ever more differentiated ways of sending and receiving feedback on its activities, its own condition, its changes of state. At first, this information is akin to noise, simply confusing. Later it becomes more refined and even becomes identified with the contents of consciousness, which, according to Freud, can be seen as the sense organ for the perception of psychic qualities.

Animals also form visual, auditory, tactile, etc. pictograms, which translate the activation of underlying neural patterns, but presumably only have a "primary" or "nuclear" consciousness, not true self-awareness. It is like being a film director who has all the footage shot during the day, the so-called rushes, but is unable to edit the material. We can do the editing every day because we have developed the language. This is how we imagine the future, plan our actions, and remember the past. Thanks to language, pictograms similar to those of animals (as far as we can surmise) become for us dream and thought.[1] Our pictograms are also a social/cultural product and are not only neurological/innate.

When it arrives, "extended" consciousness represents a significant evolutionary advantage for man. Consciousness makes the discrimination between emotions more fine-grained and the organism's response to the turbulence that presses upon it more effective. In the immediate context of experience, the primacy of the emotions is self-evident. On the neuro-anatomical level there are significantly more projections from the amygdala to the cortex than the other way round. The less evolved consciousness is never outlawed, but works in conjunction with the other, albeit within a range of variability that runs from almost instinctive reactions to the more abstract performances of thought. Formal-logical thinking is in continuity with the emotions that arise from the body, although we do not know how these are transformed into images or why they turn into certain images and not into others. As Special Agent Dale Cooper is fond of repeating, we do not know how to explain clearly the passage from body to mind, how α elements come to be formed from dynamic neural patterns. It's the same problem we encounter when in Freud's metapsychology we try to grasp the status of the psychic representatives of the drive in relation to memory traces.

For Bion, the function that corresponds to this missing link is the α function. It is no accident that this is an empty concept, but it is one whose existence it is necessary and timely to postulate in order to frame a model of how to pass from the bodily to the mental. The β elements[2] are proto-images, precursors or "image schemata" (Lakoff & Johnson, 1980), "dispositions" (Damasio, 1999) that emerge from perceptions and movement, from the *whole* body, and act as a conduit between the physical reality of the organism and the immaterial reality of the mind. They are pre-reflexive and unconscious emotional states that anticipate and influence cognition. With the concept of β elements Bion gives back theoretical centrality to the emotions, which it does not have in Freud's theory, which links it indissolubly to cognitive processes. An emotion is alphabetised when it is interpreted cognitively, even only in the sense of implicit and not reflective knowledge. This is the delicate juncture which determines its effectiveness or otherwise with respect to the body's vital purposes. It is legitimate to think that the "interpretation" is made both unconsciously (where it will be a pre-reflexive assessment) and consciously.

The α elements thus define a first level at which the brain is able, in the form of images, to process data that reflect its own functioning or state at any given moment, since it is immersed in a certain environment. The α elements are alphabetised emotions (or rather, emotions in the process of being alphabetised, since here the staging is no more than conventional), that is to say, they are already transformed, and not purely sensorial, pictograms or emotions.

If the "imaginative faculty" that coincides with the α function is to be regarded as a higher evolutionary stage (albeit continuous with the functional meaning of the proto-emotions), as a reaction to a stimulus or solution to a problem, nonetheless it is still first and foremost a bodily response to stimuli, and implies the totality of being of the individual, not just his mind.

In Bion's theory of thought reveries and dreams are ways of getting closer to the level of the unconscious mind that corresponds to the formation of α elements and their concatenation in dream thoughts (Damasio's *proto-self*?). It is obvious that these forms of mental activity need to be understood as ways of adapting to the moment being experienced, which then go on upwards to the level of abstract thinking. Even the most abstract thought is always in some way rooted in the body and in the connective tissue that gives it emotional meaning on the basis of fundamental biological values. However, since it implies the maximum degree of clarity in self-consciousness, and to the extent that the immediate needs of the organism have within certain bounds already been met, it is able to free itself from the constraints of the present and to represent the past and the future. In short, it is as if at any time a kind of triage of requests from the organism were carried out.

So we can consider everything that comes to mind as a way of adapting to the environment and adjusting tension (this is simply the point of view that is reflected in the concepts of "forced association" and "psychic determinism", "becoming O", etc.). Some responses are long-lasting: for example, when emotions become sentiments. Consequently, like emotions, dream images too have the prime meaning of being direct responses to the current needs of the organism to relieve tension in order to survive, necessities that initially are always imposed by immediate existence.

While awake the individual may act, while asleep the muscular system is disconnected. The mind contemplates, it does not act. If it does, it does so virtually or in the concreteness of psychic reality.[3] The restorative function of sleep is evidently primary—"its end is the conservation of animals [...] sleep belongs of necessity to each animal," writes Aristotle (2013)—and one can still think of dreams, as did Freud, as (indirectly) the guardians of sleep. However, I imagine them not only as the hallucinatory satisfaction of a repressed childish desire, but as an action-response to stimuli (from the most urgent to the most deferrable), which remains in a virtual state, but still achieves the most current and urgent ultimate goal. Expanded consciousness allows one to plan a response in the future, but this decision will still have its roots in the irreflexive body and will always be a response to an immediate current problem. Not only that, but expanded consciousness can only operate if it starts from the products of nuclear consciousness.

For example, if the stimulus is the emotion aroused by the image of a situation of danger that emerges from memory, this may produce a dream in which the "film" of an escape on the Bat-mobile (*The Dark Knight*, Nolan, 2008) is the way to reduce the tension that has been generated and, in an indirect way, to preserve sleep, or else the nightmare of being at the mercy of the Joker, the failed attempt to put this response into effect.

In sleep, stimuli start mainly from the memory system, but the activity of dreaming does not entail reorganising an archive of generic, abstract, and purposeless memories and not even, as has been suggested, a method that, like applying varnish to paint on a canvas, only serves to fix them—because a *new meaning is created*. If they are fixed, it is for this reason. What matters is the "poetic" response to the stimuli coming from the immediate context of experience, including understanding the memory of the past and of the future (and thus also those that do not come from the concrete environment in which the person currently finds himself), in the state of sleep, in a kind of stand-by state of the organism that is obviously essential to life. This perspective has the advantage of uniting body and mind, if we see α elements, dream images and reveries as functionally continuous with emotions, as a more differentiated stage of evolution.[4]

La rêve *or the customs house of dreams*

Something can go wrong in the delicate transition from emotions[5] to α elements, and this can create a kind of a logjam. The problem arises in the province of the *rêve*, in the space where psychic transformations are negotiated. It can be the tensions that originate metaphorically in conflicts, trafficking, natural disasters, totalitarianism, terrorism, and religious fanaticism, etc.—all events that require borders to be closed.

So, what does it mean to say that dreams or *rêveries* think, as Bachelard (1960) contends? It means that they are the result of an unconscious, involuntary and unaware thought, which in itself represents a reaction or solution to a problem facing the organism. Analysts are then like the blue helmets of a UN interposition force brought in to impose a truce and to re-establish lines of communication, or electricians called in to restore the line of connection that goes from emotions → images → thoughts at the precise points where the malfunction has occurred.

Often, in the disorders we deal with, these critical points are where non-alphabetised bodily reactions (β elements) become α elements (proto-images) and then enter the inter-human pre-reflexive and reflexive realm of the symbolic. To preserve sleep, in the dream the specific action that transforms the internal environment must be performed in order to return to a state of balance. From a certain point of view it matters little whether it is the fulfilment of a desire or something else. The action may also only remain in a virtual state, but it still leaves traces in the memory. Although it may seem counterintuitive, all we have of the future are the memories of how we dreamt it.

The specific nature of the α function is to be located on philo- and ontogenetic levels and on levels of more primitive functioning than the apparatuses for dreaming and thinking; hence it is closer to the body. Night-time (and daytime) dreaming, which is the stage closest to the α function, can be seen as the way that has become differentiated in the organism to reconstruct the link between body and mind, to give the body back to the mind (or vice versa) each time.

Like the aesthetic object, the dream works ceaselessly at the psychosomatic reintegration of the subject. Similarly at birth, the mother's capacity for reverie, the expression of her α function, helps the infant to become integrated physically and mentally, to settle the mind in the body. What founds self-consciousness is language, that is, sociality, relationships. On this level, too, malfunctions can occur which lead to disorders of the mind. Ferro distinguishes between two main sites of pathology, one a deficiency of the α function and the other a malfunction of the apparatus for dreaming/thinking: according to Grotstein (2007), "mentalisation" and "thinking" proper, respectively.

The ego therefore only emerges from a relationship, and the dream as a human product is a matter of language. That's where the feeling of existence comes into being. If this is true, every dream, in its linguistic and non-linguistic component parts, is always a reflection of an inter-subjective dimension of the mind, which always contains an implicit communicative intention. The images that the mind pretends are reality are never pure or original. Rather, they are always touched by the symbolic. One problem with the use of the term "image" is that it makes one think only of the visual.

Dreamt dreams are different from recounted dreams. Dream images make sense at the moment they appear. However, it is true that from Freud's point of view, in order to protect sleep, dream images result from all the tensions that build up in the body and in the memory, so it is possible to infer those tensions from the memory of the dream. If, though, we regard dreams this way, we lose sight of the relational meaning they have at the moment when they are recounted. We should distinguish proto-emotions from the emotions that are already also images/pictograms, even though this would be a bit like trying to halt the intimate dialectic of a process. The unconscious, whether repressed or not, cannot be thought of unless in relation to the other. The subject is constitutively trans-individual; for Bion the mind can only be seen at the group level. No person, in short, can exist unless they are part of a field of relationships. The ego is not master in its own house, but it finds a house in the other. For the same reason we can say that not even the unconscious is master in its own house. The decentring of the ego is a recentring on the other and the relationship. In his Seminars XVI Lacan (2002) introduces the neologism *extimité* (foreign intimacy/internal externality), which also brings together externality and intimacy as a way of pointing up the problematic nature of the distinction between subject and object, outside and inside. Interiority is as external, intersubjective, or social as is exteriority, just as that to which the subject belongs is also real.

For Freud "A dream does not want to say anything to anyone. It is not a vehicle for communication; on the contrary, it is meant to remain ununderstood" (1916, p. 231); "It does not think, calculate or judge in any way at all; it restricts itself to giving things a new form" (1900, p. 507); "it follows that the dream work is not creative, that it develops no phantasies of its own, that it makes no judgements and draws no conclusions; it has no functions whatever other than condensation and displacement of the material and its modification into pictorial form, to which must be added as a variable factor the final bit of interpretive revision" (1901, p. 667). The dream, in short, is "a completely asocial mental product; it has nothing to communicate to anyone else; it arises within the subject as a compromise between the mental struggling in him, it remains unintelligible to the subject himself and is for that reason totally uninteresting to other people" (1905, p. 179). To explain Freud's position, Pontalis (1988, p. 312) notes that faced with "two theoretically possible options—the model of translation […] and the expression pattern—Freud did not hesitate: the first is the one that is imposed". Against the background of this decision, comments Bezoari (2011), "there was, probably, this concern to guarantee the psychoanalytic interpretation of the dream a status that is not arbitrary, because it is a re-translation to recover meanings already existing in the unconscious."

The verb "to dream" should really only be conjugated in the passive; so, not: "I dreamed" but "It was dreamed", "Il a été rêvé", as Valéry says (quoted in Pontalis, 2003). The dreamer's position vis-à-vis the dream is one of waiting. Consciousness and the images it feeds on must be seen not as in opposition to the emotions but as continuous with them. The dream is the theatre where one passes from raw emotion, pure sensoriality, to already alphabetised emotions, and then on to images that have an emotional component. Unlike conscious thinking, which implies the possibility of actively manipulating symbols, dream thought is an automatic and spontaneous activity of the mind, involuntary thinking. But even when weakened, consciousness is always present (or perhaps, as hypothesised by Denton (2005), who traces it back to primordial emotions, it is as if every night a kind of fount of consciousness were reborn out of the dream).

In fact, corresponding to the zero degree of meaning of each word (and even before each sound uttered with particular intensity and strong emotional character) there is an elementary translation (Derrida, 1967b), a metaphor (according to others, a metonymy), a translation, a transference. Algebraic symbols also perform this elementary substitution when, in the words of Nietzsche, the equal is equated with the unequal. As Bion ironically pointed out, one plus one does not always equal two. The dimension of dream-thought is never entirely set aside, and even the most abstract calculation is made against an emotional background that determines its meaning. In short, not even logic manages to be entirely consistent with its own premises. Even the most abstract thought can be said to be to a certain extent "thought (dreamt)". Just as dream work is not incompatible with the finest performances of the intellect, so in wakefulness even the most abstract thoughts are rooted in the unconscious.

The analyst with curlers

Mario says:

> Dr Civitarese, I dreamt of you! I was hiding in the room, behind the bookcase. You were the patient and the analyst was a seventy-year-old woman with curlers. She was either English or American,

and she also had an assistant. You were very calm and spoke of your childhood memories, that your mother had died, and you were grief-stricken and in tears. I watched with admiration and I said to myself: "Look how good he is at expressing his emotions! I couldn't do it even if someone pointed a gun at my head!" The analyst said to you bluntly that inside you there was a desperate child. You protested that you would never say such a thing to a patient of yours! The analyst was unmoved and replied that the adult was getting mixed up with the sad child. Meanwhile, I'm hiding at the back and I feel both awe and respect: "Look how they manage to face up to each other!" For me you were both worthy of dignity. Unfortunately I don't remember what was said. Nonetheless, I felt a very strong sense of wonder.

Then he continues:

On Monday I had my first supervision with A. I wondered if age was what he had in common with the old lady. This dream made a deep impression on me. I really wanted to remember the dialogues. I was reminded of those costume drama films set in the eighteenth century where children would come into the room where their father worked. Dammit ... how well you manage to show your weakness! I just can't do it! I have forgotten how to cry. It's years since I last cried, it was when my grandfather died ... The lack of embarrassment in crying ... when you told me, "Why be embarrassed about going to a supervision and talking about the problems one has?" ... I felt a sense of deep honesty and also safety.

I ask him what he thinks of the analyst's interpretation of the dream. He says:

I was almost annoyed. As if it were not very welcoming. This woman interpreted your reaction as a resistance to getting in touch with the fact that there was a child involved. At the beginning I sided with you but in the end this woman with curlers (not that she actually had them on at the time) made me think. I remembered about my love for cooking. When I can, I watch cookery programmes on TV, like *Ramsay's Kitchen Nightmares*. It's about restaurant owners who are in trouble, maybe because they are in debt, and so they call on this chef, who spends some days at the restaurant and then suggests ways of getting out of the situation. In one episode there was a woman who looked English (light-skinned, blonde), and who rejected all the solutions that Gordon Ramsay suggested. She was stubborn. The analyst in the dream had similar features to this woman. So you call a person who wants to help and then you reject them! Following the discussion that you have in the dream, the old lady even acquired a certain authority. It became a fight among equals. The trainee at her side was silent; she just wrote and took notes. Deep down this woman in the dream was urging you on. She was annoyed by your crying because it was as if you were hiding behind the child who had been abandoned. She wanted to stimulate your capacities as an adult. It was hard. Maybe it has to do with A., who is always rather brusque with me.

This dream is a dream of the therapy or of the analyst and also resembles a dream within a dream. In the opening scene Mario is just an observer hiding behind the bookcase and then the second scene is what he observes. The very structure, even without the interpretation that the patient has given himself, puts them in relation to each other: the second scene sheds light on what happens in the first and in his inner life. It is a sophisticated construction, pointing to a developing capacity for self-reflexivity. Mario sees himself reflected in his analyst, replacing him in turn on the couch and then comparing his technique with that of the severe analyst with curlers. Evidently two schools of psychoanalytic thought are at play here: one based more on the superego and also prepared to engage in a confrontation, and the other more willing to be welcoming. One speaks more to the adult (ego), the other is more concerned with the child (unconscious). At first Mario envies the certainty with which his analyst (and "father") is able to express his frailty and his pain, which he compares with his own inhibitions, and he feels some discomfort about the female analyst, but then he begins to look on her with respect.

Numerous themes interweave dizzyingly in this dream, some of which I have to leave out for obvious reasons of confidentiality. However, a rapid examination of the dream (more like the "analyst with curlers") clearly shows the following: a primal scene situation, a complex relationship in the face of the strength/weakness of the father, the emergence of an infantile neurosis that turns into a transference neurosis, a reflection of real life events, in other words the clash of schools of thought between the supervisor and his analyst (the entrepreneur of the day residue to whom the capitalist of dream desire offers its funding: between mother and father).

The dream obviously comes close to being a nightmare: Mario as restaurateur feels in debt (guilty) to the *imago* of his parents, he calls another chef (actually two) to help him and he does not understand how he dare reject their suggestions. (Besides, a curler is a rather complex piece of equipment.) He wonders if his difficulties might not have something to do with the analyst's hairstyle: punk or bouffant?

From a perspective that privileges listening to the dream of the session one would give more importance to the arousing of emotions reflected in the images of the dream story. Through these Mario maps out a complex and dynamic emotional geography where sadness, admiration, envy, astonishment, embarrassment, despair, respect, and shame all appear. The trainee taking notes could stand for his mental notebook and a growing reflective and self-reflective function.

When he mentions films set in the eighteenth century, I think of Stanley Kubrick's *Barry Lyndon* and in particular of the *andante* by Schubert that accompanies one of the saddest moments in the film: the protagonist is by now in disgrace and has lost his son, the thing he loved most in the world. I liked the music so much that I bought the record of the soundtrack. Recalling the notes of that piece of music during the session tells me what words cannot say. It gives me a possible interpretive key to understanding the emotional content of the patient's dream and of the session through a poignant sense of loss and the end of all things. Mario, among other things, had at that point just mentioned a family bereavement. Again, it is not a question of the analyst explaining the content of the reverie to the patient (except in exceptional cases) but of talking (or remaining silent) about the emotional experience it registers and relaunches at the same time.

The dream as a function of the poetic mind

In this section I shall briefly summarise what I have said so far.

The emotions express reactions that are part of the mechanisms of regulating the organism designed to ensure survival. The proto-images (α elements), dream images and reveries, including those that can be triggered actively, have the same evolutionary significance. In relation to the turmoil arising from the friction with the real registered by the emotions, emotional pictograms (including those that are visual, auditory, tactile, etc.), the most complex dream scenes that are already the result of the montage of the dream work (to which is delegated "the apparatus to dream dreams"), and also the ability to represent conscious and intentional scenarios, are subsequent steps in the ability to relate successfully to the life environment.

When primitive emotions are mapped, recognised, and alphabetised, the discriminating power of the ego increases with regard to the potential benefit or harmfulness of a certain stimulus. The organism's responses have a better chance of being adaptive and it also becomes possible to predict the future consequences of one's actions.

In mental illness, however, the transition from β to α, from proto-emotions and proto-sensoriality to pictograms, may encounter dysfunctions. The mysterious α function, the function that governs the crucial passage from the body to the mind, may be deficient or may even flow in the opposite direction.

Paying attention to reveries and dreams is a way of servicing this function, of reconnecting feeling with abstract thinking and restoring the body to the mind (and to dreams). This is one of the most invaluable aspects of Bion's theory, the fact, namely, that it is based on the centrality of emotions in psychic life. It is essential to make clear that reveries can be the means to reintegrate an indivisible somatopsychic unit, independently of all dualisms.

Now, could this also be the meaning of dream activity? To preside over this unity? To keep the channel of communication between mind and body permeable? In doing so, pre-oneiric images and properly oneiric dreams would have the same role as emotions. They would only be more clearly distinguished and there would be the same difference as that between blurred and focused vision. However, the advantage of seeing things clearly and distinctly is obvious.

Like emotions, images can be seen as reactions, even solutions and answers, to stimuli that otherwise disturb the homeostasis of the organism, which admits only a very narrow range of fluctuation in its parameters in the immediate context of experience—or in the broader context that is still represented by the complex of current memories—even if one can think of stimuli and responses of varying lengths, for example, emotions that become feelings and passions. So, both during wakefulness and sleep, their function is the same. The needs of the organism may, however, vary—if not on the strategic level of survival (and I am leaving aside the question of the so-called selfish gene and individual/species differentiation), then on the tactical level. At this latter level, during wakefulness the gradient that goes from proto-emotions to more abstract images mostly triggers actions. At night the tactical goal is to recover energy by resting.

By preserving sleep, dreams carry out their function of regulating the homeostasis of the body, while actions remain on a virtual plane. In reality, just as a level of "sleep" is active in the waking state, in sleep a level of wakefulness is active and sensory channels are never completely closed. It is a matter of critical *thresholds*. Freud's idea of the dream as the guardian of sleep would then still be valid because it would be part of a wider concept, but so would Bion's notion of continuous waking and sleeping dream, and the dream's function of transforming sensoriality into thought ($\beta \rightarrow \alpha$).

At night, the most important source of stimuli is memory; during wakefulness it is perception. From a theoretical point of view, the fact that many dreams represent wish-fulfilment is no problem, nor is the existence of anxiety dreams, which can be thought of as the virtual equivalent of the acts of fight-flight which in other cases are performed in material reality. In both cases these are transformations of emotions, which of course are provoked not only by external stimuli, but also by the drives and needs of the body. They have the same function as emotions and the same meaning as sense-making (or order-making) and not sense destruction. This process, however, may be linked to the first, that is to say, it is not clear why dreams cannot hide disturbing thoughts as they create order. The problem becomes one of what is tactical and what is strategic; it becomes a question of hierarchy.

It follows from this theoretical model that dreams too make sense at the moment they are generated and the dreamt dream is different from the recounted dream, which is instead a waking dream. From a biological and evolutionary perspective, what matters is that the dream enables the organism to protect itself from the trauma of the real and to remain in a state of sleep when this activity is produced. This is its prime purpose.[6] It is true that in doing so, dream work recycles the materials that it has available: film clips, snippets from the day before, documentaries etc. Just as in *The Mirror*, in which Tarkovsky (1974) employs not only the film material that he shot for that specific purpose but also old newsreel footage, so too dream uses the dictionaries it finds in its library. It is also true that it reacts to unassimilated quotas of β elements that have accumulated during the day and still need to be digested. Likewise, waking dreams also serve to maintain sleep, but this time we are talking about waking sleep, about the lies or falsification of consciousness that act as an anti-traumatic screen against the real. In general, by night and by day, the dream is, in the words of *The Iliad*, "the breast that makes us forget our anguish" (Homer, 1991); in other words, the shield of meaning that protects us from the truth that would hurt our eyes.

Dreaming is digesting the real. When digestion proceeds smoothly, it goes unnoticed, and so we sleep at night or in the naive realism of waking. The other vital functions can carry on undisturbed. Constantly supplying the mind with tolerable truth/meaning, which has the same nutritional function as glucose to our cells, dreaming protects not only sleep but also, in the form of dream thought or the poetic function of the mind, even waking; and in both cases it does so indirectly.

(In one way or another all patients in therapy have to some extent lost the link with the body (with their emotional life). When the analyst makes an association or creates an image (reverie) from the analysand's discourse, he is trying to find a way to restore the lost or never completely acquired connection with the body; he is the plumber trying to take action at the point where something has blocked the pipe.)

Why else would Bion be obsessed with unthought emotions as β elements?

A patient who does not dream is not in contact with the real needs of his own body and its biological values; he does not know how to interpret them. The importance of the dream in analysis arises from the fact that the problem lies precisely at the point where β becomes α and the body is transformed into the mind and less, for example, at the level of the manipulation of abstract symbols. Otherwise, to help our patients we would have to solve mathematical equations, in other words we would take a hyper-rational approach. But this would not put them in contact with the needs of the body, which cannot be ignored for a long time without causing suffering.

If interventions in analysis have a specific quality, this is true on the level of emotions rather than rational knowledge, on the level of being rather than of knowing. This is why we should privilege the here and now, because it amounts to a kind of focusing on primary consciousness, the specific locus where the transition takes place from emotions to images. The main goal of therapy is to repair or to develop the α function, and this is why we pay attention to sleeping dreams and waking dreams.

It seems to me that psychoanalytic literature fails to focus adequately on this close link between dreams and the body. The dream world, according to Dodds (1951, p. 102, cited in Bolognini, 2000, p. 279), the famous scholar of the culture of ancient Greece, "offers the chance of intercourse, however fugitive, with our distant friends, our dead, and our gods. For normal men it is the sole experience in which they escape the offensive and incomprehensible bondage of time and space. Hence it is not surprising that man was slow to confine the attribute of reality to one of his two worlds, and dismiss the other as pure illusion."

This point of view can, however, be reversed. Unlike wakefulness, the dream, in which consciousness is diminished, may give the impression of eluding the limitations of time and space, but in actual fact it is more of a slave to the present. It is closer to the senses and the emotions, and less close to the spiritual side of human beings. It is for this reason that we are able to valorise its meaning as a bridge between body and mind and as an intermediate world in which consciousness can seek to catch up with the unconscious.

Notes

1. In *The Ego and the Id* Freud (1923b) writes that the ego can be considered as the psychic projection of the surface of the body. This statement is intriguing in many respects: it (theoretically) gives back body to the mind and also suggests the metaphor of the mind as film. The body is seen here as the device that projects images on to the screen of the mind. Usually we understand projection to mean the psychic mechanism whereby the subject expels from himself and locates in another person or thing qualities, feelings, desires, and even objects that he does not acknowledge he has, or which he rejects: so it is a movement that goes from the centre to the periphery. The projection Freud speaks of, on the other hand, goes from the periphery of the body to the centre of the psyche, and precedes the other. It precedes it in an ontological sense, during the development of the ego, but then always remains the first stage in the functioning of thought. I refer to the continual transformation of external and internal proto-emotional or proto-sensorial elements, those we call β elements, into α elements, pictograms, visual images that then go on to form dream images, become deposited in the archives of memory, and can be used for dreaming and thinking.

2. The term emotion is by no means understood unequivocally by the various researchers, and can mean different things along a continuum that goes from responses to stimuli that are completely physical to those that are social in nature.

3. According to the theory of "mirror neurons", perceptions themselves are translated into movements or actions even though they are virtual.

4. See Vanzago (2012, pp. 77–78, italics are mine): "Night is not the most surprising experience of the unreal, because the montage carried out during the day usually survives, and in any case it is situated in the general context of nature. But in dreams its phantasies reveal even better the general spatiality in which clear space and observable objects are encrusted. In the dream there are events, such as flying or falling, which take on unusual values, bringing to light the inherent symbolism of spatiality that pervades waking life even though it is normally not noticed. So *the dream somehow returns the subject to the more general life of his body,* which daytime thinking conceals with light. In a sense, Merleau-Ponty here reverses the usual relationship between sleep and waking: in sleep we best see those symbolic links in the perceptual world that waking reduces to shadow." From another perspective Hartmann (2011)—and I fully agree with him—regards dreaming as a mode of psychic functioning in continuity with purposeful thought. Similar to artistic activity, dreams seek to stage and solve the existing emotional problems of the individual. Bachelard, Valery, Foucault, and others also basically take a similar view of dreams.

5. It goes without saying that this is an extremely inaccurate term, which comprehends non-alphabetised stimuli, emotions that are already visual pictograms, and the lasting emotions we call feelings.

6. Botella (2012, my italics) notes that in 1932 Freud abandoned the theory of the dream as the fulfilment of a repressed infantile wish, seeing it instead as *"an urgent need* for mental life to work through unrepresented or a-historical trauma, the urgent need to make sense of them through the creation of links; indeed, transformative processes are at work".

FILMOGRAPHY

Altieri, Mitchell and Flores, Phil, (2006) *The Hamiltons*, USA.
Bay, Michael, (2005) *The Island*, USA.
Bergman, Ingmar, (1957) *Wild Strawberries*, Sweden.
Brooks, Peter, (1963) *Lord of the Flies*, UK.
Coen, Joel and Ethan, (1984) *Blood Simple*, USA.
Coen, Joel and Ethan, (1987) *Arizona Junior*, USA.
Coen, Joel and Ethan, (2007) *No Country for Old Men*, USA.
Craven, Wes, (1984) *Nightmare—Dal profondo della notte*, USA.
Demme, Jonathan, (1991) *The Silence of the Lambs*, USA.
Emmerich, Roland, (1998) *Godzilla*, USA.
Fellini, Federico, (1962) *Le tentazioni del dottor Antonio*, Italia.
Gondry, Michel, (2006) *The Science of Sleep*, France-Italy.
Harmon, Robert, (2002) *They—Incubi dal mondo delle ombre*, USA.
Herzog, Werner, (1979) *Nosferatu the Vampyre*, France-Germany.
Hitchcock, Alfred, (1945) *Spellbound*, USA.
Hitchcock, Alfred, (1958) *Vertigo*, USA.
Hogan, Paul, (2003) *Peter Pan*, USA.
Huston, John, (1962) *Freud: The Secret Passion*, USA.
Joanou, Phil, (1992) *Final Analysis*, USA.
Kurosawa, Akira, (1950) *Rashomon*, Japan.
Kurosawa, Akira, (1990) *Dreams*, Japan-USA.

Losey, Joseph, (1963) *The Servant*, UK.
Losey, Joseph, (1970) *The Go-Between*, UK.
Lynch, David, (1992) *Fire Walk with Me*, USA.
Lynch, David, (1997) *Lost Highway*, USA.
Lynch, David, (2001) *Mullholland Drive*, France-USA.
Lynch, David and Frost, Mark, (1990–1991) *Twin Peaks*, USA.
Lyne, Adrian, (1987) *Fatal Attraction*, USA.
Moretti, Nanni, (1998) *April*, Italy.
Murnau, Friedrich Wilhelm, (1922) *Nosferatu*, Germany.
Nolan, Christofer, (2008) *The Dark Knight*, USA.
Proyas, Alez, (1998) *Dark City*, USA.
Ruben, Joseph, (1986) *Dreamscape*, USA.
Satoshi, Kon, (2006) *Paprika*, Japan.
Schrader, Paul, (1980) *American Gigolo*, USA.
Sekula, Andrzej, (2002) *Cube 2: Hypercube*, Canada.
Singh, Tarsem, (2000) *The Cell*, USA-Germany.
Spielberg, Steven, (2002) *Catch Me If You Can*, USA.
Stanton, Andrew, (2008) *Wall-E*, USA.
Tarkovsky, Andrei, (1972) *Solaris*, URSS.
Tarkovsky, Andrei, (1974) *The Mirror*, URSS.
Tsukamoto, Shinya, (2006) *Nightmare Detective*, Japan.
von Trier, Lars, (2003) *Dogville*, Denmark-Sweden-France.
Wachowski, Larry and Andy, (1999) *The Matrix*, USA.
Weir, Peter, (1998) *The Truman Show*, USA.

REFERENCES

Albano, L. (2004). *Lo schermo dei sogni. Chiavi psicoanalitiche del cinema.* Venezia: Marsilio.

Amigoni, F., & Pietrantonio, V. (Eds.) (2004). *Crocevia dei sogni. Dalla "Nouvelle Revue de sychanalyse".* Firenze: Le Monnier.

Andreas-Salomé, L. (1987). *The Freud Journal.* London: Quartet.

Anzieu, D. (1959). *Freud's Self-Analysis.* London: The Hogarth Press and the Institute of Psycho-Analysis, 1986.

Aristotle (2013). *On Sleep and Sleeplessness.* http://ebooks.adelaide.edu.au/a/aristotle/sleep/ Translated by J. I. Beare (published online 2013).

Bachelard, G. (1960). *The Poetics of Reverie.* Boston, MA: Beacon Press, 1992.

Badoni, M. (2011). Corpo e sogno. In: G. De Giorgo, F. Petrella & S. Vecchio (Eds.), *Sogno o son desto? Senso della realtà e vita onirica nella psicoanalisi odierna* (pp. 54–63). Milano: FrancoAngeli.

Barile, E. (2007). *Dare corpo alla mente. La relazione mente/corpo alla luce delle emozioni e dell'esperienza del sentire.* Milano: Mondadori.

Barthes, R. (1984). *The Rustle of Language.* Berkeley and Los Angeles, CA: University of California Press, 1989.

Barthes, R. (2002). *Le Neutre: Cours au Collège de France (1977–1978).* Paris: Seuil.

Benjamin, W. (1966). *Sul concetto di storia.* Torino: Einaudi, 1997.

Berman, L. H. (1985). The primal scene significance of a dream within a dream. *International Journal of Psychoanalysis, 66*: 75–76.

Bertetto, P. (2007). *Lo spettacolo e il simulacro. Il cinema nel mondo diventato favola*. Milano: Bompiani.

Bezoari, M. (2011). Ambiente onirico e ambiente analitico. Centro Psicoanalitico di Pavia, 15 Novembre.

Bezoari, M., & Ferro, A. (1994). Il posto del sogno all'interno di una teoria del campo analitico. *Rivista di Psicoanalisi, 2*: 251–272.

Bion, W. R. (1962). *Learning from Experience*. London: Heinemann.

Bion, W. R. (1963). *Elements of Psycho-Analysis*. London: Heinemann.

Bion, W. R. (1965). *Transformations. Change from Learning to Growth*. London: Heinemann.

Bion, W. R. (1967). *Second Thoughts*. London: Heinemann.

Bion, W. R. (1970). *Attention and Interpretation*. London: Tavistock.

Bion, W. R. (1975). *A Memoir of the Future: Book 1: The Dream*. Rio de Janeiro: Imago Editora.

Bion, W. R. (1978). *Four Discussions with W. R. Bion*. Perthshire: Clunie Press.

Bion, W. R. (1992). *Cogitations*. London: Karnac.

Bléandonu, G. (1995). *L'analyse des rêves et le regard mental*. Bruxelles: Mardaga.

Bleger, J. (1967). *Symbiosis and Ambiguity: A Psychoanalytic Study*. London: Routledge, 2012.

Bodei, R. (1991). Il desiderio e la lotta. In: A. Kojève, *La dialettica e l'idea della morte in Hegel* (pp. vii–xxiv). Torino: Einaudi.

Bollas, C. (1987). *The Shadow of the Object: Psychoanalysis of the Unthought Known*. London: Free Association Books.

Bolognini, S. (Ed.) (2000). *Il sogno cent'anni dopo*. Torino: Bollati Boringhieri.

Bonaminio, V. (2009). The psyche in-dwelling in the body: States of integration, un-integration and the primary identification. 13th Frances Tustin Memorial Lecture, Los Angeles, USA, 6–7 November 2009.

Botella, C. (2012). Per un ampliamento del metodo freudiano. ASP Conference, Milano, Febbraio.

Bott Spillius, E., Milton, J., Garvey, P., Couve, C., & Steiner, D. (2011). *The New Dictionary of Kleininan Thought* [based on *A Dictionary of Kleinian Thought* by R. D. Hinshelwood]. London: Karnac.

Borges, J. L. (1964). *Labyrinths: Selected Stories & Other Writings*. New York: New Directions Books.

Borges, J. L. (1979). The Cypress Leaves (Translated by Alastair Reid). *New England Review, II(1)*: 1–2.

Borges, J. L. (2010). *The Sonnets*. London: Penguin.

Borutti, S. (2006). *Filosofia dei sensi. Estetica del pensiero tra filosofia, arte e letteratura*. Milano: Raffaello Cortina.

Brenan, G. (1975). *St. John of the Cross: His Life and Poetry*. Cambridge: Cambridge University Press.

Bromberg, P. (2006). *Awakening the Dreamer: Clinical Journeys*. Mahwah, NJ: The Analytic Press.

Campari, R. (2008). *Sogni in celluloide. Reale e immaginario al cinema*. Venezia: Marsilio.

Campra, R., & Amaya, F. R. (Eds.) (2005). *Il genere dei sogni*. Bergamo: Edizioni Sestante.

Cartwright, D. (2005). β-Mentality in *The Matrix* trilogy. *International Journal of Psychoanalysis, 86*: 179–90.

Civitarese, G. (2004). Symbiotic bond and the setting. In: *The Intimate Room: Theory and Technique of the Analytic Field* (pp. 22–49). London: Routledge, 2010.

Civitarese, G. (2006). Dreams that mirror the session. *International Journal of Psychoanalysis, 87*: 703–723.

Civitarese, G. (2007). Metalepsis, or the rhetoric of transference interpretation. In: *The Intimate Room: Theory and Technique of the Anaytic Field* (pp. 50–71). London: Routledge, 2010.

Civitarese, G. (2008a). 'Caesura' as Bion's discourse on method. *International Journal of Psychoanalysis, 89*: 1123–1143.

Civitarese, G. (2008b). Immersion versus interactivity and analytic field. *International Journal of Psychoanalysis, 89*: 279–298

Civitarese, G. (2010a). Abjection and aesthetic conflict in Boccaccio's (L) *Isabetta. Journal of Romance Studies, 3*: 11–25.

Civitarese, G. (2010b). Le parentesi di Ogden ovvero della continuità dell'esperienza cosciente e inconscia: A proposito di … Thomas Ogden (2009) "Riscoprire la psicoanalisi. Pensare e sognare, imparare e dimenticare." *Rivista di Psicoanalisi, 56*: 771–780.

Civitarese, G. (2010c). Do cyborgs dream? Post-human landscapes in Shinya Tsukamoto's *Nightmare Detective* (2006). *International Journal of Psychoanalysis, 91*: 1005–1016.

Civitarese, G. (2011a). *The Violence of Emotions. Bion and Post-bionian Psychoanalysis*. London: Routledge, 2013.

Civitarese, G. (2011b). Exploring core concepts: Sexuality, dreams and the unconscious. *International Journal of Psychoanalysis, 92*: 277–280.

Civitarese, G. (2011c). Il riparo della quasi-morte e l'analista come detective degli incubi. In: A. Ferro et al., *Psicoanalisi in giallo. L'analista come detective* (pp. 149–171). Milano: Raffaello Cortina.

Civitarese, G. (2011d). Il sognato del sogno. In: G. De Giorgo, F. Petrella & S. Vecchio (Eds.), *Sogno o son desto? Senso della realtà e vita onirica nella psicoanalisi odierna* (pp. 70–77). Milano: FrancoAngeli, 2011.

Civitarese, G. (2012a). *Perdere la testa. Abiezione, conflitto estetico e critica psicoanalitica*. Firenze: Clinamen.

Civitarese, G. (2012b). L'intermedietà come paradigma epistemologico in psicoanalisi. *L'Educazione Sentimentale, 17*: 40–55.

Civitarese, G. (2013). The grid and the truth drive. *Italian Psychoanalytic Annual, 7*: 91–114.

Civitarese, G. (2014). Between "other" and "other": Merleau-Ponty as a precursor of the analytic field. *Fort Da*, in press.

Collovà, M. (2007). Per una psicoanalisi sostenibile. In: A. Ferro et al., *Sognare l'analisi. Sviluppi del pensiero di Wilfred R. Bion* (pp. 59–85). Torino: Bollati Boringhieri.

Damasio, A. R. (1999). *The Feeling of What Happens: Body, Emotion in the Making of Consciousness*. New York, NY: Mariner Books.

De Man, P. (1971). *Blindness and Insight: Essays in the Rhetoric of Contemporary Criticism*. London: Routledge, 1983.

Denton, D. (2005). *The Primordial Emotions: The Dawning of Consciousness*. Oxford: OUP, 2009.

Derrida, J. (1967a). *Writing and Difference*. London: Routledge, 2001.

Derrida, J. (1967b). *Of Grammatology*. Baltimore MD: John Hopkins University Press, 1998.

Derrida, J. (1972). *Margins of Philosophy*. Chicago: University of Chicago Press, 1985.

Derrida, J. (1988). *Limited Inc*. Evanston, IL: Northwestern University Press.

Derrida, J. (1990). *Memoirs of the Blind: The Self-Portrait and Other Ruins*. Chicago: University of Chicago Press, 1993.

Dodds, E. D. (1951). *The Greeks and the Irrational*. Berkeley and Los Angeles, CA: University of California Press.

Dubois, J. et al. (1970). *A General rhetoric*. Chicago, IL: Johns Hopkins University Press, 1981.

Eco, U. (1980). Metafora. In: *Enciclopedia* (pp. 191–236), Vol. IX. Torino: Einaudi, 1980.

Edelman, G. M. (1992). *Bright Air, Brilliant Fire: On the Matter of the Mind*. New York: Basic Books.

Edelman, G. M. (2004). *Wider Than the Sky: A Revolutionary View of Consciousness*. London: Penguin.

Ehrenburg, I. (1931). *Die Traumfabrik: Chronik des Films*. Berlin: Malik.

Etchegoyen, H. (1986). *The Fundamentals of Psychoanalytic Technique*. London: Karnac, 1991.

Fairbairn, W. R. D. (1952). *Psychoanalytic Studies of the Personality*. London: Routledge, 1994.

Ferro, A. (1992). *The Bi-Personal Field: Experiencing Child Analysis*. New York: Routledge, 1999.

Ferro, A. (1996). *In the Analyst's Consulting Room*. London: Routledge, 2002.

Ferro, A. (1998). *Supervision in Psychoanalysis: The Sao Paulo Seminars.* London: Routledge, 2013.

Ferro, A. (1999). *Psychoanalysis as Therapy and Storytelling.* London: Routledge, 2006.

Ferro, A. (2002). *Seeds of Illness, Seeds of Recovery.* London: Routledge, 2004.

Ferro, A. (2008). *Rêveries.* Torino: Antigone.

Ferro, A. (2009). Transformations in dreaming and characters in the psycho-analytic field. *International Journal of Psychoanalysis, 90:* 209–230.

Ferro, A. (2010). *Tormenti di anime. Passioni, sintomi, sogni.* Milano: Raffaello Cortina.

Ferro, A. et al. (2011). *Psicoanalisi in giallo. L'analista come detective.* Milano: Raffaello Cortina.

Fornaro, M. (1991). *Psicanalisi tra scienza e mistica. L'opera di Wilfred R. Bion.* Roma: Studium.

Foucault, M. (1994). *Il sogno.* Milano: Raffaello Cortina, 2003.

Freud, E. L. (1961). *Letters of Sigmund Freud 1873–1939.* London: The Hogarth Press.

Freud, S. (1900). *The Interpretation of Dreams. S. E., 4 & 5.*

Freud, S. (1901). On dreams. *S. E., 5:* 629–686.

Freud, S. (1905). Jokes and their relation to the unconscious. *S. E., 8:* 1–247

Freud, S. (1905). Fragment of an analysis of a case of hysteria (1905 [1901]). *S. E., 7:* 1–122.

Freud, S. (1911a). Formulations on the two principles of mental functioning. *S. E., 12:* 213–226.

Freud, S. (1915). On Transformations of Instinct, as Exemplified in Anal Erotism. *S. E., 17:* 125–134.

Freud, S. (1916). *Introductory Lectures on Psycho-Analysis. S. E., 15:* 1–240

Freud, S. (1918). From the history of an infantile neurosis. *S. E., 17:* 1–124.

Freud, S. (1920). *Beyond the Pleasure Priciple. S. E., 18:* 7–64.

Freud, S. (1922). Some neurotic mechanisms in jealousy, paranoia and homosexuality. *S. E., 18:* 221–232

Freud, S. (1923a). Remarks on the theory and practice of dream-interpretation. *S. E., 19:* 107–122.

Freud, S. (1923b). *The Ego and the Id. S. E., 19:* 1–66.

Freud, S. (1925). *An Autobiographical Study. S. E., 20:* 1–74.

Freud, S. (1930). *Civilization and its Discontents. S. E., 21:* 59–145.

Freud, S. (1933). *New Introductory Lectures On Psycho-Analysis. S. E., 22:* 1–182.

Freud, S. (1937). Constructions in analysis. *S. E., 23:* 255–270.

Freud, S. (1950). *A Project for a Scientific Psychology* [1985]. *S. E., 1:* 283–391.

Freud, S., & Abraham, K. (2002). *The Complete Correspondence of Sigmund Freud and Karl Abraham 1907–1925* (Ed. Ernst Falzeder, Trans. Caroline Schwarzacher). London: Karnac.

Gabbard, G. O., & Gabbard, K. (1999). *Psychiatry and the Cinema*. Washington, DC: American Psychiatric Publishing, Inc.

Gallese, V. (2006). La molteplicità condivisa. Dai neuroni mirror all'intersoggettività. In: S. Mistura (Ed.), *Autismo. L'umanità nascosta* (pp. 207–270). Torino: Einaudi.

Gallo, F. (2004). *Nietzsche e l'emancipazione estetica*. Roma: Manifestolibri.

Garma, A. (1966). *The Psychoanalysis of Dreams*. New York, NY: J. Aronson, 1974.

Genette, G. (1972). *Figure III. Discorso del racconto*. Torino: Einaudi, 1976.

Genette, G. (2004). *Métalepse: De la figure à la fiction*. Paris: Seuil.

Ginzburg, C. (1979). Morelli, Freud, and Sherlock Holmes: Clues and scientific method. In: U. Eco & T. Sebeok (Eds.), *The Sign of Three: Dupin, Holmes, Peirce* (pp. 81–118). Bloomington, IN: History Workshop, Indiana University Press.

Girard, M. (2010). Winnicott's foundation for the basic concepts of Freud's metapsychology? *International Journal of Psychoanalysis, 91*: 305–324.

Green, A. (2000). The primordial mind and the work of the negative. In: P. Bion Talamo, F. Borgogno & S. A. Merciai (Eds.), *W. R. Bion Between Past and Future* (pp. 108–128), London: Karnac.

Grinstein, J. (1983). The dramatic device: A play within a play. *Journal of the American Psychoanalytic Association, 4*: 49–52.

Grosskurth, P. (1980). *Melanie Klein: Her World and Her Work*. London: Karnac Books, 1987.

Grotstein, J. S. (2000). *Who Is the Dreamer, Who Dreams the Dream?: A Study of Psychic Presences*. London: Routledge.

Grotstein, J. S. (2007). *A Beam of Intense Darkness: Wilfred Bion's Legacy to Psychoanalysis*. London: Karnac.

Hartmann, E. (2011). *The Nature and Functions of Dreaming*. Oxford: OUP.

Hegel, G. W. F (2009). *The Phenomenology of Spirit*. Boston, MA: Digireads.com.

Hinshelwood, R. D. (1989). *A Dictionary of Kleinian Thought*. London: Free Association.

Homer (1991). *The Iliad* (trans. R. Fagles). London: Penguin.

Horovitz, M. (2008). Personal communication.

Isakower, O. (1954). Spoken words in a dream—a preliminary communication. *Psychoanalytic Quarterly, 23*: 1–6.

Johnson, M. (1987). *The Body in the Mind. The Bodily Basis of Meaning, Imagination and Reason*. Chicago, IL: The University of Chicago Press.

Journot, M. -T. (2002). *Le vocabulaire du cinéma*. Paris: Nathan.

Khan, M. M. R. (1962). Dream psychology and the evolution of the psychoanalytic situation. *International Journal of Psychoanalysis, 43*: 21–31.

Khan, M. M. R. (1972). The use and abuse of dream in psychic experience. In: M. M. R. Khan, *The Privacy of the Self* (pp. 306–315). London: Hogarth, 1974.

King, P., & Steiner, R. (Eds.) (1991). *The Freud–Klein Controversies 1941–45.* London: Routledge.

Klein, M. (1923). The rôle of the school in the libidinal development of the child. In: *Contributions to Psycho-Analysis 1921–1945* (pp. 68–86). London: The Hogarth Press, 1948.

Klein, M. (1926). The psychological principles of infant analysis. In: *Contributions to Psycho-Analysis 1921–1945* (pp. 141–151). London: The Hogarth Press, 1948.

Klein, M. (1927). Criminal tendencies in normal children. In: *Contributions to Psycho-Analysis 1921–1945* (pp. 185–201). London: The Hogarth Press, 1948.

Klein, M. (1928). Early stages of the Oedipus conflict. In: *Contributions to Psycho-Analysis 1921–1945* (pp. 202–214). London: The Hogarth Press, 1948.

Klein, M. (1930). The importance of symbol-formation in the development of the ego. In: *Contributions to Psycho-Analysis 1921–1945* (pp. 236–250). London: The Hogarth Press, 1948.

Klein, M. (1932). The Psycho-Analysis of Children. *The International Psycho-Analytical Library,* 22:1–379. London: The Hogarth Press.

Klein, M. (1933). The early development of conscience in the child. In: *Contributions to Psycho-Analysis 1921–1945* (pp. 267–278). London: The Hogarth Press, 1948.

Klein, M. (1940). Mourning and its relation to manic-depressive states. In: *Contributions to Psycho-Analysis 1921–1945* (pp. 311–338). London: The Hogarth Press, 1948.

Kojève, A. (1947). *Introduction to the Reading of Hegel: Lectures on the "Phenomenology of Spirit".* Ithaca, NY: Cornell University Press, 1980.

Kristeva, J. (1980). *Powers of Horror: An Essay on Abjection.* New York, NY: Columbia University Press, 1984.

Kristeva, J. (2003). *Melanie Klein.* New York, NY: Columbia University Press, 2002.

Lacan, J. (2002). *The Seminar of Jacques Lacan XVI: From an Other to the Other (1968–1969).* London: Karnac.

Lakoff, G., & Johnson, M. (1980). *Metaphors We Live By.* Chicago, IL: University of Chicago Press 1981.

Laplanche, J., & Pontalis, J. -B. (1967). *The Language of Psychoanalysis.* New York: W. W. Norton, 1974.

Lipschitz, F. (1990). The dream within a dream—Proflection vs. reflection. *Contemporary Psychoanalysis,* 26: 716–731.

Mahon, E. J. (2002). Dreams within dreams. *Psychoanalytic Study of the Child,* 57: 118–130.

Mancia, M. (2006). Memoria implicita e inconscio precoce non rimosso: loro ruolo nel transfert e nel sogno. *Rivista di Psicoanalisi, 52*: 629–655.

Masson, J. M. (1984). *The Assault on Truth: Freud's Suppression of the Seduction Theory.* New York: Farrar, Strauss, Giroux.

Masson, J. M. (1985). *The Complete Letters of Sigmund Freud to Wilhelm Fliess, 1887–1904.* Cambridge, MA: The Belknap Press of Harvard University Press.

Masson, J. M. (1990). *Final Analysis: The Making and Unmaking of a Psychoanalyst.* Reading, MA: Addison-Wesley.

Mazzacane, F. (2007). L'analista e i contenuti killer. In: A. Ferro, G. Civitarese, M. Collovà, G. Foresti, F. Mazzacane, E. Molinari & P. Politi, *Sognare l'analisi. Sviluppi clinici del pensiero di Wilfred R. Bion* (pp. 109–130). Torino: Bollati Boringhieri.

Mazzarella, A., & Risset J. (Eds.) (2003). *Scene del sogno.* Roma: Artemide.

Meltzer, D. (1967). *The Psycho-Analytical Process.* London: Karnac, 2008.

Meltzer, D. (1973). *Sexual States of Mind.* London: Karnac, 2008.

Meltzer, D. (1978). *The Kleinian Development.* Karnac, 2008.

Meltzer, D. (1981). *La comprensione della bellezza e altri saggi.* Torino: Loescher.

Meltzer, D. (1984). *Dream-Life: A Re-Examination of the Psycho-analytical Theory and Technique.* London: Karnac.

Meltzer, D., & Williams, M. H. (1988). *The Apprehension of Beauty: The Role of Aesthetic Conflict in Development, Art and Violence.* London: Karnac, 2008.

Merleau-Ponty, M. (1945). *Phenomenology of Perception.* London: Routledge, 2002.

Merleau-Ponty, M. (1969). *Prose of the World.* Evanston, IL: Northwestern University Press, 1973.

Mills, J. (2000). Hegel on projective identification: Implications for Klein, Bion, and beyond. *Psychoanalytic Review, 87*: 841–874.

Nietzsche, F. (1975). *Frammenti postumi 1884–1885.* OFN, vol. 7, tomo 3. Milano: Adelphi.

Nietzsche, F. (1991). *The Gay Science, With a Prelude in Rhymes and an Appendix of Songs.* New York, NY: The Random House.

Nietzsche, F. (1992). *Frammenti postumi. Estate 1872-Autunno 1873.* OFN, vol. 3. Milano: Adelphi.

Ogden, T. H. (1989). *The Primitive Edge of Experience.* Northvale, NJ: Jason Aronson.

Ogden, T. H. (1994). *Subjects of Analysis.* London: Karnac.

Ogden, T. H. (1997). *Reverie and Interpretation: Sensing Something Human.* Northvale, NJ: Jason Aronson.

Ogden, T. H. (2001a). *Conversations at the Frontier of Dreaming*. Northvale, NY: Jason Aronson.

Ogden, T. H. (2001b). Reading Winnicott. *Psychoanalytic Quarterly, 70*: 299–323.

Ogden, T. H. (2005a). Foreword. In: A. Ferro, *Seeds of Illness and Seeds of Recovery: The Genesis of Suffering and the Role of Psychoanalysis* (IX–XIII). New York: Brunner-Routledge.

Ogden, T. H. (2005b). *This Art of Psychoanalysis: Dreaming Undreamt Dreams and Interrupted Cries*. London: Routledge.

Ogden, T. H. (2007). On talking-as-dreaming. *International Journal of Psychoanalysis, 88*: 575–589.

Ogden, T. H. (2009). *Rediscovering Psychoanalysis: Thinking and Dreaming, Learning and Forgetting*. London: Routledge.

Petrella, F. (2000). Estetica del sogno e terapia a cento anni dalla *Treaumdeutung*. In: S. Bolognini (Ed.), *Il sogno cent'anni dopo* (pp. 29–48). Bollati Boringhieri, Torino.

Pontalis, J. -B. (1988). *Perdere di vista*. Roma: Borla, 1993.

Pontalis, J. -B. (2003). Il a été rêvé. In: A Mazzarella & J. Risset (Eds.), *Scene del sogno* (pp. 11–24), Roma: Artemide.

Proust, M. ([1927] 2003). *Finding Time Again* (Volume 6 of *In Search of Lost Time*, translated by Ian Petterson). London: Penguin Classics, 2003.

Quignard, P. (1995). *Rhétorique spéculative*. Paris: Gallimard, 1997.

Reis, B. E. (1999). Thomas Ogden's phenomenological turn. *Psychoanal Dialogues, 9*: 371–393.

Riefolo, G. (2006). *Le visioni di uno psicoanalista*. Torino: Antigone.

Rodley, C. (Ed.) (1997). *Lynch on Lynch*. London: Faber & Faber.

Sabbadini, A. (2003). *The Couch and the Silver Screen: Psychoanalytic Reflections on European Cinema*. London: Routledge.

Sandler, P. C. (2005). *The Language of Bion*. London: Karnac.

Schneider, J. A. (2010). From Freud's dream-work to Bion's work of dreaming: The changing conception of dreaming in psychoanalytic theory. *International Journal of Psychoanalysis, 91*: 521–540.

Schreber, D. P. (1903). *Memoirs of My Nervous Illness*. New York, NY: The New York Review of Books, 2000.

Segal, H. (1957). Notes on symbol formation. *International Journal of Psychoanalysis, 38*: 391–397.

Segal, H. (1979). *Klein*. New York, NY: Other Press LLC, 1989.

Segre, C. (2003). *La pelle di san Bartolomeo. Discorso e tempo dell'arte*. Torino: Einaudi.

Sharpe, E. F. (1937). *Dream Analysis*. London: Routledge, 1978.

Silber, A. (1983). A significant "dream within a dream." *Journal of the American Psychoanalytic Association, 31*: 899–915.

Sperling, M. (1958). Pavor nocturnus. *Journal of the American Psychoanalytic Association, 6*: 79–94.

St. John of the Cross (2005). *The Dark Night of the Soul*. New York, NY: Barnes & Nobles.

Stein, M. H. (1989). How dreams are told: Secondary revision—the critic, the editor, and the plagiarist. *Journal of the American Psychoanalytic Association, 37*: 65–88.

Steiner, J. (1993). *Psychic Retreats: Pathological Organizations in Psychotic, Neurotic and Borderline Patients*. London: Routledge.

Stern, D. B. (2009). *Partners in Thought: Working with Unformulated Experience, Dissociation, and Enactment*. London: Routledge.

Stokes, A. (1963). *Painting and the Inner World*. London: Tavistock.

Vanzago, L. (2012). *Merleau-Ponty*. Roma: Carocci.

Vitale, S. (2005). *La dimora della lontananza. Saggi sull'esperienza dello spazio intermedio*. Bergamo: Moretti & Vitali.

Vitale, S. (2007). *Si prega di chiudere gli occhi. Esercizi di cecità volontaria*. Firenze: Clinamen.

Waelder, J. (1935). Analyse eines Falles von Pavor Nocturnus. *Zeitschrift für psychoanalytische Pädagogik, 9*: 1–70.

Wilder, J. (1956). Dream analysis within dreams. *Psychoanalytic Review, 43*: 42–56.

Winnicott, D. W. (1945). Primitive emotional development. In: *Through Paediatrics to Psycho- Analysis* (pp. 145–156). London: Karnac, 1975.

Winnicott, D. W. (1947). Hate in the countertransference. In: *Through Paediatrics to Psycho- Analysis* (pp. 194–203). London: Karnac, 1975.

Winnicott, D. W. (1961). Further remarks on the theory of the parent-infant relationship. In: *Psycho-Analytic Explorations* [1989] (pp. 73–75). London: Karnac, 2010.

Winnicott, D. W. (1965). *The Maturational Processes and the Facilitating Environment*. London: The Hogarth Press and the Institute of Psycho-Analysis.

Winnicott, D. W. (1971). *Playing and Reality*. London: Tavistock Publications.

INDEX